800 Years of
Women's Letters

800 Years of
Women's Letters

OLGA KENYON

FOREWORD BY P. D. JAMES

SUTTON PUBLISHING LIMITED

First published in the United Kingdom in 1992
Alan Sutton Publishing Ltd · Phoenix Mill · Stroud · Gloucestershire

Paperback edition, with corrections, first published 1994

Reprinted 1995 (4 times), 1996 (twice)
Reprinted 1997
Copyright © Olga Kenyon, 1992

British Library Cataloguing in Publication Data

800 Years of Women's Letters
I. Kenyon, Olga
808.86

ISBN 0-7509-0725-8

Typeset in 10/13 pt Sabon.
Typesetting and origination by
Alan Sutton Publishing Limited.
Printed in Great Britain by
WBC Limited, Bridgend.

Contents

'Women find under their pens turns of phrases and expressions which in us men are the result only of long labour and painful searching. It is women who can make an entire emotion be read in a single word.'

La Bruyère

Foreword

by P.D. James

No literary form is more revealing, more spontaneous or more individual than a letter. Long before women were writing novels they were expressing their emotions, aspirations, hopes and fears in epistolary form, and those letters from past centuries which have survived can give us a more vivid and realistic portrait of the age in which they were written than many more portentous literary forms.

This fascinating anthology reveals a richness of experience which will be of interest not only to social historians but to all those fascinated by the way in which, throughout the centuries, women have responded to the opportunities as well as to the frustrations of daily living, and the way, too, in which the changing style of letter-writing has reflected the spirit and concerns of the age. It is through letters that women, parted from family and friends by catastrophes such as war, civil strife or rebellion, or by marriage and travel, kept each other informed of those details of everyday life, those small and large satisfactions, those trials and calamities on which the interest and happiness of daily living so much depends, as well as of the great rites of passage: death, birth and marriage.

As Jane Austen writes in *Northanger Abbey*, published in 1818, 'Everybody allows that the talent of writing agreeable letters is peculiarly female'. In gathering together some of the most agreeable as well as the most notable of women's letters covering a period of eight hundred years, Olga Kenyon has performed a service to all who are interested not only in the written word, but in the changing lives of women and the way in which they themselves have perceived these changes. Some of the women who appear in her book were close to the heart of great national events, were the wives or associates of great men, or themselves have names which are part of history: Empress Maria Theresa, Florence Nightingale, Queen Victoria. Others are virtually unknown but come alive in lines which reveal the infinite variety and interest of their daily lives. Some were women of considerable erudition and intelligence, famed for their wit and political acumen; others lived apparently ordinary lives and wrote about more personal family concerns in letters which, in their directness, intimacy and sympathy, are even more fascinating than the epistles of famous and well-known women. Most were written with no thought of publication. Here is the intimacy of heart and mind speaking to heart and mind across distance and across time. In the words of Dorothy Wordsworth to her brother William, we 'see the beating of the inmost heart upon paper'.

Olga Kenyon has provided a scholarly and perceptive introduction to her anthology which adds to our interest in the letters themselves. In the words of Héloïse:

> If a picture, which is but a mute representation of an object, can give such pleasure, what cannot letters inspire? They have souls, can speak, have in them all that force which expresses the transports of the heart.

Introduction

My aim is to show that women's letters are a valid form of literature. This book revalues a wealth of previously ignored female writing from the Middle Ages to today. In recent years, novels and poetry written by women have been reprinted (mainly by women's presses) and acclaimed. Women as letter-writers have been comparatively neglected, though often the letter was their main literary outlet. Such writing was merely esteemed for its information on the famous, or the world of men. No previous anthology has presented the richness to be found in women's letters, of interest both for historians and the general reader.

These letters are valuable for many reasons, including the range of topics discussed, and variety of styles. They show women using one of the few forms of writing open to them with wit and skill. Already in the earlier centuries women's correspondence matches the expressiveness if not erudition of mens'. By the sixteenth century their scope has increased and they use the more complex, gravely formal discourse of the Tudor age, to draw attention to female needs. Lively conversational modes developed in the eighteenth century, when women were famed for their wit and political acumen. They prefigure the direct, sometimes colloquial registers of today.

This wealth demonstrates that a tradition of female letter-writing has existed for at least eight centuries. It had many functions: to inform; to instruct (children, even monarchs at times); to entertain family and friends with descriptions of society or daily life (by writers as amusing as Madame de Sévigné and Fanny Burney); to keep up relationships (a female quality); to convey news, before newspapers were widespread; to recount travels, before the time of the 'foreign correspondent'; to give advice on many issues, from personal to public; to explore psychological problems, often with wisdom and insight, before counselling was thought of; to keep in touch, before the days of the telephone or cheap travel; to offer love and express caring.

More implicitly, and perhaps even more interestingly, these letters explore female experiences, viewpoints and emotions. The writer, and the recipient, gain a clearer sense of identity in cultures which underestimate their abilities by stereotyping their needs.

This study cannot be fully comprehensive, yet shows many women reaching eminently sensible or provocative conclusions on a vast array of topics, including both national issues and domestic concerns. They offer thoughtful solutions to deeply personal issues, from how to deal with family and health problems, to how to make life bearable, even when isolated or poverty-stricken. There is heartfelt sympathy in response to fear of sickness and dying, the burden of mental depression, the boredom of monotonous routine. The many ideas for coping with children and work, difficult husbands, money, are well worth reading still. In a world which seldom listened, letters provided a sharing of dilemmas, an early process of therapy attempts at a constructing of a positive female identity.

Letters have one considerable advantage over conversation in that they are written with time for reflection, allowing choice of apt wording. They prove more subtle than talk in strategies for subverting patriarchal limitations. Because letters were the one form of writing which men did not find threatening (according to Virginia Woolf) they could both explore the sexist devaluation of female values and aid consciousness-raising.

Of course, there are many parallels with men's letters, in attitudes to topics and manner of expression. Nevertheless, women did not learn Latin and Greek. The training of men in the rhetoric of dead languages could have brilliant effects, as is well known, but it could be stultifying. Leonard Woolf testifies to the dreariness of translating for seven hours each day at a school as good as Westminster, even in this century, and Shakespeare's schoolboy crawled unwillingly to school. Women, not allowed this education, had to listen more carefully to adults to gain learning (even listening outside doors while their brothers were tutored, as in *The Mill on the Floss*, quite possibly George Eliot's own experience). This ear for real conversation, the power of oracy, enriches these remarkable missives.

My geographical range is wider than most anthologies, from America to Europe. I have lived and worked in France and Spain, which made me keen to include writers considered great there, still underappreciated here, such as Madame de Sévigné and George Sand, St Teresa and La Pasionaria. I enjoy their special tone and have made my own translations from the original.

Some of the writers have been continuously read since their own time, such as Lady Mary Wortley Montagu, in my view the most interesting letter-writer in the English language. Not one volume of her letters is at present available in print. This sad fact is yet more evidence of the relative neglect of some outstanding female writers, which at last I can redress a little with long extracts from three of her many books. Other writers in this volume, whose names are better known, yet still not fully appreciated include Héloïse (to Abelard); Margaret Paston, Dorothy Osborne, Emily Eden, Isabella Bird, Empress Maria Theresa, Mrs Gaskell, Florence Nightingale, Edith Wharton and Anaïs Nin and Jean Rhys. Of course, most of us have looked at some letters by Queen Victoria, who wrote an average of six a day. At such a production rate some are unpolished, but many offer both her speaking voice and good advice. Recently, the actress Maria Perry collected all the letters and speeches of Elizabeth I in a delightfully illustrated volume, which displays her tremendous skill with words and arguments. On a par is Queen Isabella of Castile. She married Ferdinand of Aragon, probably a model for Machiavelli's *The Prince*, in 1469. Together they united Spain, Isabella accounted the more skilful politician of the two. It was she, and no other leader in Europe at the time, who had the sense to grant Columbus the small fund he requested to discover the spice routes to the Indies.

My aim is also to bring to a wider public women only recently 'rediscovered' by feminist historians and critics. These include Hildegard of Bingen (1154–1201), the Mystic Abbess, respected by emperors; Christine de Pisan, the first woman professional writer, in fourteenth-century Paris; Aphra Behn (1640–89), now established as one of our great women writers, who virtually invented the novel with *Oroonoko, or the Royal Slave* (1688) and the scandalous *Love Letters Between a Nobleman and his Sister* (1684–7), from which I include passionate extracts.

Fanny Burney was celebrated in her own time, even by the demanding Dr Johnson. Yet she was neglected until re-read by feminists, specifically Dale Spender in *Mothers of the Novel: 100 Great Women Novelists Before Jane Austen*. Her epistolary novels reveal detailed study of society, and lively characterization through the speaking voice, qualities noticeable in epistolary novels today, of which the outstanding is Alice Walker's *The Color Purple*. Burney's witty letters about Dr Johnson, about life at court when she was lady-in-waiting, her meeting with Madame de Staël and her reactions to her weakness are all worth attention.

This book opens with the twelfth century, because in Paris and Germany women there began to write with assurance, and their letters have been preserved. It is only too possible that the majority of women's letters were thrown away, as even happened to some of Bach's manuscripts. The earliest letter-writer in English (as opposed to Latin) was Margaret Paston. She was the efficient, affectionate manager of her husband's estate while he practised law in London during the Wars of the Roses. Her description of facing attacks from neighbouring barons is so dramatic that it is now quoted in schoolbooks.

The main timespan of this study is, therefore, from the Wars of the Roses to the beginning of the Second World War. I also include two ancient Greek epistles, to prove that women were more vital then than is commonly supposed, and some present-day letters, mainly from women friends, to show the continuing power of female correspondence in analysing ideas, feelings and social issues.

In the Middle Ages letters were often dictated, especially by women, to scribes or secretaries. However by Tudor times public schools increased the literacy of the rising yeoman class. In 1660 an Act of Parliament set up a national Post Office. Twenty years later the service was enlarged and stamping introduced. This new penny post service set up 334 houses for receiving letters, which reached 200 towns outside London. Foreigners admired the efficiency of our service, an achievement which enhanced the social, and business, life of the middle classes. Writers such as Daniel Defoe praised the 'utmost safety and Dispatch' of letters within the capital, up to 'Four, Five, Six to Eight times a Day, according as the Distance of the Place makes it practicable'.[1] It cost one penny inside London, to the person receiving the letter. Outside London both sender and receiver paid one penny each. Even money could be sent safely by post. France developed a service for the rich, of great help to writers such as Madame de Sévigné.

By the eighteenth century educated people were expected to be able to write elegant letters. In fact, some schools trained pupils by making letter-writing into a standard composition exercise. Students were often made to study and copy Greek, and especially Latin, letters. Recently established newspapers such as *The Tatler* (1709) and *The Spectator* (1711) received many letters, which soon became – and remain – a feature. Their editors, Addison and Steele, wrote that they had 'Complaints from Lovers, Schemes for Projectors, Scandal from Ladies, Congratulations,

Compliments and Advice in Abundance'.[2] Editor John Dunton initiated a popular item of the editor's reply to these 'anonymous' widely read letters.

So much paper was being bought that the government hit on the cunning idea of taxing it, to obtain more revenue in order to finance the War of Spanish Succession in Europe, which ended in 1713 with the Treaty of Utrecht. The Stamp Act of 1711 imposed a tax on stamped vellum, parchment and paper and upon certain printed papers, pamphlets and advertisements. Clearly business was using far more paper, and many more people were corresponding with each other.

It was aristocratic women who gave social acceptability to the public letter-writing of women. The Duchess of Newcastle (1623–94) was protected by a rich and powerful husband who had fought for Charles I and was rewarded by Charles II. She longed for fame, wrote a great deal in many genres and in 1664 brought out virtually the first volume of collected letters: *Sociable Letters*. Her aim was not modest: 'I have endeavoured under the Cover of Letters to Express the Humour of Mankind.' She describes the communion of two female friends who are happiest when reading and writing to each other. Her preface states that if she were empress of the world, she would advance people of learning and wit, not just men. One of the correspondents is said to be fit to be an empress because 'Nature had Crown'd her Soul with a Celestial Crown, made of a Poetical Flame of Understanding. Judgement and Wit, also with clear Distinguishings, and sparkling Fancies'.[3] She used the genre of letter writing to portray real life, to present actual problems and even propose solutions. The drawback of discursiveness was overcome by providing narrative; thus the epistolary novel started life.

Her admiration for knowledge *and* the imagination also distinguishes the writing of many women of her time and the following century. Thanks to the success of Restoration women, especially playwrights such as Aphra Behn, far more women felt able to take up the pen. Even if not encouraged by their menfolk, letter-writing was allowed, since it was done unobtrusively. Jane Austen sometimes pretended to be writing letters in the drawing room when in fact she was creating fiction.

The letter-writing of women was seldom taken seriously, as it posed no threat to the male-dominated literary establishment, which never counted it as 'real' writing, though male letters were considered 'literature'. Indeed, letters became a significant part of our culture. They are autobiographical, based on intimate experience, yet not opposed to the Puritan tradition of noting the facts of an individual's life. Many were encouraged by the notion that God's Divine Purpose could be discerned in the recounting of events – and emotions. Letters deepen self-inspection, at a time when Puritan divines considered self-examination a healthy step towards salvation.

Many of these letter-writers were upper-middle-class women who felt able, by the middle of the eighteenth century, to display their prowess in literature. The group known as the bluestockings provided a network of wealthy women with salons (like those of seventeenth-century France), encouraging the intellectual activity of women without disturbing the hierarchies of gender and class. Their letters to each other were frequently witty and honest. In 1782 Elizabeth Montagu (named 'Queen of the Blues' by Dr Johnson) wrote about a friend:

> I really believe she was just like Eve before she ate the apple, at least she answers to Milton's description of her. She would have preferred her husband's discourse to the angels. I am afraid you and I my dear friend should have entered some metaphysical disquisitions with the angel, we are not so perfectly the rib of man as woman ought to be.[4]

That century has given us some outstanding letters from women. We have now rediscovered amusing, emotional, informed and well-argued letters which both influenced newly emerging fiction and were influenced by it. The most striking collections come from bluestockings with both the leisure and the learning for long correspondence. They often shared ideas and discussed projects, such as women's education. At times they recounted scandals in court, which could be salacious; at times they described the latest Paris fashions, providing a need for information only fulfilled much later by women's magazines.

Middle-class women were usually more preoccupied with their emotions, and used letters for self-analysis, an occupation encouraged by the Protestant Church with its emphasis on the individual conscience. In this letter of 1744, for example, salon topics are rejected in favour of a discourse of feeling, suitable both for the sharing of friendship – and for epistolary fiction:

> There are times when even the magnificence of the sky, the fair extensions of a flowery lawn, the verdure of the groves, the harmony of rural sounds, and the universal fragrance of the balmy air, strike us with no agreeable sensations, nothing surely but the ungrateful perverseness of

one's own humour. This reflection throws human happiness in a most mortifying light.[5]

Women who needed to earn money now took to publishing collections of letters, often with a moral aim, sometimes with the didactic message transformed into an epistolary novel. Among these, one of the most successful was Eliza Haywood (1693–1756). Prolific and versatile, she developed sentimental, realistic, didactic and epistolary novels – and books on how to conduct oneself. She even set up a newspaper for women and composed its agony column! Booksellers co-operated with her in declaring that every epistolary work was genuine. The preface usually claimed that the letters had never been intended for publication, had been stolen or lost and only printed at great risk to the bookseller. Amazingly, letters became one of the most bought genres, perhaps because they seemed truthful. They proved a suitable vehicle for travel reports, and even for tales of adventures in distant countries. They also conveyed contemporary news reports, and public scandals; in fact, newspapers were often composed of topical letters. Hack writers tended to disguise their sensational accounts as eyewitness reports. The now respected 'foreign correspondent' began work in this half-fictional letter form.

Letters on conduct served as manuals to the rising bourgeoisie. Designed as a guide through the complexities of social life, they explained morals, discourse and etiquette. Daniel Defoe went further in his *The Family Instructor* (1715) with advice on problematic situations between relatives and do-it-yourself counselling for parents and offspring. His *Conjugal Lewdness* (1727) even warned partners against indulgence in the sexual aspects of their marriages. The saleability of letters proved an asset to women. It was one of the few forms of writing familiar to them, unlike the epic poem or academic treatise.

Who was buying these letters? Respectable women could not easily enter bookshops, or the new coffee shops where newspapers were read; but by the middle of the eighteenth century they could subscribe, through catalogues. Publishers were as disinclined then as now to take risks, so readers were asked to subscribe in advance. Thus women with a little money of their own could exercise some influence and encourage wealthy friends, in both their reading – and writing.

By the time of the French Revolution the tone of women's letters became bolder on social issues, during a short-lived belief in the possibility of equality. The Romantic Movement was beginning to affect sensibility, and many writers felt able to discuss emotions at length. Both these aspects are present in the correspondence of the feminist Mary Wollstonecraft, whose *Vindication of the Rights of Women* (1792) remains a skilfully argued, path-breaking contribution to feminist thought. When she fell in love with an American businessman, Gilbert Imlay, she wrote passionate letters to him, particularly once she realized he was deceiving her. Nevertheless, she bore his child and agreed to go on a business journey for him round Scandinavia. Her travel letters range from philosophical, social and personal reflection to brilliant description, an example variously followed by a wide variety of Victorian women travellers, from the well-born Emily Eden, whose brother was Viceroy of India, to Mary Kingsley who funded her innovative studies of the Congo by useful, small-scale trading.

Though Victorian women had few legal and no voting rights, the slow increase in education allowed wider access to literacy. Isolated governesses wrote to friends, schoolteachers described their lot, while educated mothers found momentary release from large families. By the middle of the nineteenth century more men are proposing that their women write, from Shelley and George Lewes to Mr Gaskell. Though the motives may have been therapeutic and financial, the results are outstanding novels – and letters.

The example of well-known women publishing with impunity (from the time of Jane Austen's later novels, praised by the Prince Regent) made lesser-known females less inhibited about attempting to write, demonstrated in the many letters to novelists such as Mrs Gaskell and George Eliot requesting advice. These two deeply moral writers exemplify the social conscience of some intellectual Victorians. Concern with lack of welfare provision led many women to campaign publicly, through talks and above all letters, to redress wrongs. Caroline Norton worked for fairer divorce laws, attempting to free wives from overtly tyrannical husbands. Josephine Butler spent ten years in persuading men to repeal the repressive Contagious Diseases Acts, which discriminated against prostitutes and poorer women. Octavia Hill campaigned for better living conditions in the East End of London. And, of course, Florence Nightingale spent most of her life, while ostensibly resting on a couch, in her celebrated correspondence, which improved the standard of nursing care and education not only in Britain but worldwide.

Thanks to the penny post, reducing costs considerably, women's friendships were able to flourish in correspondence. There are many examples of talented wives, such as the undervalued Jane Carlyle and Geraldine

Jewsbury, who shared insightful reflections on their society in remarkable epistles. A few decades later, well-known writers such as Virginia Woolf and Vita Sackville-West sound more self-consciously literary, more openly emotional. They had achieved a standing in the twentieth century which gave them greater confidence in their worth and in their lesbian love.

In our century obviously there are far more women writing. Primary school education allowed many working-class women to write, virtually for the first time. Evidence of their letters, particularly during the enforced separations of the two World Wars, lies in the collections of the Imperial War Museum, London. Women have now resumed the eighteenth-century occupation of publishing books of their letters in order to earn a living, from travel writers such as Freya Stark, to novelists, including Françoise Sagan and Fay Weldon.

The telephone is often blamed for what some consider a dearth of good letter-writing today. For this reason I include letters written to me, by friends, on topics such as living alone, travelling in India, coping with a small boy while studying, and on how to live a full life on a tiny income. They testify to the continuing qualities of women's letters.

Although these letters, written over eight centuries, display a variety of concerns, they also reveal similarities which can now be seen as forming a tradition of women's writing. Certain aspects stand out. First, the need to use writing to communicate with a wider circle than the family, or small community, in which the women lived. Writing was obviously of tremendous importance in replacing lack of freedom to move physically with this freedom to correspond with the outside world.

The women letter-writers' ability to use many types of discourse is evident. They include the conversational, the descriptive, the dramatic, the caring, the spiritual – some of which may be termed 'feminine' – and rational, philosophical discourse, sometimes termed 'patriarchal', since it was too frequently the preserve of males in power, in law and in the Church. With many women, skill in using the pen to persuade was highly developed. This can be seen, for instance, in the missives of Hildegard of Bingen to Popes, Elizabeth I's letters to her father, and in recent epistolary novels.

The warmth of female relationships, which male society scarcely recognized until recently, can also be seen significantly in sisters, such as Lady Mary Wortley Montagu, Fanny Burney, and Jane Austen, who developed close lasting friendships with their sisters. Their letters, despite radical differences, reveal honesty, love, compassion, truthful analysis and humility

– values extolled by ethical and religious codes but seldom seen in the more public world of men. Furthermore these letters form a precious new primary source for study of the past. Women's letters give us a new type of history. The lost voices of the past are restored to the reader of this book.

Notes

1. *Women, Letters and the Novel*, Ruth Perry, A.M.S. Press, N.Y., 1980.
2. Ibid.
3. Preface to *Sociable Letters*, Margaret Cavendish, Duchess of Newcastle, 1664.
4. To Elizabeth Carter, 1782. *Mrs Montagu 'Queen of the Blues': Her Letters and Friendships from 1762 to 1800*, ed. R. Blunt (Constable n.d.) pp. 11, 119.
5. 'A Series of Letters between Mrs Elizabeth Carter and Miss Catherine Talbot from 1741 to 1770'. London 1809 (pub. n.k.)

Further Reading

Writing the Female Voice: Essays on Epistolary Literature, Elizabeth C. Goldsmith, Northeastern Univerity Press, Boston, 1989.

Women's Letters: The Feminist Approach

Recent criticism offers varied and skilful ways to analyse these letters: post-modernism, post-colonialism, deconstruction, Black feminist criticism, French literary criticism and New Historicism.

Post-modernism uncovers the non-masterful voice of much recent writing – and of many of these letters. Since the Middle Ages women have disclaimed the master narrative of history, the imposition of over-arching theory to explain multifarious 'reality'. Women generally refuse to be an 'authority' on topics such as moral wisdom, unlike Lord Chesterfield in his letters to his son. They show there is another cognitive space, a less arrogant, less definitive way of inscribing the 'I' of the defining self.

Women who enjoyed power, such as Saint Teresa of Avila, Catherine the Great and La Pasionaria, demonstrate the ability to deploy many discourses. These can be read as constant difference and plurality, because they considered themselves the equals of male leaders when angered, but knew when to exploit female wiles to persuade. When discussing topics they had considered in depth, such as politics or religion, they wrote with clarity of argument and moral perspective. Many less powerful women also possess rich diversity of register, including Mrs Gaskell, Madame de Staël and Rosalía de Castro (in nineteenth-century Spain). This diversity undermines the concept of the unified self. It supports the deconstructive view of identity as a cultural construct, never finalized, constantly shifting.

Jacques Derrida has pointed out the inadequacy of Western construction of the 'Other'. How far has the hegemonic conceptual framework prevented culture from discovering the genuine 'otherness' of women's letters? Derrida claims the other cannot be invented; it must 'come upon us' (*in-venire*) after we have deconstructed our habitual categories for apprehending the world (*Psyche*, '*Inventions de l'autre*,' Galilée, Paris, 1987, pp. 11–16). Even when patriarchal artists consider they 'invent', they are merely re-inscribing their own concepts. These letter-writers display the diversity of possible definitions of the other. Hildegard of Bingen, Elizabeth I, George Sand, Fanny Burney, George Eliot, offer a wide range of discourses in their letters, from dominating to passionate, from meditative to reasoning on public issues. They can be read as disruptive texts, blurring binary definitions of gender attributes, between 'high' and 'low' registers, between culture and subcultures.

Another way of approaching these letters is to analyse them according to Julia Kristeva's three categories in her 1969 study of the 'subject-in-process' in *Women's Time*. She outlined three generations of women: the first she defined as those who work *within* the symbolic, male order; the second counter-identify, while the third undo fixed notions of gender identity. This third category is seen by some critics, even Terry Eagleton, as disturbing. I would argue, like Kristéva, that it allows us to envisage a new space for women.

Women's letters show evidence of all three categories since the twelfth century. And close reading of *some* of these letters reveals Kristéva's third category of the undoing of fixed notions of gender. That is implicit in some of the wording of women in power, such as Queens and Abbesses.

Study of letters is in the forefront of comparative literature studies, which have developed beyond the comparing of literature in two distinct languages. Now differing cultural conceptions, approaches and impositions are analysed. The novelist Angela Carter and Professor Susan Basnett look at ways in which hegemonic languages have 'colonized' minds. They are de-colonizing in showing up male attempts to 'feminize' the unknown. In an era of post-colonialism, it is not far-fetched to see parallels between the physical liberating of countries and the metaphorical freeing of women's minds from at least some areas of patriarchal power, when they take up their pens to inscribe their ideas.

Letters are written in the first person, which can resemble the first person of narrative fiction, and also include 'realistic' and idealizing modes. As in autobiography, the 'I' ranges from the singular to the third person plural. We all possess multiplicity, frequently stifled by patriarchy. Many unknown young letter-writers, such as Stéphanie Jullien (see p. 19), resemble novelists like Marguerite Duras, who, in semi-autobiographical novellas, cannot fix 'self', finds no centre. This 'deconstruction' of her situation is addressed to a male reader, like many female narratives. Duras often apostrophizes a 'you' who is implicitly male. Jullien's male is explicit, the bourgeois patriarch who has obviously criticized her dilemma as 'indecision', the social refusal of meaningful work as 'leisure'. She demonstrates that it is in and by language that we define identity. This young female's identity is fractured, exceedingly fragile, imposed by males; her use of different discourses strives to free her 'I' from the 'I' of classifying patriarchy.

Jullien's questioning, and some of her vocabulary, may be called 'feminine'. This word is problematic, though frequently used in the sense of 'different from the masculine' and/or 'culturally constructed'. In literary criticism it often incorporates Cixous' definition of '*écriture féminine*' as being less fixed than male, with more fluid sentences, linked with bodily rhythms, our sexuality. Thus the long parentheses of a Dorothy Richardson are 'feminine' but so are many sentences of avant-garde male writers such as James Joyce and Proust. We still need a satisfactory definition of 'feminine' writing which struggles to enunciate identity while UNdoing categories. I tentatively propose 'uncovering new levels of meaning' and/or 'linking conscious and unconscious elements'.

Letters such as George Eliot's, on page 24, can be analysed as '*écriture féminine*', as they are an outpouring on many levels. Cixous maintains that women include the semiotic and the symbolic, the freedom of early childhood expression and the greater rigidity of the 'law of the father', of culturally determined norms. 'Semiotic' can be defined as the pre-oedipal, pre-imaginary rupturing of meaning, while the 'symbolic' represents the order of patriarchal language and culture.

Conclusion

We read *past* texts from the perspective of present-day knowledge and concerns, yet there is a significant difference between those who attempt to read them in their historical difference from the present, and those who merely seek to convert them into current categories. Both attitudes are valid, ever since Barthes pronounced the 'the author is dead'. However contemporary re-readings may lead us to judge limitations of past women, rather than place them in the context of their restricting cultures. Where possible, it is more productive to read for historical meanings rather than relevance to our expectations. Studying these past letters for their difference from the present, both historical and sexual, underlines both historical relativity and cultural construction. Such a process should help toward our understanding of the past *and* of gender formation.

A further fruitful way to analyse women's letters is the New Historicist approach. New Historicism, inspired by Professor Greenblatt in America, stresses that the artist functions within *many* processes, representing society to itself. The literary and the non-literary cannot be divided – as we notice in these letters. This new school of criticism asks us to grasp the social presence of the text in the world more sensitively, as Black feminist literary critics do also. They both point out that history is not purely descriptive, nor static; historical documents can be considered for their discourses, symbolism, etc., like literature. New Historicists maintain that 'Literature is a primary document' and I maintain that these letters form a vital primary source, certainly for historical and women's studies. The relationship between literature and history is notoriously problematic, so a study of the synchronic text, as part of a whole culture, is to be welcomed. I have tried to show, as Professor Greenblatt proposed, that there are no hierarchies, and 'to make the past live'.

one

How Women View Their Roles

Too little is still known about how women in the past differed from women today. The letters that follow give insights into explicit and implicit attitudes and how far gender division was accepted by most women. Did four walls and long skirts restrict the mind more than the body? When ideas of the inferiority of women were enshrined in religion and legislation, how many felt able to express their discontent?

There appear times when women have unselfconsciously used the language of patriarchy, even adopted the approach of males. Patriarchal discourse and assumptions are present in the letters of twelfth-century Hildegard of Bingen, Elizabeth I, and Anaïs Nin in the twentieth century. This could be partially explained by their upbringing, or by a temporary increase in equality. Feminists such as Dale Spender argue that history is cyclical, that women's movements have recurred, been suppressed, only to resurface in another period. These letters provide primary source material on this contentious issue of possible progress.

Also highlighted are the many different ways in which women reacted to cultural constructing of 'femininity'. The very fact of being literate, being able to pick up a pen to manipulate words may have given them a sense of self-worth. Nevertheless, throughout the centuries dependent girls, from medieval Dorothy Plumpton to nineteenth-century Stéphanie Jullien, reveal themselves in more anxious and pleading registers than the few who exercised power (see pp. 39–40, 89–90).

In each century writing ranges from the forceful deployment of reason and argument to a variety of affectionate, emotional, dramatic and descriptive registers or styles, from Héloïse in the twelfth century to the present.

More is now available from the Middle Ages, thanks to feminist historians. The letters of Hildegard of Bingen, recently translated from the Latin, show she could be bold when writing to Popes; yet when asking for support, from Saint Bernard of Clairvaux, she used strategies suggesting the weakness of her sex, in order to beg for his much-needed male ecclesiastical support for her bold visionary preaching.

Héloïse, at roughly the same time, wrote in the scholastic language she had learnt in her uncle's house, while pleading for a letter from her adored Abelard, fusing 'feminine' attributes in religious registers. Paris proved less chauvinist than most capitals and in the late fourteenth century, the first professional woman writer emerged: Christine de Pisan. Though born in Italy, as her name suggests, her father went to work in Paris when she was young. That is where she married and wrote her seminal works, even disputing the sexism of *Le Roman de la Rose* publicly. Like many women, she published first out of economic necessity, as she was widowed at twenty-five, and had three young children to support. She explicitly offered role models in *The City of Ladies* (1405), written in praise of women.

In seventeenth-century France, under Louis XIV, aristocrats had enforced leisure, in which they could analyse their feelings, as shown in the burgeoning novels about love, and the letters of Madame de Sévigné. The short extract here stresses the unpretentiousness which is a trait noticeable in many female letters from the time of Hildegard, a humility often used as a strategy. Women were particularly praised for the 'sensibility' of their letters in seventeenth-century France, which saw the publication of anthologies of their work.

England, after the Civil War, offered less leisure. But some aristocratic women, notably Lady Margaret Cavendish, inherited money, and she was able to write as she wished, thanks to an unusually understanding husband. The public letter included is addressed 'To All Writing Women'. It exploits rhetoric in a way few women did, probably because she wished to make public statements, like the Latin orators seldom taught to girls.

From her time, women rebelled more overtly against restrictions, and by the eighteenth century were expressing themselves with striking clarity, whether writing to men or women, but especially to women they knew well, such as Lady Mary Wortley Montagu who wrote skilfully on girls' education. In this extract to her daughter she expresses clear ideas for her granddaughter, advising her against breeding 'a fine lady qualifying her for a station in which she will never appear, and at the same time incapacitating her for that retirement for which she is destined'. Such advice might seem to emanate from a poverty-stricken pen. The fact that it comes from the daughter of the Earl of Kingston, whose husband was an ambassador, is first-hand evidence of the low public esteem of even well-born women.

Mary Hays and Mary Wollstonecraft felt a little freer just before the French Revolution, when what might be called a feminist movement surfaced. They expounded public issues, the rights of women, their social position, the need for franchise, demands for education. However, Hays lived long enough to feel the backlash against feminism (and revolutionaries) in the late 1790s, and softened her political statements with her Christian beliefs.

To counteract such subversiveness, many middle-class writers, mainly men, expounded on female duties. These hierarchical, proclaimedly Christian attitudes were often interiorized by women, who wrote letters, both real and fictitious, usually to daughters, on topics such as duty towards husbands, female education, and proper behaviour. From the 1740s there were attempts to define women's roles and determine sexual ethics. Mary Astell had already written on wifely submission, in 1700, but with irony; whereas Hannah More, in 1799, stressed obedience, while advocating education ('industry and humility are worth more than splendour'). Lady Pennington (1761) advised 'discreet improvement' of indifferent males, and education of daughters – strategies of subversion and adaptation, a frequent necessity.

The nineteenth century saw an increase in the availability of education, though slowly. There was a wider spectrum of female letter-writers, from middle-class wives with enforced leisure, to girls forced to support themselves in one of the few new professions, teaching. Village schools, ragged schools and Sunday schools were being founded, generally underfunded, but at least keeping some children out of factory work while imparting a modicum of literacy. Primary education for all was not introduced in England until 1873, later than in France and Germany, and cost a penny a week, even from the unemployed. Capitalism was also producing industrialists who employed governesses for their offspring, hoping to resemble the aristocracy. Many letters from lonely, underpaid young middle-class women testify to their usually undignified treatment, and misery in old age.

By the 1850s, with Victoria securely on a now respected throne, more women felt able to lead public campaigns against the harsh treatment of their sex, of poor children, and of the working class. The letters of Caroline Norton are impressive, since her arguments are both reasoned and forceful. She campaigned for years, and finally brought about some improvement for brutally treated wives. Women like her devoted years of their lives to fighting for women's rights. They succeeded in alleviating various harsh laws (against prostitutes, etc.), in creating the first colleges of higher education for women, and in winkling an opening to some of the professions, such as medicine. This struggle was pursued far more publicly by the suffragettes, though even they had little success till after the First World War.

The letter here from Millicent Fawcett, who campaigned for women's suffrage, is a private one, showing her sense of perspective, tact and humour, despite setbacks. Women are allowed to reveal their sense of fun and wit far more publicly in the late twentieth century. One of my aims with these letters is to show that women always enjoyed humour, in areas where not repressed by patriarchal mores. Fay Weldon, one of whose semi-fictional letters to her niece is also included, commented to me that women were inhibited until very recently by the need not to displease the men on whom they were economically dependent. Weldon exemplifies the freedom of economically in dependent twentieth-century women to state what they really think about male behaviour. The extract here is ostensibly from a work of fiction, but used polemically to broadcast one of her feminist messages.

As there is little from virtually silent majorities such as Muslim women, I have included a letter from an African epistolary novel. The author voices the stoicism necessary to ill-treated wives. The chapter ends on a completely new tone, a lesbian proud of her love, examining the potential of lesbian relationships. It is significant that these three letters were published in the early eighties. Three vastly different twentieth-century attitudes to women's predicaments are voiced, all skilful, all individual, yet preoccupied with the lot of other women and with working out strategies for survival – by wielding the pen.

'Your Superior Wisdom'

This letter is from Héloïse to her beloved Abelard, in twelfth-century Paris. Abelard was in the church, and it would have ruined his promising career if churchmen in power learned that he was having a passionate love affair. Here she claims she would rather be his 'whore' than his wife, in order to allow him to pursue his studies. Her selflessness was not rewarded, because her uncle, an ecclesiastic, put a cruel end to their love by castrating Abelard, and shutting her in a convent. She proved so able that she soon became Abbess.

Twelfth Century

Your superior wisdom knows better than our humble learning of the many serious treatises which the holy Fathers compiled for the instruction or exhortation or even the consolation of holy women, and of the care with which these were composed. And so in the precarious early days of our conversion long ago I was not a little surprised and troubled by your forgetfulness, when neither reverence for God nor our mutual love nor the example of the holy Fathers made you think of trying to comfort me, wavering and exhausted as I was by prolonged grief, either by word when I was with you or by letter when we had parted. Yet you must know that you are bound to me by an obligation which is all the greater for the further close tie of the marriage sacrament uniting us, and are the deeper in my debt because of the love I have always borne you, as everyone knows, a love which is beyond all bounds.

You know, beloved, as the whole world knows, how much I have lost in you, how at one wretched stroke of fortune that supreme act of flagrant treachery robbed me of my very self in robbing me of you; and how my sorrow for my loss is nothing compared with what I feel for the manner in which I lost you. Surely the greater the cause for grief the greater the need for the help of consolation, and this no one can bring but you; you are the sole cause of my sorrow, and you alone can grant me the grace of consolation. You alone have the power to make me sad, to bring me happiness or comfort; you alone have so great a debt to repay me, particularly now when I have carried out all your orders so implicitly that I was powerless to oppose you in anything, I found strength at your command to destroy myself. I did more, strange to say – my love rose to such heights of madness that it robbed itself of what it most desired beyond hope of recovery, when immediately at your bidding I changed my clothing along with my mind, in order to prove you the sole possessor of my body and my will alike. God knows I never sought anything in you except yourself; I wanted simply you, nothing of yours. I looked for no marriage-bond, no marriage portion, and it was not my own pleasures and wishes I sought to gratify, as you well know, but yours. The name of wife may seem more sacred or more binding, but sweeter for me will always be the word mistress, or, if you will permit me, that of concubine or whore. I believed that the more I humbled myself on your account, the more gratitude I should win from you, and also the less damage I should do to the brightness of your reputation.

I beg you, think what you owe me, give ear to my plea for a word from you, and I will finish with a brief ending:

farewell, my only love

ED. AND TRANS. B. RADICE, *EPISTOLA* (1974)

'Provide Your Servant-Girl With Comfort'

Hildegard of Bingen was respected by many churchmen in the twelfth century for her preaching and her visions. In 1141 she felt commanded by God to record her mystical visions. However she needed support and here writes to the authoritative Bernard of Clairvaux, currently preaching the Second Crusade.

1147

Reverend Father Bernard, the great honours you have attained through the power of God are a source of wonder; you are truly to be feared by the lawless folly of this world. Under the banner of the Holy Cross, you draw men in exalted devotion, burning with love for the Son of God, to do battle in Christ's army against the savagery of the heathens. I beg you, father, through the living God, to listen to me as I question you. I am greatly troubled by this vision which has appeared to me through the inspiration of divine mystery. I have never seen it with the outer eyes of the flesh. Wretched as I am (and more than wretched in bearing the name of woman) I have seen, ever since I was a child, great miracles, which my tongue could not utter had the Spirit of God not shown me them so that I might believe. Most true and gentle Father, answer in your goodness, your unworthy maidservant. For never, since I was a child, have I lived an hour free from care. Provide your servant-girl with comfort from your heart.

For in the text, I understand the inner meaning of the exposition of the Psalms and Gospels and the other books which are shown to me by this vision. The vision touches my heart and soul like a burning flame, showing me these depths of interpretation. Yet it does not show me writings in the German tongue – these I do not understand. I only know how to read the words as a single unit – I cannot pull the text apart for analysis.

So tell me please what all this seems to you to signify – for I am someone untaught by any schooling in external matters (though I have been taught within, in my soul), so that I speak, as though in doubt. But having heard of your wisdom and your holiness, I know that I will be comforted. For I have not dared to tell these things to anyone (since I have heard that there are many schisms in the world) except to a certain monk whose conduct in the community won my approval. To him I revealed all my secrets and he did indeed reassure me that these were great and worthy of reverence. Father, for the love of God, I want you to comfort me, and I will be certain.

Two years ago, I saw you in this vision as one who looked into the sun without being frightened – a truly brave man. And I wept because I blush so deeply and am so timorous.

Noble and most gentle Father, I depend upon your soul. Make it clear to me, if you will, through this exchange, whether I should say these things in the open or maintain my silence. For it costs me great pains to say what I have seen and heard in this vision. Yet, because I have kept silent, I have been laid out by this vision all this time on my bed, in great sickness, unable even to lift myself up. And so I wail before you, in sorrow. For I am prone to the motion of the wine-press lever in my nature – the nature sprung from the root that rose from the Devil's promptings, which entered into Adam, and made him an outcast in an alien world. But now, rising up, I run to you. I tell you: You are not moved by that lever but are always lifting it up. You are a vanquisher in your soul, raising not just yourself, but the world as well, towards salvation.

Farewell. Be strong in your soul Amen.

ED. M. FOX, *LETTERS OF HILDEGARD OF BINGEN* (1987)

'Be Pure, Simple and Serene'

At the end of the fourteenth century Christine de Pisan offered this advice for girls and women. It comes from the prefatory open letter at the beginning of her magnificent City of Ladies *where she praises the little recognized virtues of women, in an imaginary city without men. Though from Italy, she lived and wrote in Paris for most of her life.*

1405

And you, virgin maidens, be pure, simple, and serene, without vagueness, for the snares of evil men are set for you. Keep your eyes lowered, with few words in your mouths, and act respectfully. Be armed with the strength of virtue against the tricks of the deceptive and avoid their company.

And widows, may there be integrity in your dress, conduct, and speech; piety in your deeds and way of life; prudence in your bearing; patience (so necessary!) strength, and resistance in tribulations and difficult affairs; humility in your heart, countenance, and speech; and charity in your works.

In brief, all women – whether noble, bourgeois, or lower-class – be well-informed in all things and cautious in defending your honor and chastity against your enemies! My ladies, see how these men accuse you of so many vices in everything. Make liars of them all by showing forth your virtue, and prove their attacks false by acting well, so that you can say with the Psalmist, 'the vices of the evil will fall on their heads.' Repel the deceptive flatterers who, using different charms, seek with various tricks to steal that which you must consummately guard, that is, your honor and the beauty of your praise. Oh my ladies, flee, flee the foolish love they urge on you! Flee it, for God's sake, flee! For no good can come to you from it. Rather, rest assured that however deceptive their lures, their end is always to your detriment. And do not believe the contrary, for it cannot be otherwise. Remember, dear ladies, how these men call you frail, unserious, and easily influenced but yet try hard, using all kinds of strange and deceptive tricks, to catch you, just as one lays traps for wild animals. Flee, flee, my ladies, and avoid their company – under these smiles are hidden deadly and painful poisons. And so may it please you, my most respected ladies, to cultivate virtue, to flee vice, to increase and multiply our City, and to rejoice and act well. And may I, your servant, commend myself to you, praying to God who by His grace has granted me to live in this world and to persevere in His holy service. May He in the end have mercy on my great sins and grant to me the joy which lasts forever, which I may, by His grace, afford to you. Amen.

TRANS. E.V. RICHARDS, *CITY OF LADIES* (1982)

Elizabeth I Rejects Erik of Sweden

Elizabeth I skilfully rejected the proposal of King Erik of Sweden, who set out to woo her in August 1560.

25 February 1561

Most Serene Prince Our Very Dear Cousin,

A letter truly yours both in the writing and sentiment was given us on 30 December by your very dear brother, the Duke of Finland. And while we perceive therefrom that the zeal and love of your mind towards us is not diminished, yet in part we are grieved that we cannot gratify your Serene Highness with the same kind of affection. And that indeed does not happen because we doubt in any way of your love and honour, but, as often we have testified both in words and writing, that we have never yet conceived a feeling of that kind of affection towards anyone. We therefore beg your Serene Highness again and again that you be pleased to set a limit to your love, that it advance not beyond the laws of friendship for the present nor disregard them in the future. And we in our turn shall take care that whatever can be required for the holy preservation of friendship between Princes we will always perform towards your Serene Highness. It seems strange for your Serene Highness to write that you understand from your brother and your ambassadors that we have entirely determined not to marry an absent husband; and that we will give you no certain reply until we shall have seen your person.

We certainly think that if God ever direct our heart to consideration of marriage we shall never accept or choose any absent husband how powerful and wealthy a Prince soever. But that we are not to give you an answer until we have seen your person is so far from the thing itself that we never even considered such a thing. But I have always given both to your brother, who is certainly a most excellent prince and deservedly very dear to us, and also to your ambassador likewise the same answer with scarcely any variation of the words, that we do not conceive in our heart to take a husband, but highly commend this single life, and hope that your Serene Highness will no longer spend time in waiting for us.

God keep your Serene Highness for many years in good health and safety. From our Palace at Westminster, 25 February
Your Serene Highness' sister and cousin,

Elizabeth

MARIA PERRY, *THE WORD OF A PRINCE: A LIFE OF ELIZABETH I* (1990)

A True and Constant Friendship

Madame de Sévigné is, I consider, the greatest French letter-writer. She spent part of her time in the Court of Louis XIV, about whom we learn a great deal. She was a beauty, but preferred to devote her love to her children, especially her daughter, when she was widowed in her twenties. She had the ability to keep the friendship of many men who admired her. Here she writes to a now-forgotten poet, Ménage. He gained a name at court, wooed her, and later married another. However he did not forget her, wrote to her again in their forties, and received this warm, honest reply:

23 June 1656

Your remembrance of me is a real joy: it has renewed all the pleasure of our old friendship. Your verses have reminded me of my youth, and I wonder why the loss of such a good thing does not make me sad. The verses have given me pleasure, while I think they should have made me weep. But without going into the question of where the feeling comes from, I like whatever it is makes me feel thankful for your gift. You will readily understand that it is pleasant to have one's self-love so much flattered and to be celebrated in this way by the best poet of one's time. But it would have been better for your honour as a poet if I had been more worthy of all you have said about me. However, whatever I have been and whatever I am, I shall never forget your true and constant friendship, and all my life I shall be the most grateful as well as the oldest of your very humble servants.

TRANS. L. TANCOCK, *MADAME DE SÉVIGNÉ: SELECTED LETTERS* (1982)

The Need for Learning

Lady Mary Wortley Montagu lived at the time of Pope, Dr Johnson and Addison. She became well known for her lively interest in intellectual and social concerns, particularly women's rights and education. Her lively correspondence appears in various chapters of this study, as she wrote in many registers on people, places and, above all, ideas. Her husband proved dull and once her children were adult she decided to live in Italy. She was delighted to hear that her daughter, the Countess of Bute, was enjoying the company of her own daughters. In this letter she gives unusual advice on the need for developing interests, since even a rich woman is 'destined' for a retiring life.

To the Countess of Bute

Louvere, Jan. 28, N.S., 1753

DEAR CHILD, – You have given me a great deal of satisfaction by your account of your eldest daughter. I am particularly pleased to hear she is a good arithmetician; it is the best proof of understanding: the knowledge of numbers is one of the chief distinctions between us and brutes. If there is anything in blood, you may reasonably expect your children should be endowed with an uncommon share of good sense. Mr Wortley's family and mine have both produced some of the greatest men that have been born in England. I will therefore speak to you as supposing Lady Mary not only capable, but desirous of learning: in that case by all means let her be indulged in it. You will tell me I did not make it a part of your education: your prospect was very different from hers. As you had much in your circumstances to attract the highest offers, it seemed your business to learn how to live in the world, as it is hers, to know how to be easy out of it. It is the common error of builders and parents to follow some plan they think beautiful (and perhaps is so), without considering that nothing is beautiful which is displaced. Hence we see so many edifices raised that the raisers can never inhabit, being too large for their fortunes. Vistas are laid open over barren heaths, and apartments contrived for a coolness very agreeable in Italy, but killing in the north of Britain; thus every woman endeavours to breed her daughter a fine lady, qualifying her for a station in which she will never appear, and at the same time incapacitating her for that retirement, to which she is destined. Learning, if she has a real taste for it, will not only make her contented, but happy in it. No entertainment is so cheap as reading, nor any pleasure so lasting. She will not want new fashions, nor regret the loss of expensive diversions, or variety of company, if she can be amused with an author, in her closet. To render this amusement complete, she should be permitted to learn the languages. I have heard it lamented that boys lose so many years in mere learning of words: this is no objection to a girl, whose time is not so precious: she cannot advance herself in any profession,

11

and has therefore more hours to spare; and as you say her memory is good, she will be very agreeably employed this way. There are two cautions to be given on this subject: first, not to think herself learned, when she can read Latin, or even Greek. Languages are more properly to be called vehicles of learning than learning itself, as may be observed in many schoolmasters, who, though perhaps critics in grammar, are the most ignorant fellows upon earth. True knowledge consists in knowing things, not words. I would no farther wish her a linguist than to enable her to read books in their originals, that are often corrupted, and are always injured by translations. Two hours' application every morning will bring this about much sooner than you can imagine, and she will have leisure enough beside, to run over the English poetry, which is a more important part of a woman's education than it is generally supposed. This subject is apt to run away with me. I'll trouble you no more with it.

Your mother M. Wortley
ED. R. HALSBAND, *THE SELECTED LETTERS OF LADY MARY WORTLEY MONTAGU* (1971)

A Poet's Dream

We have too little from working class or peasant women, though feminists have now discovered a tradition of those responding to a fashion for 'primitive' poetry. The most famous is Ann Yearsley, encouraged by Hannah More in the eighteenth century. Another underestimated poet was Mary Leapor (1722–46), daughter of a gardener. This extract is from a poem written to other women about fears of the illness which led to her death at the age of twenty-four. It is particularly moving, since she knew she was about to die and had no hope of being noticed as a poet, being a poor man's daughter. Written only a few months before her death, she refers to herself as 'Mira' and recounts a dream which she contrasts to her kitchen work in 'dusty walls' with merely 'sliding joys'.

I include two extracts from verse epistles, because this form became fashionable in the Renaissance, when it was imported from Italy. It was popular among aristocrats able to make the Grand Tour through France and Italy. Women soon showed their proficiency at this demanding form, though they had to learn the skill on their own, unlike men. It is striking that Mary Leapor was able to master the demands of rhyming couplets at such a young, untutored age.

Yet Mira dreams, as slumb'ring poets may,
And rolls in treasures till the breaking day,
While books and pictures in bright order rise,
And painted parlours swim before her eyes:
Till the shrill clock impertinently rings,
And the soft visions move their shining wings:
Then Mira wakes – her pictures are no more,
And through her fingers slides the vanished ore.
Convinced too soon, her eye unwilling falls
On the blue curtains and the dusty walls:
She wakes, alas! to business and to woes,
To sweep her kitchen, and to mend her clothes.
But see pale Sickness with her languid eyes,
At whose appearance all delusion flies:
The world recedes, its vanities decline,
Clorinda's features seem as faint as mine:
Gay robes no more the aching sight admires,
Wit grates the ear, and melting music tires.
Its wonted pleasures with each sense decay,
Books please no more, and paintings fade away,
The sliding joys in misty vapours end:
Yet let me still, ah! let me grasp a friend:
And when each joy, when each loved object flies,
Be you the last that leaves my closing eyes.
But how will this dismantled soul appear,
When stripped of all it lately held so dear,
Forced from its prison of expiring clay,
Afraid and shiv'ring at the doubtful way?
Yet did these eyes a dying parent see,
Loosed from all cares except a thought for me,
Without a tear resign her short'ning breath,
And dauntless meet the ling'ring stroke of death.
Then at th' Almighty's sentence shall I mourn,
'Of dust thou art, to dust shalt thou return'?
Or shall I wish to stretch the line of fate,
That the dull years may bear a longer date,
To share the follies of succeeding times,
With more vexations and with deeper crimes?

Ah no – though heav'n brings near the final day,
For such a life I will not, dare not pray:
But let the tear for future mercy flow,
And fall resigned beneath the mighty blow.

EDS. D. SPENDER AND J. TODD, *ANTHOLOGY OF BRITISH WOMEN WRITERS*
(1989)

'Vain Regret'

Apprehension about the reception of their writing has worried women from the time of Hildegard to today's young novelists, such as Maggie Gee. Here, Charlotte Smith uses the verse epistle to bemoan the fate of her novel Emmeline, *intended for print, then suppressed in 1782. Smith (1749–1806), a prolific poet and novelist, was forced to support her many children when her husband was imprisoned for debt. Her long Gothic novels were relatively successful, especially the first,* Emmeline, *finally published in 1788. She pleased the Romantic taste: 'I wrote mournfully because I was unhappy.'*

1787

O'erwhelm'd with sorrow, and sustaining long
'The proud man's contumely, th'oppressor's wrong,'
Languid despondency, and vain regret,
Must my exhausted spirit struggle yet?
Yes! – Robb'd myself of all that fortune gave,
Even of all hope – but shelter in the grave,
Still shall the plaintive lyre essay its powers
To dress the cave of Care with Fancy's flowers,
Maternal Love the fiend Despair withstand,
Still animate the heart and guide the hand.
– May you, dear objects of my anxious care,
Escape the evils I was born to bear!
Round *my* devoted head while tempests roll,
Yet there, where I have treasured up my soul,
May the soft rays of dawning hope impart
Reviving Patience to my fainting heart: –
And when its sharp solicitudes shall cease,
May I be conscious in the realms of peace

That every tear which swells my children's eyes,
From sorrows past, not present ills arise.
Then, with some friend who loves to share your pain,
For 'tis my boast that *some* such friends remain,
By filial grief, and fond remembrance prest,
You'll seek the spot where all my sorrows rest.

Charlotte Smith, Emmeline (1788)

Mary Hays Appeals to Men on behalf of Women, in a Range of Discourses, from Ironic to Rationalist

Mary Hays was born in 1760 of a Dissenting family. Her fiancé died before the wedding and her later passion for a philosopher was not requited, which made her well aware of the sufferings of women, to which she draws public attention in 1798:

Dear generous creatures!

Of all the systems which human nature in its moments of intoxication has produced – if indeed a bundle of contradictions and absurdities may be called a system – that which men have contrived with a view to forming the minds, and regulating the conduct of women, is perhaps the most completely absurd. And, though the consequences are often very serious to both sexes, yet if one could for a moment forget these, and consider it only as a system, it would rather be found a subject of mirth . . .

How great in some parts of their conduct, how insignificant upon the whole, would men have women to be! For one example – when their love, their pride, their delicacy; in short, when all the finest feelings of humanity are insulted and put to the rack, what is expected? When a woman finds that the husband of her choice, the object of her most sincere and constant love, abandons himself to other attachments, infinitely cutting to a woman of sensibility and soul, what is expected of a creature declared weak by nature – and who is rendered weaker by education?

They expect that this poor weak creature, setting aside in a moment love, jealousy, and pride, the most powerful and universal passions interwoven in the human heart, and which even men, clothed in wisdom and fortitude, find so difficult to conquer, that they seldom attempt it – that she shall notwithstanding lay all these aside as easily as she would her gown and petticoat, and plunge at once into the cold bath of prudence, of which though the wife only is to receive the shock, and make daily use of, yet if she does so, it has the virtue of keeping both husband and wife in a most agreeable temperament. Prudence being one of those rare medicines which affect by sympathy; and this being likewise one of those cases, where the husbands have no objections to the wives acting as principals, nor to their receiving all the honors and emoluments of office; even if death should crown their martyrdom, as has been sometimes known to happen.

For, there are no vices to which a man addicts himself, no follies he can take it into his head to commit, but his wife and his nearest female relations are expected to connive at, are expected to look upon, if not with admiration, at least with respectful silence, and at awful distance. Any other conduct is looked upon, as a breach of that fanciful system of arbitrary authority, which men have so assiduously erected in their own favor; and any other conduct is accordingly resisted, with the most acrimonious severity.

A man, for example, is addicted to the destructive vice of drinking. His wife sees with terror and anguish the approach of this pernicious habit, and by anticipation beholds the evils to be dreaded to his individual health, happiness, and consequence: and the probable misery to his family. Yet with this melancholy prospect before her eyes, it is reckoned an unpardonable degree of harshness and imprudence, if she by any means whatever endeavour to check in the bud, this baleful practice; and she is in this case accused at all hands of driving him to pursue in worse places, that which he cannot enjoy in peace at home. And, when this disease gains ground, and ends in an established habit, she is treated as a fool for attempting a cure for what is incurable.

M. HAYS, *LETTERS AND ESSAYS, MORAL AND MISCELLANEOUS* (1793)

Mary Wollstonecraft to Talleyrand: Votes for Women

Mary Wollstonecraft (1759–97) was a novelist, essayist, travel writer, and a leading feminist and radical. She lived in France for two years, just after the French Revolution. It proclaimed 'Liberty, Fraternity and Equality', but did not extend these rights to women. Here she writes in 'patriarchal' registers to a leading French politician, Talleyrand, to persuade him of the wisdom of giving women the right to vote. In the new Constitution of 1791, only men *over twenty-five were considered citizens and allowed the vote. French women did not get the vote till 1944.*

1791

Consider, I address you as a legislator, whether, when men contend for their freedom, and to be allowed to judge for themselves respecting their own happiness, it be not inconsistent and unjust to subjugate women, even though you firmly believe that you are acting in the manner best calculated to promote their happiness? Who made man the exclusive judge, if women partake with him the gift of reason?

In this style, argue tyrants of every denomination, from the weak king to the weak father of a family; they are all eager to crush reason; yet always assert that they usurp its throne only to be useful. Do you not act a similar part, when you *force* all women, by denying them civil and political rights, to remain immured in their families groping in the dark? For surely, Sir, you will not assert, that a duty can be binding which is not founded on reason? If indeed this be their destination, arguments may be drawn from reason: and thus augustly supported, the more understanding women acquire, the more they will be attached to the duty – comprehending it – for unless they comprehend it, unless their morals be fixed on the same immutable principle as those of man, no authority can make them discharge it in a virtuous manner. They may be convenient slaves, but slavery will have its constant effect, degrading the master and the abject dependent.

But, if women are to be excluded, without having a voice, from a participation of the natural rights of mankind, prove first, to ward off the charge of injustice and inconsistency, that they want reason – else this flaw in your NEW CONSTITUTION will ever shew that man must, in some shape, act like a tyrant, and tyranny, in whatever part of society it rears its brazen front, will ever undermine morality.

I have repeatedly asserted, and produced what appeared to me irrefragable arguments drawn from matters of fact, to prove my assertion, that women cannot, by force, be confined to domestic concerns; for they will, however ignorant, intermeddle with more weighty affairs, neglecting private duties only to disturb, by cunning tricks, the orderly plans of reason which rise above their comprehension.

Noted for her path-breaking Vindication of the Rights of Woman, *Wollstonecraft had many intellectual men friends, including Dissenters. In 1787 she was befriended by her publisher, Johnson. He was a middle-aged bachelor and suggested she marry a young acquaintance to prevent gossip. She replied angrily in completely distinct discourses:*

1787

I will not be insulted by a superficial puppy – His intimacy with Miss —— gave him a privilege, which he should not have assumed with me – a proposal might be made to his cousin, a milliner's girl, which should not have been mentioned to me. Pray tell him that I am offended – and do not wish to see him again! – When I meet him at your house, I shall leave the room, since I cannot pull him by the nose. I can force my spirit to leave my body – but it shall never bend to support that body – God of heaven, save thy child from this living death!

I scarcely know what I write. My hand trembles – I am very sick – sick at heart.

Through Johnson she met the poet-painter Blake and the painter Fuseli, with whom she had an obsessive, unpromising relationship. She travelled alone to revolutionary France in 1792, and met Gilbert Imlay, an American writer and businessman. They fell in love, and later had a daughter in Le Havre. To her grief, he soon lost interest, and she attempted suicide. She despised Imlay's affairs with 'beings whom I feel to be my inferiors', yet to hate his behaviour would be to lose her dignity as a rational human being. However she could not prevent herself from expressing her hurt to him, while emphasizing her 'feminine' needs.

1794

Gracious God! It is impossible to stifle something like resentment, when I receive fresh proofs of your indifference. What I have suffered this last year, is not to be forgiven.

Love is a want of my heart. I have examined myself lately with more care than formerly, and find, that to deaden is not to calm the mind – Aiming at tranquility, I have almost destroyed all the energy of my soul . . . Despair, since the birth of my child, has rendered me stupid . . . the desire of regaining peace (do you understand me?) has made me forget the respect due to my own emotions – sacred emotions that are the sure harbingers of the delights I was formed to enjoy – and shall enjoy, for nothing can extinguish the heavenly spark.

CLAIRE TOMALIN, *The Life and Death of Mary Wollstonecraft*
(1974)

'An Excess of Moroseness'

Middle-class girls in the nineteenth century wanted some fulfilment in marriage. They also wanted to please their families, to help if possible. The Parisian Stéphanie Jullien was twenty-two when she wrote this to her father. Her worries about whether to marry make her anxious about her whole life and exacerbate her self-doubt.

Feb. 20, 1836

You want an answer to your letter and I believe, in reality, that this is the best way to express a thousand things that one can lose sight of during a conversation in which one speaks only with difficulty and embarrassment. . . . I don't want to enumerate my anxieties about the future, the discord in my family that I felt more than anyone else, the vexations my mother endured and to which I was the only witness and consolation, the six months passed in anguish and despair over her deathbed. . . . I only want you to understand that I know grief. You men have a thousand occupations to distract you: society, business, politics, and work absorb you, exhaust you, upset you. But all these things also help you forcibly. As for us women who, as you have said to me from time to time, have only the roses in life, we feel more profoundly in our solitude and in our idleness the sufferings that you can slough off. I don't want to make a comparison here between the destiny of man and the destiny of women: each sex has its own lot, its own troubles, its own pleasures. I only want to explain to you that excess of moroseness of which you complain and of which I am the first to suffer. My life has been sad, and my character shows it. But even now, when I do appear to be calm and happy, what anxieties, what worries about the future don't I have? I am not able to do anything for myself and for those around me. I am depriving my brothers in order to have a dowry. I am not even able to live alone, being obliged to take from others, not only in order to live but also in order to be protected, since social convention does not allow me to have independence. And yet the world finds me guilty of being the only person that I am at liberty to be; not having useful or productive work to do, not having any calling except marriage, and not being able to look by myself for someone who will suit me, I am full of cares and anxieties.

Is it astonishing that since any work that I could do would be *null* and *useless* for others as well as for myself, since it would not lead to anything, that I let myself be lazy, that I try to prolong my sleep in order to escape life? This laziness that you seem to reproach me for is really a means of discharging an excess of energy that has no outlet. If you believe that this *laziness* prevents me from doing anything, you are mistaken. I would quickly find courage and ardor again if I had some mission to fulfill or if some goal were proposed to me. But that is not the case. I don't have any calling, nor could I have one. That has been the most ardent of my wishes and no one will let me do it. I don't understand the reasons, and I'm not accusing anyone if I don't have a calling. I hope that one gives me the same benefit of a doubt, because it is not my fault. As for the sadness that I am accused of, one should not be astonished by it. This awkward position in which I find myself, my memories, my fears, my anxieties, often the delicacy of my health, are enough cause for it. . . . Would one be just if one reproached you for the annoyed and sad air that you often have?

EDS. E.O. HELLERSTEIN, L.P. HUME AND K.M. OFFEN, *VICTORIAN WOMEN*
(1981)

'How a Woman Cares for a Man'

Geraldine Jewsbury (1812–80) published six novels and contributed to Westminster Review *and* Household Words. *She spent many years housekeeping for her father and brother. Fortunately she met Jane Carlyle, who found a publisher for her first novel* Zoë *(1845). These two women had a great deal in common and when not in London both wrote lively, thoughtful, long letters. They express warmth, intelligent reflection on life and skill with words that deserve a wider audience. Here Jewsbury comments on the different attitudes men and women bring to relationships.*

15 June 1841

Dearest Jane,

There is a great deal I want to say to you, but when I begin it seems difficult, almost impossible, to put it down as it really is . . . How much I wish you would give me some of your own philosophy! One day, whilst at Seaforth, a youth I have known a long time took it into his head to be very confidential, and preached his own gospel for the space of a whole afternoon! He had been thrown on the world very young to shift for himself, and a real little youth of the world he had become. He looked so young – though he is twenty-five – that one could not call him a man! The mere facts that he told me were not disguised and beautified, yet the *morale* that stood out clear was to the effect that men cannot afford to be very long or very much in earnest in their intercourse with women: that when a woman got thoroughly earnest and engrossed, a man who had any regard for himself or her would break off at once! That *une grande passion* was an embarrassing affair, and was very dangerous to people who had to get a living, and that he had always broken off as soon as he came to his senses: that women seemed to think it was the only object of interest in life, and it was a desperate thing to let them go too far. One thing specially struck me – though this was not said to me, only repeated to me – viz., that all men who have received an English education hate a woman in proportion as she commits herself for them, though a woman cares for a man exactly in the proportion in which she has made sacrifices for him, evidently thinking and showing, he thought, that all that was in the world – business and riches and success and so forth – were the only realities, and the only things worth making objects! He is neither better nor worse, but an average specimen of the generality of men. He once did me a material piece of kindness, and he was not in love with me: he had taken a fit of kindness to a friend of mine, and he raised himself in my opinion, and showed more real feeling that I had supposed in him. To be sure, the fact that my friend did not care about him would account for his good behaviour; it was not in his power to behave ill! This will seem stupid to you, not knowing the people and the circumstances: but it had a great interest for me, and it set me moralising to think how much more miserable we should be than we are if we had our eyes opened to discern always true from make-believe. I have great sympathy with that prayer of the Ancient Mariner, 'O let me be awake, my God, or let me sleep away!' There is something else I long very much to tell you, but I dare not in a letter.

I wish there were some photographic process by which one's mind could be struck off and transferred to that of the friend we wish to know it, without the medium of this confounded letter-writing!

A poor lady of my acquaintance is in great trouble; she has just lost a daughter, of whom I was very fond, under most painful circumstances, and I must go and see her. It makes my heart sick to see her. Her husband is a great scoundrel; he left his family, after tormenting them to death, and now he increases their trouble by all sorts of vexations, and it makes me mad to hear people coolly say, 'I understand Mrs —— has a violent temper,' as if a woman was to be steel and marble under the most unprovoked outrages! I wish I might say my say about matrimony. This is a tremendously long letter.

God bless you, dear love. Take care of yourself, and write as soon as you can.

Ever yours G.E.J.

ED. A. IRELAND, *SELECTION FROM THE LETTERS OF GERALDINE E. JEWSBURY TO JANE WELSH CARLYLE* (1892)

A Married Woman Has No Legal Existence

In 1855, Caroline Norton, granddaughter of Sheridan and a fairly successful writer, wrote a letter to Queen Victoria on the Marriage and Divorce Bill. She had married the Honourable George Norton in 1827. He proved violent and mean, to the extent of refusing her access to their three children. She played a leading role in the agitation to reform the law, which made wives suffer so greatly when their husbands were unfaithful, cruel or unbalanced. This extract is taken from a lengthy, well-argued letter to the Queen, analysing skilfully the humiliations that many wives had to undergo. At last, in 1857, Parliament passed the Matrimonial Causes Act, which set up civil divorce courts.

1855

A married woman in England has *no legal existence.*

An English wife may not leave her husband's house. Not only can he sue her for 'restitution of conjugal rights,' but he has a right to enter the house of any friend or relation with whom she may take refuge, and who may 'harbour her,' – as it is termed, – and carry her away by force, with or without the aid of the police.

If the wife sue for separation for cruelty, it must be 'cruelty that endangers life or limb,' and if she has once forgiven, or, in legal phrase, '*condoned*' his offenses, she cannot plead them; though her past forgiveness only proves that she endured as long as endurance was possible.

If her husband takes proceedings for a divorce, she is not, in the first instance, allowed to defend herself. She has no means of proving the falsehood of his allegations. She is not represented by attorney, nor permitted to be considered a party to the suit between him and her supposed lover, for 'damages.' . . .

If an English wife be guilty of infidelity, her husband can divorce *her* so as to marry again; but she cannot divorce the husband, *a vinculo*, however profligate he may be. No law court can divorce in England. A special Act of Parliament annulling the marriage is passed for each case. The House of Lords grants this almost as a matter of course to the husband, but not to the wife. In only four instances (two of which were cases of incest) had the wife obtained a divorce to marry again.

She cannot prosecute for a libel. Her husband must prosecute; and in cases of enmity and separation, of course she is without a remedy. . . .

She cannot claim support, as a matter of personal right, from her husband. The general belief and nominal rule is, that her husband is 'bound to maintain her.' That is not the law. He is not bound to *her*. He is bound to his country; bound to see that she does not cumber the parish in which she resides. If it be proved that means sufficient are at her disposal, from relatives or friends, her husband is quit of his obligation, and need not contribute a farthing: even if he have deserted her; or be in receipt of money which is hers by inheritance. . . .

Separation from her husband by consent, or for his ill usage, does not alter their mutual relation. He retains the right to divorce her *after* separation, – as before, – though he himself be unfaithful.

Her being, on the other hand, of spotless character, and without reproach, gives her no advantage in law. She may have withdrawn from his roof knowing that he lives with 'his faithful housekeeper': having suffered personal violence at his hands; having 'condoned' much, and being able to prove it by unimpeachable testimony: or he may have shut the doors of her house against her: all this is quite immaterial: the law takes no cognisance of which is to blame. As *her husband*, he has a right to all that is hers: as *his wife*, she has no right to anything that is his. As her husband, he may divorce her. For his wife, the utmost 'divorce' is permission to live alone – married to his name. [Her husband spent the money she earned from writing, even when he had left her destitute. It was not illegal for him to do so – nor to take their three children.]

C. NORTON, 'A LETTER TO THE QUEEN ON LORD CHANCELLOR
CRANWORTH'S MARRIAGE AND DIVORCE BILL' (1855)

George Eliot Comforts a Friend

George Eliot wrote to a close friend, Mrs Robert Lytton, attempting to comfort her after the death of her uncle, Lord Clarendon, whom she had loved as a father. The writer offers thoughts of death as a means to help women live more independently.

8 July 1870

I did not like to write to you until Mr Lytton sent word that I might do so, because I had not the intimate knowledge that would have enabled me to measure your trouble; and one dreads of all things to speak or write a wrong or unseasonable word when words are the only signs of interest and sympathy that one has to give. I know now, from what your dear husband has told us, that your loss is very keenly felt by you, – that it has first made you acquainted with acute grief, and this makes me think of you very much. For learning to love any one is like an increase of property, – it increases care, and brings many new fears lest precious things should come to harm. I find myself often thinking of you with that sort of proprietor's anxiety, wanting you to have gentle weather all through your life, so that your face may never look worn and storm-beaten, and wanting your husband to be and do the very best, lest anything short of that should be disappointment to you. At present the thought of you is all the more with me, because your trouble has been brought by death; and for nearly a year death seems to me my most intimate daily companion. I mingle the thought of it with every other, not sadly, but as one mingles the thought of some one who is nearest in love and duty with all one's motives. I try to delight in the sunshine that will be when I shall never see it any more. And I think it is possible for this sort of impersonal life to attain great intensity – possible for us to gain much more independence, than is usually believed, of the small bundle of facts that make our own personality.

I don't know why I should say this to you, except that my pen is chatting as my tongue would if you were here. We women are always in danger of living too exclusively in the affections; and though our affections are perhaps the best gifts we have, we ought also to have our share of the more independent life – some joy in things for their own sake. It is piteous to see the helplessness of some sweet women when their affections are disappointed – because all their teaching has been, that they can only delight in study of any kind for the sake of a personal love. They have never contemplated an independent delight in ideas as an experience which they could confess without being laughed at. Yet surely women need this sort of defence against passionate affliction even more than men.

Just under the pressure of grief, I do not believe there is any consolation. The word seems to me to be drapery for falsities. Sorrow must be sorrow, ill must be ill, till duty and love towards all who remain recover their rightful predominance. Your life is so full of those claims, that you will not have time for brooding over the unchangeable. Do not spend any of your valuable time now in writing to me, but be satisfied with sending me news of you through Mr Lytton when he has occasion to write to Mr Lewes.

I have lately finished reading aloud Mendelssohn's *Letters*, which we had often resolved and failed to read before. They have been quite cheering to us, from the sense they give of communion with an eminently pure, refined nature, with the most rigorous conscience in art. In the evening we have always a concert to listen to – a concert of modest pretensions, but well conducted enough to be agreeable.

I hope this letter of chit-chat will not reach you at a wrong moment. In any case, forgive all mistakes on the part of one who is always yours sincerely and affectionately.

ED. G. HAIGHT, *THE GEORGE ELIOT LETTERS* (1954)

Millicent Fawcett to a Member of the House

Millicent Fawcett devoted her life to women's rights, for which she was often slandered publicly by men. Here she describes the tactful way she dealt with a Member of Parliament who vilified her.

Jan. 1872

A few days later a then well-known Member of Parliament, Mr C.R., referred publicly in the House of Commons to the appearance of Mrs Taylor and myself upon a platform to advocate votes for women, as 'two ladies, wives of members of this House, who had disgraced themselves,' and added that he would not further disgrace them by mentioning their names.

It so happened that a very short time after this, my husband and I were spending the week-end in Cambridge, and that most hospitable of men, Mr James Porter, of Peterhouse, [the victim of Mr Perkins's bulldog!] asked us to dine with him. What was my amusement to see Mr C.R. among the guests: this amusement was intensified into positive glee when he was asked to take me in to dinner. I could not resist expressing condolences with him on his unfortunate position. Should I ask Mr Porter to let him exchange me for some other lady who had not disgraced herself? But after we had let off steam a little in this way, I found him quite an agreeable neighbour at the table, and so far as I know, he never again publicly held up any woman to contempt for advocating the enfranchisement of her own sex. After all, what he had said was very mild compared to Horace Walpole's abuse of Mary Wollstonecraft as 'a hyena in petticoats'.

RAY STRACHEY, *MILLICENT FAWCETT* (1931)

A Muslim Wife's Stoicism

Female stoicism was harrowingly expressed in the epistolary novel So Long a Letter by Mariama Bâ, first published in French in 1980. Mariama Bâ was Senegalese. She married the Minister of Education, who divorced her after she had given him nine children.

When I stopped yesterday, I probably left you astonished by my disclosures.

Was it madness, weakness, irresistible love? What inner confusion led Modou Fall [her husband] to marry Binetou?

To overcome my bitterness, I think of human destiny. Each life has its share of heroism, an obscure heroism, born of abdication, of renunciation and acceptance under the merciless whip of fate.

I think of all the blind people the world over, moving in darkness. I think of all the paralysed the world over, dragging themselves about. I think of all the lepers the world over, wasted by their disease.

Victims of a sad fate which you did not choose, compared with your lamentations, what is my quarrel, cruelly motivated, with a dead man who no longer has any hold over my destiny? Combining your despair, you could have been avengers and made them tremble, all those who are drunk on their wealth; tremble, those upon whom fate has bestowed favours. A horde powerful in its repugnance and revolt, you could have snatched the bread that your hunger craves.

Your stoicism has made you not violent or subversive but true heroes, unknown in the mainstream of history, never upsetting established order, despite your miserable condition.

TRANS. M. BODÉ-THOMAS, MARIAMA BÂ, *So Long A Letter* (1982)

A Letter of Literary Advice

Fay Weldon is one of our most controversial novelists, partly because she criticizes patriarchal attitudes vehemently, also because she attempts to make women face their weaknesses, in prose which is often as didactic as it is inventive. In 1983 she published Letters to Alice on First Reading Jane Austen. *Although she terms it an epistolary novel, it is rather a series of open letters on the practice of reading and writing fiction. Furthermore, it is in the tradition of women writing after reading an older, influential woman's writing. This letter offers caustic late twentieth-century comments on the role of women in the late eighteenth century.*

October 1983

My dear Alice,

Jane Austen is reputed to have fainted when her father said 'We're moving to Bath.' She was twenty-five; she had lived all her life in the Vicarage at Steventon: her father, without notifying anyone, had decided to retire, and thought that Bath was as pleasant a place as any to go. None of us fainted the day my father came home and told my mother, my sister and myself that he was leaving us that day to live for ever with his sweetheart, whose existence he'd never hinted at before. What are we to make of that? That swooning has gone out of fashion? Or that a later female generation has become inured, by reason of a literature increasingly related to the realities of life, to male surprises? Jane Austen's books are studded with fathers indifferent to their families' (in particular their daughters') welfare, male whims taking priority, then as now, over female happiness. She observes it: she does not condemn. She chides women for their raging vanity, their infinite capacity for self-deception, their idleness, their rapaciousness and folly; men, on the whole, she simply accepts. This may be another of the reasons her books are so socially acceptable in those sections of society least open to change. Women are accustomed to criticism; to being berated, in fiction, for their faults. Men are, quite simply, not. They like to be heroes.

That is quite enough of this letter. If I write too much at any one time the personal keeps intruding, and I am writing a letter of literary advice to a young lady, albeit a niece, on first reading Jane Austen, not a diatribe on the world's insensitivity to her aunt's various misfortunes, or the hard time women have at the hands of men: a fact liberally attested to up and down the streets of the City of Invention.

Alice, I see in your postscript, to my alarm, that you plan to write a novel as soon as you have the time. I sincerely hope you do *not* find the time, for some years.

With best wishes

Aunt Fay

FAY WELDON, *LETTERS TO ALICE, ON FIRST READING JANE AUSTEN*
(1983)

The Twentieth-century Role

In this extract, again from a novel composed entirely of letters, Gillian Hanscombe describes a lesbian falling in love. Between Friends (1983) analyses the roles of women in the late twentieth century, the need to work, look after the home and children, while experimenting with meaningful relationships in women's groups.

What I really want to write about is seeing Jane. You know I was going to pop in for a chat after leaving you. Well, I did. And ended up staying the night. Have just rushed back down the motorway, collected Simon, paid some bills and sat down here, before even sorting out the washing. I'm behaving like some giddy young girl who is nothing but a web of impulse and irresponsibility. I'm supposed to be a sober mother and reliable friend, sorting out details about the house and Jan and Simon, but what's really happening is a set of fantasies about joining Jane's household! There – I've said it.

It is all mostly just fantasy, and due in part to my lapping up the human company after feeling so alone since Jan left, rattling round in this house. There's Simon, of course, but it's not the same as having adult company to share things with. Jane's household positively hums by comparison – they're all so busy getting a protest organized about the lack of proper sex education in schools. As well as all that, there's the normal money-earning and housework, but it seems so much easier when there are more to share it. I began to think we should all be living like they do – if women really are to become liberated from the full-time work of caring for house and children (usually in that order), the only way to do it seems to be to share it out. Anyway, I know I can't be serious about it because they would never agree to having Simon, and I don't want to give him up, even though I know Jan would take him like a shot. We discussed it, but both felt he should stay with me – at least for the moment.

Jane is such a strange mixture – a creature of moods and impulses on the one hand, and a determined hard-liner on the other. I told her that her indulgence in extreme mood changes was exactly the kind of character-istic people describe as 'feminine'. Doctors and the so-called helping pro-fessions are always describing women as hysterical and neurotic, and I told Jane (though she didn't want to hear it) that carrying on as she does simply adds fuel to the prejudice. She was pretty quiet for a while after that conversation and I think some of it may have sunk in.

Nevertheless, I find her so attractive and even think I may be half in love with her. It's fairly obvious that something similar has happened to her, though how she would describe it I can't imagine, since she vehe-mently denies that there is any such thing as 'falling in love' – says it's a load of bourgeois crap and invented by the patriarchy to keep women enslaved to ideals and dreams instead of encouraging them to live more actively. I suppose it's some variation on the Marxist argument about reli-gion, and she may be right.

But I think no one can totally escape the process of cultural condition-ing, so whether being in love is mere conditioning or whether it is some truthful human experience is a merely academic question, since there is no one enough outside the culture to answer it. What I think privately is that she may never have been in love at all, not seriously – and if that is the case, I feel sorry for her, because it will hit her hard.

I'm just speculating about all this. What is not speculation is the degree to which she fascinates me. I suppose you won't approve, but I can't help it. It's such an age since I felt passionate about Jan that I'm ready – I must be – for that sort of experience to happen again.

It was super to see you and chat. Look after yourself and don't work too hard. Whether you have six hours' sleep or eight is not likely to change anything.

Love,

Meg

GILLIAN HANSCOMBE, *BETWEEN FRIENDS* (1983)

two

Friendship

The importance of friendship in women's lives, and their ability to sustain lifelong relationships has only recently been recognized. There is little extant correspondence between friends until the time of Lady Mary Wortley Montagu, when she, her sister Lady Mar, and fellow writers shared their ideas and feelings on a range of personal and public issues. A group of wealthy eighteenth-century intellectuals, named bluestockings by Dr Johnson, displayed both political commitment and the ability to work together on many philosophical, social and governmental issues. Women in the nineteenth century continued this tradition of collaboration.

Friendship provided a rampart against solitude and incomprehension *and* against the social indignities which many spinsters were forced to undergo. Friendships between sisters proved vitally supportive, as did correspondence between writers, often isolated or underappreciated. Fanny Burney was delighted to meet Madame de Staël in 1792, as Virginia Woolf was to meet Vita Sackville-West in 1926. (However, with her novelist's honesty, Woolf realized that envy slightly undermined her response to Katherine Mansfield.)

The second part of this section deals with 'romantic friendship', a more evocative term than lesbian to describe close, loving, possibly sexual relationships between women. I concentrate on the emotional and intellectual sharing and caring of the Ladies of Llangollen at the end of the eighteenth century, and also letters between Sackville-West and Woolf in the twentieth century. Compare these with the extracts from the significantly named *Between Friends* by Gillian Hanscombe in the previous chapter, and on pages 50–2.

The third part concentrates on women's friendships with men. First George Sand, as she was skilful in maintaining emotional and intellectual relationships with a wide circle of men, often helping them, as with her advice to Flaubert in his old age (see Chapter Ten). Her powers of analysis are used to indicate where the strengths of friendship lie. In this century Anaïs Nin was supportive emotionally, and often financially. Marina Tsvetayeva and Boris Pasternak both needed their correspondence in order to share poetic ideas. This section represents the multifaceted aspects of female friendship.

The First Female Letter in Roman Britain
Celebrates Women's Friendship

The earliest letter written by a woman on British soil dates from 170, the first century AD. *It was written in Latin, on a writing-tablet in the recently excavated area of Vindolanda. The ink is unusually well preserved, so that the writing is still clear.*

The tablet contains a letter to Sulpicia Lepidina (the name appears in full on the back) from a Claudia Severa. In her letter Severa sends Lepidina a warm invitation to visit her for her (Severa's) birthday. We can confidently deduce that Lepidina was the wife of Flavius Cerialis, prefect of one of the cohorts at the fort on Vindolanda. She then adds greetings from 'Aelius Meus', who must have been her husband. In one of the other letters found in 1985 Severa is again the writer and in this letter she refers to a certain Brocchus in such a way that there can be no doubt that she means her husband; his full name, therefore, was Aelius Brocchus. We cannot locate his station or specify his rank, but we can be sure that he was a commander of another unit, presumably in north Britain.

The discovery of this tablet and of others with evidence concerning officers' wives and families is of major importance, showing conditions in north Britain at this period, so soon after the conquest of the area. Equally important is the palaeographical evidence which the tablet presents. The body of the letter is written in an elegant script, the work of a professional writer. The second hand is noticeably less elegant, indeed it may fairly be described as somewhat clumsy in appearance. It is quite certain that the writer is Severa herself, adding a brief message and the closing greeting in her own hand. Almost certainly, therefore, this is the earliest known example of writing in Latin by a woman.

Claudia Severa to her Lepidina greetings.

On the 3rd day before the Ides of September, sister, for the day of the celebration of my birthday, I give you a warm invitation to make sure that you come to us, to make the day more enjoyable for me by your arrival, if you come. Give my greetings to your Cerialis. My Aelius and my little son send you greetings. I shall expect you, sister. Farewell, my dearest soul, as I hope you prosper and hail.

BRITANNIA, vol. XVIII (1987)

This is a Vile World, Dear Sister

Lady Mary Wortley Montagu's friendship with her sister sustained them both during travels and separations. Here she remembers their unhappy childhood and shares her misery. Her son Edward, fourteen, has just run away from Westminster School for the second time. He managed to reach Gibraltar and was not returned to his wretched mother until January 1728.

September 1727

This is a vile world, dear sister, and I can easily comprehend that whether one is at Paris or London ons is stifled with a certain mixture of fool and knave that most people are composed of. I would have patience with a parcel of polite rascals or your downright honest fools. But father Adam shines through his whole progeny; he first ate the apple like a sot and then turned informer like a scoundrel. – So much for our inside. Then our outward is so liable to ugliness and distempers that we are perpetually plagued with feeling our own decays and seeing other people's – yet six pennorth of common sense divided amongst a whole nation would make our lives roll away glib enough. But then we make laws and we follow customs; by the first we cut off our own pleasures, and by the second we are answerable for the faults and extravagancies of others. All these things and five hundred more convince me (as I have the most profound adoration for the Author of nature) that we are here in an actual state of punishment. I am satisfied I have been damned ever since I was born, and in submission to divine justice don't at all doubt that I deserved it in some pre-existent state. I am very willing to soften the word damned and hope I am only in purgatory, and that after whining and grunting here a certain number of years I shall be translated to some more happy sphere where virtue will be natural and custom reasonable; that is, in short, where common sense will reign.

I grow very devout, as you see, and place all my hopes in the next life, being totally persuaded of the nothingness of this. Don't you remember how miserable we were in the little parlour at Thoresby? We thought marrying would put us at once into possession of all we wanted; then came being with child, etc., and you see what comes of being with child.

Though after all I am still of opinion that 'tis extremely silly to submit to ill fortune; one should pluck up a spirit and live upon cordials when one can have no other nourishment. These are my present endeavours, and I run about though I have 5,000 pins and needles running into my heart. I try to console with a small damsel who is at present everything that I like, but alas, she is yet in a white frock. At fourteen she may run away with the butler. There's one of the blessed consequences of great disappointment; you are not only hurt by the thing present, but it cuts off all future hopes and makes your very expectations melancholy. *Quelle vie!*

ED. R. HALSBAND, *THE COMPLETE LETTERS OF LADY MARY WORTLEY MONTAGU (1965)*

Jane Austen to her Sister Cassandra

Jane Austen's friendship with her sister Cassandra was so warm and harmonious that she could share most of her reactions. She wrote twice a week, sharing small happenings with a wit that reveals the novelist. In these extracts we feel the close bond with her sister, and her mocking at superficial concepts of friendship.

Steventon: Tuesday Janry 8 [1799]

My dear Cassandra

You must read your letters over *five* times in future before you send them, and then, perhaps, you may find them as entertaining as I do. I laughed at several parts of the one which I am now answering . . .

You express so little anxiety about my being murdered under Ashe Park Copse by Mrs Hulbert's servant, that I have a great mind not to tell you whether I was or not, and shall only say that I did not return home that night or the next, as Martha kindly made room for me in her bed, which was the shut-up one in the new nursery. Nurse and the child slept upon the floor, and there we all were in some confusion and great comfort. The bed did exceedingly well for us, both to lie awake in and talk till two o'clock, and to sleep in the rest of the night. I love Martha better than ever, and I mean to go and see her, if I can, when she gets home . . .

The friendship between Mrs Chamberlayne and me which you predicted has already taken place, for we shake hands whenever we meet. Our grand walk to Weston was again fixed for yesterday, and was accomplished in a very striking manner. Every one of the party declined it under some pretence or other except our two selves, and we had therefore a tête à tête but *that* we should equally have had after the first two yards had half the inhabitants of Bath set off with us.

It would have amused you to see our progress: we went up by Sion Hill, and returned across the fields: in climbing a hill Mrs Chamberlayne is very capital; I could with difficulty keep pace with her, yet would not flinch for the world. On plain ground I was quite her equal. And so we posted away under a fine hot sun, *she* without any parasol or any shade to her hat, stopping for nothing, and crossing the churchyard at Weston with as much expedition as if we were afraid of being buried alive. After seeing what she is equal to, I cannot help feeling a regard for her . . .

We are to have a tiny party here tonight. I hate tiny parties, they force one into constant exertion. Miss Edwards and her father, Mrs Busby and her nephew, Mr Maitland, and Mrs Lillingstone are to be the whole; and I am prevented from setting my black cap at Mr Maitland by his having a wife and ten children . . .

Affectionately yours,

J.A.

ED. R.W. CHAPMAN, *JANE AUSTEN: LETTERS* (1932)

Charlotte Brontë Sorrowfully Alone

Female friendships were supportive and enduring to many girls who needed to share their problems, their happiness or their loneliness. Here Charlotte Brontë, aged eighteen, is wretched as an assistant teacher. She writes to her lifelong, emotionally stable friend Ellen Nussey.

Feb. 20, 1837. – I read your letter with dismay, Ellen – what shall I do without you? Why are we so to be denied each other's society? It is an inscrutable fatality. I long to be with you because it seems as if two or three days or weeks spent in your company would beyond measure strengthen me in the enjoyment of those feelings which I have so lately begun to cherish. You first pointed out to me that way in which I am so feebly endeavouring to travel, and now I cannot keep you by my side. I must proceed sorrowfully alone.

Why are we to be divided? Surely, Ellen, it must be because we are in danger of loving each other too well – of losing sight of the *Creator* in idolatry of the *creature*. At first I could not say, 'Thy will be done.' I felt rebellious; but I know it was wrong to feel so. Being left a moment alone this morning, I prayed fervently to be enabled to resign myself to *every* decree of God's will – though it should be dealt forth with a far severer hand than the present disappointment. Since then, I have felt calmer and humbler – and consequently happier. . . .

I have written this note at a venture. When it will reach you I know not, but I was determined not to let slip an opportunity for want of being prepared to embrace it. Farewell; may God bestow on you all His blessings. My darling – Farewell. Perhaps you may return before midsummer – do you think you possibly can? I wish your brother John knew how unhappy I am; he would almost pity me.

EDS. T.J. WISE AND J.A. SYMINGTON, *THE BRONTËS: THEIR LIVES,*
FRIENDSHIPS AND CORRESPONDENCE IN FOUR VOLUMES (1932)

Comfort For a Friend

Geraldine Jewsbury wrote with sense and sensibility yet her name is scarcely known. Here she writes to a close friend, Jane Carlyle (the wife of writer Thomas) to comfort her after the death of her mother, for which she was grieving.

Seaforth: Friday (Postmark, May 30, 1842)
My Darling – Your note has made me very sad. There is nothing to be said to it, as you cannot be comforted, but time – time, that is the only hope and refuge for all of us! I know full well what it is to cease to see the necessity of struggling; it would puzzle the wisest of us to point it out at the best of times, but the inscrutableness does not always press upon us so heavily – it does not come till we see into some deep trouble, and then are like to go mad. To all of us life is a riddle put more or less unintelligibly, and death is the only end we can see – for we may die, and that is a strong consolation, of which nothing can defraud us. We cannot well be more dark or miserable than we are: we shall all die – no exception, no fear of

exemption. Every morning I say this to myself. When I am in sorrow, it is
the only comfort that has strength in it. Why, indeed, must we go on
struggling, rising up early and late and taking rest? 'Behold, He giveth
His beloved sleep!' And yet it is not well that you feel this so constantly
that it swallows up all other feelings. Life is not strong in you when you
are thus – it will not be so always. There is a strength in life to make us
endure it. I am astonished sometimes to find that I am glad to be alive –
that the instinct of feeling that it is a pleasant thing to behold the sun,
and that light is good. And this is a feeling that will spring up in your
heart after a while, crushed and dead as it seems now. When my father
died I cannot tell you the horrible sense of desolateness and insecurity
that struck through me. I had friends to love me, who would do anything for me, but I had no right to count on their endurance. I had lost
the one on whose love I could depend as on the earth itself – the one
whose relationship seemed to revoke the law of change pronounced
against all other things in this world. Our parents and relations are
given us by the same unknown Power which sent us into this world,
given to us like our own bodies, without our knowing how or where, and
when they are taken from us our ties to this life are loosened, and all
seems tottering – nothing can supply their place. But yet even this gets
blunted after a while; we can and do live, when we are put to it, on wonderfully little, without all we at first fancied indispensable, and then for
ever after the love of such friends as are left or raised up to us becomes
strangely precious in a way no one else can understand. We strain them to
us with all our force, to try to supply the place of that natural necessity
which united us without effort on our part to those who are gone! We
have always a fear that the friends we have made for ourselves will leave
us; we were only afraid for the others that they would be taken away.
Dear love, this present strange, stunned state you will recover from. No
fear of your sinking down into apathy – there is too much for you to do.
You are necessary to the welfare of too many, your life will take shape
again, though now it seems nothing but confused hoplessness. The
thought of you brings tears to my eyes any moment it comes. Do not be
so very wretched I can give you no comfort – there is none – but from
time to time write when you can, but don't plague yourself. I will also
write without waiting. I am most thankful the dear little cousin still stays
with you. Give my love to her. I am glad that your husband is well, and
that he has his book to busy himself in. It is like a child to him. I am here
since a week. I go home in a few days. Mrs —— sends her love to you. I

wish you could be within reach of her; she would be a comfort to you, as she has been to me. Good bye, dear love: take care of yourself for the sake of others besides yourself!

ED. A. IRELAND, *SELECTIONS FROM THE LETTERS OF GERALDINE E. JEWSBURY TO JANE WELSH CARLYLE* (1892)

Women on Women: Two Views on Madame Germaine de Staël

Madame de Staël (1766–1817), daughter of the influential Necker, became the best-known woman writer in Revolutionary France. Today, she is possibly remembered for her novel Corinne *(1807). She was also a leading critic on 'everything concerned with the exercise of thought in writing', as she said in* De la littérature considérée dans ses rapports avec les Institutiens sociales *(1800). The book which most influenced contemporaries was* De l'Allemagne *(1810), which includes a philosophy of history, ethics and politics.*

Rosalie de Constant, the favourite among Benjamin Constant's innumerable cousins and who later detested Germaine, was enchanted by her on first acquaintance (novelist Benjamin Constant was one of Germaine's lovers):

She is an astonishing woman. The feelings to which she gives rise are different from those that any other woman can inspire. Such words as *sweetness, gracefulness, modesty, desire to please, deportment, manners,* cannot be used when speaking of her; but one is carried away, subjugated by the force of her genius. It follows a new path; it is a fire that lights you up, that sometimes blinds you, but that cannot leave you cold and indifferent. Her intelligence is too superior to allow others to make their worth felt, and nobody can look intelligent beside her. Wherever she goes, most people are changed into spectators. And yet, at the same time; it is astonishing to find in this singular woman a kind of childlike good humour which saves her from appearing in the least pedantic.

J.C. HEROLD, *LIFE OF MADAME DE STAËL* (1959)

In 1792, de Staël fled France with her then lover, Narbonne, and General d'Arblay, who was to marry Fanny Burney. The novelist felt admiration

*for Madame de Staël and the cultured émigrés with whom she came over
after the French Revolution. However, her father wrote to warn her about
rumours of adultery. Her answer shows warmth of affection to her new
friends, but care about her reputation, since she needed her earnings as
lady-in-waiting.*

Mickleham, February 22, '93.

What a kind letter is my dearest father's, and how kindly speedy! Yet it is
too true it has given me very uncomfortable feelings. I am both hurt and
astonished at the acrimony of malice; indeed, I believe all this party to
merit nothing but honour, compassion, and praise. Madame de Staël, the
daughter of M. Necker – the idolising daughter – of course, and even
from the best principles, those of filial reverence, entered into the opening
of the Revolution just as her father entered into it; but as to her house
having become the centre of revolutionists before the 10th of August, it
was so only for the constitutionalists, who, at that period, were not only
members of the then established government, but the decided friends of
the king. The aristocrats were then already banished, or wanderers from
fear, or concealed and silent from cowardice; and the jacobins – I need
not, after what I have already related, mention how utterly abhorrent to
her must be that fiend-like set.

The aristocrats, however, as you well observe, and as she has herself
told me, hold the constitutionalists in greater horror than the Convention
itself. This, however, is a violence against justice which cannot, I hope, be
lasting; and the malignant assertions which persecute her, all of which she
has lamented to us, she imputes equally to the bad and virulent of both
these parties.

The intimation concerning M. de Narbonne was, however, wholly
new to us, and I do firmly believe it a gross calumny. M. de N. was of
her society, which contained ten or twelve of the first people in Paris,
and, occasionally, almost all Paris; she loves him even tenderly, but so
openly, so simply, so unaffectedly, and with such utter freedom from
all coquetry, that, if they were two men, or two women, the affection
could not, I think, be more obviously undesigning. She is very plain, he
is very handsome; her intellectual endowments must be with him her
sole attraction.

M. de Talleyrand was another of her society, and she seems equally
attached to him. M. le Viscomte de Montmorenci she loves, she says, as
her brother: he is another of this bright constellation, and esteemed of

excellent capacity. She says, if she continues in England he will certainly come, for he loves her too well to stay away. In short, her whole côterie live together as brethren. Indeed, I think you could not spend a day with them and not see that their commerce is that of pure, but exalted and most elegant, friendship.

I would, nevertheless, give the world to avoid being a guest under their roof, now I have heard even the shadow of such a rumour; and I will, if it be possible without hurting or offending them. I have waived and waived acceptance almost from the moment of Madame de Staël's arrival. I prevailed with her to let my letter go alone to you, and I have told her, with regard to your answer, that you were sensible of the honour her kindness did me, and could not refuse to her request the week's furlough; and then followed reasons for the compromise you pointed out, too diffuse for writing. As yet they have succeeded, though she is surprised and disappointed. She wants us to study French and English together, and nothing could to me be more desirable, but for this invidious report.

J.C. Herold (1959)

The openness of the relationship between Narbonne and de Staël seems to have shocked the more prudish English middle class, and unfortunately, Fanny Burney was terrified this friendship might jeopardize her pension from the Queen; she refused all further invitations. In vain Germaine tried to reassure her that far from being Jacobins, she and her friends had 'barely escaped the Jacobins' knives'. When Susan Phillips tried to explain her sister's conduct, Germaine was dumbfounded: 'Do you mean to say that in this country a woman is treated as a minor all life long? It seems to me that your sister behaves like a girl of fourteen.'

Literary Friendship

Vita Sackville-West and Virginia Woolf had an affair which lasted some months, until it changed into a literary, supportive friendship. Woolf's novel Orlando *(1928) is partly based on the flamboyant Vita, born at Knole. Here, Vita analyses her first reactions:*

Long Barn
Weald
Sevenoaks

11 October

My darling

I am in no fit state to write to you – and as for cold and considered opinions, (as you said on the telephone) such things do not exist in such a connection. At least, not yet. Perhaps they will come later. For the moment, I can't say anything except that I am completely dazzled, bewitched, enchanted, under a spell. It seems to me the loveliest, wisest, *richest* book that I have ever read, – excelling even your own *Lighthouse*. Virginia, I really don't know what to say, – am I right? am I wrong? am I prejudiced? am I in my senses or not? It seems to me that you have really shut up that 'hard and rare thing' in a book; that you have had a complete vision; and yet when you came down to the sober labour of working it out, have never lost sight of it nor faltered in the execution. Ideas come to me so fast that they trip over each other and I lose them before I can put salt on their tails; there is so much I want to say, yet I can only go back to my first cry that I am bewitched. You will get letters, very reasoned and illuminating, from many people; I can only tell you that I am really shaken, which may seem to you useless and silly, but which is really a greater tribute than pages of calm appreciation, – and then after all it does touch me so personally, and I don't know what to say about that either, only that I feel like one of those wax figures in a shop window, on which you have hung a robe stitched with jewels. It is like being alone in a dark room with a treasure chest full of rubies and nuggets and brocades. Darling, I don't know and scarcely even like to write, so overwhelmed am I, how you could have hung so splendid a garment on so poor a peg. Really, this isn't false humility; *really* it isn't. I can't write about that part of it, though, much less ever tell you verbally.

By now you must be thinking me too confused and illiterate for anything, so I'll just slip in that the book (in texture) seems to me to have in it all the best of Sir Thomas Browne and Swift, – the richness of the one, and the directness of the other.

There are a dozen details I should like to go into, – Queen Elizabeth's visit, Greene's visit, phrases scattered about, (particularly one on p. 160 beginning 'High battlements of thought, etc.' which is just what you did for *me*,) Johnson on the blind, and so on and so on, – but it is too late today; I have been reading steadily all day, and it is now 5 o'clock, and I must catch the post, but I will try and write more sensibly tomorrow. It is your fault, for having moved me so and dazzled me completely, so that all my faculties have dropped from me and left me stark.

EDS. L. DeSaho and M. Leaska, *The Letters of Vita Sackville-West to Virginia Woolf* (1984)

Friendship for another Poet

Marina Tsvetayeva admired and liked the poet Anna Akhmatova. She met her when they were young, during the Russian Revolution. Anna's early poems had excited her so much that Marina began a cycle of poems for her in 1916. Sadly, by 1921 most writers were having to learn to be less outspoken, even in Writers House and House of the Arts in Petrograd, as Marina described in this letter to her friend:

Everywhere there was silence, waiting and uncertainty. The 24 August arrived. Early in the morning, when I was still in bed, Ida Nappelbaum came over. She came to tell me that on the street corners were posted the announcements: all had been shot . . . sixty-two persons in all. . . .

ELAINE FEINSTEIN, *Marina Tsvetayeva* (1989)

The passion that went into Marina's letter to Akhmatova of 31 August, offering her loyalty, was characteristically reckless:

31 August 1921

Dear Anna Andreyevna,

Of late, gloomy rumours have been circulating about you, becoming more persistent and unequivocal with every hour that passes. I write to you about this because you will hear in any case. I want you to be correctly informed, at least. I can tell you that, to my knowledge, your only friend among poets (a friend indeed!) turned out to be Mayakovsky, as he wandered among the billboards of the 'Poets Café' looking like a slaughtered bull.

I have, in the hope of finding out about you, spent these last few days in the Poets' Café. What monsters! What squalid creatures! What curs they are! Everything is here: homunculi, automotons, braying stallions and lip-sticked sleeping-car attendants from Yalta . . .

ELAINE FEINSTEIN (1989)

A few days later, after a meeting at Writers Union, she wrote again.

Dear Anna Andreyevna,

To understand what yesterday evening was for me, to understand Aksyonov's nod to me, one would have to know how I lived the previous three *unspeakable* days. A horrible dream. I want to wake up, but I cannot. I confronted everybody, beseeching your life. A little longer and I would have actually *said* 'Gentlemen! See to it that Akhmatova be alive!'. . . Alya comforted me: 'Marina! She has a son!'

   At the end of yesterday's proceedings, I asked Bobrov's permission to make an official journey – to Akhmatova. Laughter all round.

ELAINE FEINSTEIN (1989)

Literary Rivals

The literary friendship between Katherine Mansfield and Virginia Woolf was disturbed by rivalry and disease. After Mansfield's early death from tuberculosis, Woolf tried to analyse what she had felt for this woman friend. She wrote to Vita Sackville-West:

1922

Katherine has been dead a week, & how far am I obeying her 'do not quite forget Katherine' which I read in one of her old letters? Am I already forgetting her? It is strange to trace the progress of one's feelings. Nelly said in her sensational way at breakfast on Friday 'Mrs Murry's dead! It says so in the paper!' At that one feels – what? A shock of relief – a rival the less? Then confusion at feeling so little – then, gradually, blankness & disappointment; then a depression which I could not rouse myself from all that day. When I began to write, it seemed to me there was no point in writing. Katherine won't read it. Katherine's my rival no longer. More generously I felt, But though I can do this better than she could, where is she, who could do what I can't! Then, as usual with me, visual impressions kept coming & coming before me – always of Katherine putting on a white wreath, & leaving us, called away; made dignified, chosen. And then one pitied her. And one felt her reluctant to wear that wreath, which was an ice cold one. And she was only 33. And I could see her before me so exactly, & the room at Portland Villas. I go up. She gets up, very slowly, from her writing table. A glass of milk & a medicine bottle stood there. There were also piles of novels. Everything was very tidy, bright, & somehow like a doll's house. At once, or almost, we got out of shyness. She (it was summer) half lay on the sofa by the window. She had her look of a Japanese doll, with the fringe combed quite straight across her forehead. Sometimes we looked very steadfastly at each other, as though we had reached some durable relationship, independent of the changes of the body, through the eyes. Hers were beautiful eyes – rather doglike, brown, very wide apart, with a steady slow rather faithful & sad expression. Her nose was sharp, & a little vulgar. Her lips thin & hard. She wore short skirts and liked 'to have a line round her' she said. She looked very ill – very drawn, & moved languidly, drawing herself across the room, like some suffering animal. I suppose I have written down some of the things we said. Most days I think we reached that kind of certainty, in talk about books, or rather about our writings, which I thought had something durable about it. And then she was inscrutable. Did she care for me? Sometimes she would say so – would kiss me – would look at me as if (is this sentiment?) her eyes would like always to be faithful. She would promise never never to forget. That was what we said at the end of our talk. She said she would send me her diary to read, & would write always. For our friendship was a real thing we said, looking at each other quite straight. It would always go on whatever happened. What happened was, I suppose, faultfindings & perhaps gossip. She never answered my letter. Yet I still feel, somehow that friendship persists. Still there are things about writing I think of & want to tell Katherine. If I had been in Paris & gone to her, she would have got up & in three minutes, we should have been talking again. Only I could not take the step. The surroundings – Murry & so on – and the small lies and treacheries, the perpetual playing & teasing, or whatever it was, cut away so much of the substance of friendship. One was too uncertain. And so one let it all go. Yet I certainly expected that we should meet again next summer, & start afresh. And I was jealous of her writing – the only writing I have ever been jealous of. This made it harder to write to her; & I saw in it, perhaps from jealousy, all the qualities I disliked in her . . . I have the feeling that I shall think of her at intervals all through life. Probably we had something in common which I shall never find in anyone else . . .

CLAIRE TOMALIN, KATHERINE MANSFIELD: A SECRET LIFE (1987)

Comfort For a Friend Abandoned

A Senegalese divorced woman comforts her great friend Aissatou, who has been abandoned by her husband. This modern epistolary novel So Long A Letter, *written in 1982 by Mariama Bâ displays the same caring and wisdom that Geraldine Jewsbury showed to Jane Carlyle.*

Leave! Draw a clean line through the past. Turn over a page on which not everything was bright, certainly, but at least all was clear. What would now be recorded there would hold no love, confidence, grandeur or hope. I had never known the sordid side of marriage. Don't get to know it! Run from it! When one begins to forgive, there is an avalanche of faults that comes crashing down, and the only thing that remains is to forgive again, so keep on forgiving. Leave, escape from betrayal! Sleep without asking myself any questions, without straining my ear at the slightest noise, waiting for a husband I share.

I counted the abandoned or divorced women of my generation whom I knew.

I knew a few whose remaining beauty had been able to capture a worthy man, a man who added fine bearing to a good situation and who was considered 'better, a hundred times better than his predecessor'. The misery that was the lot of these women was rolled back with the invasion of the new happiness that changed their lives, filled out their cheeks, brightened their eyes. I knew others who had lost all hope of renewal and whom loneliness had very quickly laid underground.

The play of destiny remains impenetrable. The cowries that a female neighbour throws on a fan in front of me do not fill me with optimism, neither when they remain face upwards, showing the black hollow that signifies laughter, nor when the grouping of their white backs seems to say that 'the man in the double trousers' is coming towards me, the promise of wealth. 'The only thing that separates you from the man and wealth, is the alms of two white and red cola nuts.' adds Farmata, my neighbour.

She insists: 'There is a saying that discord here may be luck elsewhere. Why are you afraid to make the break? A woman is like a ball; once a ball is thrown, no one can predict where it will bounce. You have no control over where it rolls, and even less over who gets it. Often it is grabbed by an unexpected hand . . .' I looked at myself in the mirror. My eyes took in the mirror's eloquence. I had lost my slim figure, as well as ease and quickness of movement. My stomach protruded from beneath the wrapper that hid the calves developed by the impressive number of kilometers walked since the beginning of my existence. Suckling had robbed my breasts of their round firmness. I could not delude myself: youth was deserting my body.

Whereas a woman draws from the passing years the force of her devotion, despite the ageing of her companion, a man, on the other hand, restricts his field of tenderness. His egoistic eye looks over his partner's shoulder. He compares what he had with what he no longer has, what he has with what he could have.

I had heard of too many misfortunes not to understand my own. There was your own case, Aissatou, the cases of many other women, despised, relegated or exchanged, who were abandoned, worn-out.

To overcome distress when it sits upon you demands strong will. When one thinks that with each passing second one's life is shortened, one must profit intensely from this second; it is the sum of all the lost or harvested seconds that makes for a wasted or a successful life. Brace oneself to check despair and get it into proportion! A nervous breakdown waits around the corner for anyone who lets himself wallow in bitterness. Little by little, it takes over your whole being.

Oh, nervous breakdown! Doctors speak of it in a detached, ironical way, emphasizing that the vital organs are in no way disturbed. You are lucky if they don't tell you that you are wasting their time with the ever-growing list of your illnesses – your head, throat, chest, heart, liver – that no X-ray can confirm. And yet what atrocious suffering is caused by nervous breakdowns!

TRANS. M. BODÉ-THOMAS, MARIAMA BÂ, *So Long a Letter* (1982)

A 'Romantic' Friendship

Women in patriarchal cultures have seldom expressed public understanding of the intense love of Sappho for other women.

In 1790 Mrs Piozzi (formerly Mrs Thrale, whom Dr Johnson loved) wrote that the 'Queen of France is at the Head of a Set of Monsters called by each other Sapphists, *who boast her example; and deserve to be thrown with the He Demons that haunt each other likewise, into Mount Vesuvius'. (Thraliana 1776–1809, ed. K. Balderston, 1951, p. 740). In 1795 she returned to this topic, still upholding views preached by the church and the majority of men: ''Tis now grown common to suspect impossibilities (for such I think 'em) whenever two Ladies live too much together' (op. cit. p. 949). English social history had scarcely mentioned this topic. It was alluded to as 'romantic friendship', a far wider, less scornful term. Fanny Hill, forty years before, had mentioned 'secret bias', but there are few allusions to lesbianism. Havelock Ellis wrote in* Studies in the Psychology of Sex, *Vol. 2, p. 261) that a Miss Hobart was mentioned in the court of Charles II, which shows us 'how rare was the exception'. A century later, however, homosexuality among English women seems to have been regarded by the French as common, and Bacchaumont, on 1 January 1773, recording that Mlle Heinel of the Opera was settling in England, added, 'Her taste for women will there find attractive satisfaction, for it is said that London is herein superior to Paris'.*

In the eighteenth century, middle-class daughters, sisters, aunts and some wives were gaining a little leisure to read and study. The notable correspondents reveal that terms often associated today with sexual relationships were mostly confined to literary friendships between women: tenderness, sensibility, shared tastes, even coquetry. For example, a clergyman's daughter, Miss Carter, who corresponded with Mrs Montagu and Dr Johnson, wrote of a clever girl at Oxford: 'Miss Talbot is absolutely my passion; I think of her all day, dream of her all night and one way or other introduce her into every subject I talk of' (Mrs Carter's Letters Vol. 1 p. 2). Like the Ladies of Llangollen, these women agreed to strict planning of their time, and shunning of town life. They all rose early, to pursue a rigourous course of reading and study of foreign languages, alleviated by long walks or rides, gardening and preserving or embroidery.

'Romantic friendship' is a term now lost, yet less marginalizing than 'lesbian' to describe a relationship which includes tenderness, lifelong devotion, shared tastes, probably passion and shared beds. One of the best known, at the end of the eighteenth century is that of the Ladies of Llangollen, Eleanor Butler and Sarah Ponsonby, who ran away to set up house together in 1778. They first had to fight their families, then public opinion, but succeeded in leading the intellectual life they sought together. Their friends and admirers included Wellington and Wordsworth.

Wedgwood, Darwin and Sheridan, among many others, visited their 'gothick' cottage in Llangollen.

They were both from aristocratic families, Butler thirty-nine, and Ponsonby twenty-three when they eloped together. Butler was considered eccentric as she was tall, clever and disinclined to marry. Ponsonby was considered pretty. When orphaned, she was taken in by her uncle who soon turned his unwelcome eyes on her.

Sarah Ponsonby wrote many lively letters of complaint, to women relations and secretly to her friend Eleanor Butler:

neither my pride, resentment, nor any other passion shall ever be sufficiently powerful to make me give Lady Betty any uneasiness in my power to spare her, and I sometimes laugh to think of the earnestness with which she presses me to be obliging to him, for I have adopted the most reserved mode of behaviour . . . taking no pains when she does not perceive it, to show my disgust and detestation of him. I would rather die than wound Lady Betty's heart.

E. MAVOR, *LADIES OF LLANGOLLEN: A STUDY IN ROMANTIC FRIENDSHIP*
(1971)

Butler's mother had attempted to persuade Eleanor to enter a convent, but the girl no longer felt the happiness in Catholicism which she had experienced when younger. The two girls left their homes on the last day of March 1778. The following day, Sir William's men caught up with the girls and brought them home, but a few weeks later, they succeeded in escaping together and bought a small cottage in Llangollen. There they developed a 'system' to devote their minds to self-improvement. Sarah described it to her aunt Mrs Tighe:

11 April 1783

. . . my B[eloved] has a Book of (I think) very well chosen Extracts from all the Books she has read since we had a home. We record elegant extracts, recipes, nostrums, garden plants, anecdotes, and in a special book, our future projects. We wish to eschew the vanity of society, never to leave home, and to better, in so far as we can, the lot of the poor and unfortunate . . .

TIGHE MS

48

The daughter of Mrs Tighe, Caroline Hamilton, wrote of their friendship:

I have no cause to think that Lady Eleanor Butler ever repented the steps she had taken, but from a letter I suspect that Miss Ponsonby sometimes expressed regret at having left Ireland. The two ladies continued to the last devoted to each other, and if they had a difference of opinion, they discussed it in a particular walk where they could not be overheard, for as they felt themselves bound to give to the world, an example of perfect friendship, the slightest appearance of discord would have tarnished their reputation.

NLI. MS 4811

Friendships with Men

George Sand, the French novelist, not only fell in love with many men, she maintained lifelong friendships with men even more than with women. To François Rollinat, one of her most intimate and valued friends, a young barrister, practising in Châteauroux, the town near Nohant, she wrote:

Nohant, 1834

I have never felt *love* for you of any kind, neither moral nor physical; but from the very first day we met I felt for you one of those rare sympathies, those deep unconquerable attractions which no force can alter, because the more deeply one explores then the more one identifies one's own soul with the being who inspires this attraction, and shares in it.

I never found you superior to myself either mentally or morally, if I had, perhaps I should have regarded you with that glowing enthusiasm which leads to love.

In a way you were worth more than I, because you were younger, because you had lived less than I in torment, because God had sent you from the first upon a better more firmly marked road than mine. But you come from His creative hand with the same number of virtues and failings, of great qualities, and of miseries as I did.

I know many men who are superior to you, but I shall never have the same depth of affection (it comes from the depths of my being) for them as I have for you. I should never be able to walk with any one of them under the stars all night, as I can with you, without feeling one moment of disagreement or antipathy. And yet we often prolonged these walks and talks until dawn and never without awakening an identical transport in the souls of both of us; and did the confession of some misery fall from my lips, it never failed to drawn an echo of the same sorrow from yours.

We had for each other the profound indulgence and the almost cowardly tenderness that one feels for oneself. We felt for each other that kind of besotted confidence which one feels for one's own ideas, and we felt that confident pride, that one has in one's personal force, for one another.

We have never *once* quarrelled or disagreed on any subject bad or good. What one suggests is adopted by the other immediately, and not out of complaisance or devotion, but because of necessity and inevitable sympathy.

ED. E. DREW, *LETTERS OF GEORGE SAND* (1930)

A Poet in Exile

The great Russian poet Marina Tsvetayeva found life in exile tough, mentally and physically. Though she was happier in Czechoslovakia, from where she wrote this letter, than in Paris, she desperately needed the friendship of other writers. Her correspondence with Pasternak was important to them both.

Mokropsy, 19 November 1922

My dear Pasternak,

My favourite mode of communication is in the world beyond: a dream, to see in a dream.

My second favourite is correspondence. A letter is, as a form of other-worldly communication, less perfect than a dream, but the rules are the same.

Neither can be ordered. We dream and write not as *we* want, but as *they* want. A letter *has* to be written: a dream *has* to be seen. (My letters *always* want to be written!)

Now about Weimar [where Pasternak had suggested that they meet in two years' time]. Pasternak, don't joke. I shall live by this for two years running . . . Pasternak, I was just returning along the rough country road . . . I was feeling my way. Dirt, potholes, dark lamp posts. Pasternak, with what force did I then think of you; no, not of you; of myself without you, of these street lamps and roads without you. Oh Pasternak, my feet will walk milliards of verses before we meet! (Forgive me for such an explosion of truth; I am writing as if about to die.)

Now the prospect of massive insomnia. Springs and summers – I know myself – every tree that my eyes single out will be you. How can one live with this? It is not that you are there, while I am here; the point is that you will be *there*, that I shall never know whether you exist or not. Yearning for you and fear for you, wild fear; I know myself . . .

Do not be afraid. There will be only one letter like this . . .

My Pasternak, perhaps I shall, one day, really and truly become a major poet – thanks to you! I do have to speak without bounds to you, to unfold my heart. In conversation this is done through silence. But I have only a pen! . . .

Pasternak, how many questions I have to put to you! We have not talked about anything yet. In Weimar we shall have a long conversation.

ELAINE FEINSTEIN, *MARINA TSVETAYEVA* (1989)

Mokropsy, 9 March 1923

Dear Pasternak,

I have nothing, except my fervour for you, and that will not help. I kept waiting for your letter, not daring to ask for a visa to visit you without your permission. And I did not know whether you needed me or not. I simply lost heart. (I write in a cheerful fatal fever.) It's too late.

On receipt of your *Themes and Variations* – no, earlier, from the news of your arrival – I said: 'I shall see him.' With your lilac-coloured book, this came to life, turned visible (blood) and I started on a large book of prose (correspondence!) counting on finishing by the end of April. I worked every day without a break.

I have just received your letter at 6.30 in the morning. And this is the dream you fell into the middle of. I make you a gift of it: I am walking across some sort of a narrow bridge. Constantinople. Behind me, a little girl in a long dress. I know that she will not fall behind, and that it is she who is guiding. But as she is so small, she cannot keep pace, and I take her by the hand. Through my left hand runs a flood of striped silk: the dress. Steps. We climb them (I, in my dream: 'A good omen' . . .). Striped planks on piles, and below – black water. The girl has crazed eyes, but will do me no harm, as she was sent, she loves me . . .

It was summer then, and I had my own balcony in Berlin. Stone, heat, your green book [*My Sister Life*. 1922] in my lap. (I used to sit on the floor.) I lived by it then for ten days as if on the high crest of a wave. I surrendered to it and did not choke. I had exactly enough breath for those eight lines which to my great joy, you liked.

I do not like meetings in real life. Foreheads knocking together. Two walls. You just cannot penetrate. A meeting should be an arch. Then the meeting is *above*. Foreheads tilted back! That's how I'm writing to you. I live in Czechia near Prague, at Mokropsy, in a village hut. The last house in the village. There is a stream under the hill, and I carry water from it. A third of the day goes on stoking the huge tiled stove. Life, as far as its everyday routines is concerned, differs little from Moscow. Possibly it's even poorer! But there is a bonus for my poetry: the family, and nature. There are wonderful hills here . . . I write and walk all morning.

ELAINE FEINSTEIN (1989)

The Irresponsible Life

Anaïs Nin, daughter of Spanish composer Joaquín Nin was taken to live in New York in 1923. The ten volumes of her Journals *are fascinating, as she explores personal, psychological and philosophical themes from many angles. Here she reproduces one of her letters to Jim Herlihy:*

The fascinating problem of the irresponsible life. Just as we discussed it more openly, and clearly, I realized that we live our irresponsible life in secret. Danger of exposure creates our violent attacks of guilt. Our desire to live everything out will always meet with the obstacle of guilt. The unwillingness to cause pain as well as the unwillingness to accept the judgment of others. One of the most inspiring things about our friendship is that we never pass judgment. I should not even state it as negatively as that: we accepted each other's unconscious self, the hidden one. This gives an elating sense of freedom. Now I solved the problem of not hurting any-one, or hurting with amnesia and chloroform. But I never solved the prob-lem of guilt, which is proved by masochism. I can only get rid of the guilt by atonement. Analysis only helped me to shorten the periods of atone-ment. When you wrote to me about your restlessness and the guilt you feel for even wishing to be free, I wanted to help you. For that is the real drama, the real tragedy. It might account for all the masochism in the world, the sacrifices, the self-destruction. Guilt is at the core, the toxic effect of Christianity. I have often referred to the history of the Caesars. That is even a greater mystery as they were not religious. They felt all-powerful. They were convinced of their omnipotence and godlessness. They considered themselves the only gods. They all committed abominations. And each one of them died of guilt, not from sensual excesses, not from war, not from illness but of a madness brought on by guilt. So guilt is even older than Christianity. In your case guilt presents itself in a more subtle form. When success grows near you begin to feel uneasy. You see a more obvious form of atoning for success in Bill and his destructive drinking. You are too clever, people like you too much for you to ruin anything, but you can spoil your enjoyment, and that is more subtle to detect and to cure. Watch for it. It is the real enemy, the real incubus, succubus, the only demon and the only voodoo.

ANAÏS NIN, *JOURNALS* (1970)

three

Childhood and Education

Childhood

Childhood defies satisfactory definition, because views vary from seeing it as an age of innocence to one of original sin. Christ said 'Suffer little children to come unto me' while St Augustine opined that sin must be beaten out. The Greeks, like many today, divided childhood into three stages:

– *infantia*, infancy, from birth to seven, when parents should nurture and train;

– *pueritia*, which lasted until fourteen for boys, only twelve for girls, since it was realized that girls matured faster. In this period children began to deploy written language;

– *adolescentia*, which lasted until adulthood. Boys were often expected to establish themselves in a job, but marriage was the career of the girl.

Until very recently historians followed the ideas of Frenchman Philippe Ariès in *Centuries of Childhood* (1960), in which he maintained that there was no concept of childhood in the Middle Ages, partly because of the high mortality rate, which reduced parental affection, and because we see so few children in early pictures. However, recent research suggests that parental caring for offspring was widespread. Putting children in apprenticeships, or in orphanages when the mother was starving, may be interpreted as having attempted to give a slightly better life to offspring in an imperfect world.

In most families, children had to grow up very fast, and help their parents. They were 'allowed' to work in factories from the age of five in Victorian England, which may account for the increase of interest in the psyche of children, highlighted by the novels of Dickens and Charlotte Brontë, whose fiction pointed out, virtually for the first time, that the emotional suffering of children is different in kind from that of many adults.

Paintings enable us to guess the place of children in the past. Scarcely a child occurs in the Middle Ages, apart from a stylized baby Jesus. By Tudor times they appear in the background, dressed as tiny adults. They proliferate in the seventeenth century, mainly as rubicund angels or cupids, seldom as valid in their own right. By the eighteenth century children take part in family life and parents express joy in being with their offspring.

A Daughter to her Mother at Home

Girls, like boys in the late Middle Ages, might be sent to complete their worldly education in the household of another aristocratic family. When monarchs still possessed parts of France, there was the benefit of learning a foreign language. The main advantage lay in the wider circle of marriageable people to meet.

Lord and Lady Lisle sent their daughter Mary to a Lady Bours in Calais when she was eleven. She grew very fond of her adoptive mother. The formal Tudor language does not quite convey either her real affection for Lady Lisle nor for Madame Bours, but her many letters give proof of it.

5 September 1537

Madame, I recommend me most humbly to the good favour of my lord my father and to you.

Madame, I am right heavy at being so long without tidings of your welfare. And glad am I indeed that Madame de Bours now sendeth to you. It was told me at Abbeville that you had sent me a letter; but the messenger lost it, which grieveth me sore. Madame, I most humbly thank you for that which you sent me by Jehan Semit. I am waiting till he must pass again by Abbeville in order that I may send you tidings of myself.

Madame, I entreat you to be so good lady to me as to send me a pair of sleeves to give to Madame, and a pair for me. She hath very little that is from England. If it please you to send her something I should be very glad. There is a gentleman, who is a good friend of mine, who hath begged a pair of me, and a pair of shoes. I should be very glad to make him a present of them. This bearer will tell you who he is . . .

Mademoiselle d'Agincourt recommendeth her very humbly to your favour.

Your very humble and most obedient daughter,

Marie Basset

ED. M. ST CLARE BYRNE, *THE LISLE LETTERS* (1983)

Lady Mary Wortley Montagu Advises her Daughter on her Granddaughter's Upbringing

Although Lady Mary Wortley Montagu recommends education as the 'amusement of solitude' and 'to moderate the passions' she cautions her 'to conceal whatever learning she attains'.

1753

You should encourage your daughter to talk over with you what she reads; and as you are very capable of distinguishing, take care she does not mistake pert folly for wit and humour, or rhyme for poetry, which are the common errors of young people, and have a train of ill consequences. The second caution to be given her (and which is most absolutely necessary) is to conceal whatever learning she attains, with as much solicitude as she would hide crookedness or lameness: the parade of it can only serve to draw on her the envy, and consequently the most inveterate hatred, of all he and she fools, which will certainly be at least three parts in four her acquaintance. The use of knowledge in our sex, beside the amusement of solitude, is to moderate the passions, and learn to be contented with a small expense, which are the certain effects of a studious life; and it may be preferable even to that fame which men have engrossed to themselves, and will not suffer us to share. You will tell me I have not observed this rule myself; but you are mistaken: it is only inevitable accident that has given me any reputation that way. I have always carefully avoided it, and ever thought it a misfortune. The explanation of this paragraph would occasion a long digression, which I will not trouble you with, it being my present design only to say what I think useful for the instruction of my granddaughter, which I have much at heart. If she has the same inclination (I should say passion) for learning that I was born with, history, geography, and philosophy will furnish her with materials to pass away cheerfully a longer life than is allotted to mortals. I believe there are few heads capable of making Sir Isaac Newton's calculations, but the result of them is not difficult to be understood by a moderate capacity.

ED. R. HALSBAND, *THE COMPLETE LETTERS OF LADY MARY WORTLEY MONTAGU* (1965)

A 'Frivolous' Household

Upbringing could be neglected in an upper-class eighteenth-century home. Viscount Kingsborough was the biggest landowner in Ireland. His exceedingly rich wife Caroline produced many children, in whom she took virtually no interest. However an exceptional governess was employed by them in the year 1787 – Mary Wollstonecraft. Here one of the daughters, Margaret, describes her upbringing and the impact of the great feminist in a 'frivolous, injudicious' household, in a letter to her two illegitimate daughters in 1818.

1818

My father Robert King Earl of Kingston, was married very young to his relation Caroline Fitzgerald. . . . I was the second of their twelve children and being born in that rank of life in which people are too much occupied by frivolous amusements to pay much attention to their offspring I was placed under the care of hirelings from the first moment of my birth – before three years old I was subjected to the discipline of governesses and teachers whose injudicious treatment was very disadvantageous to my temper. As I was advanced in years I had various masters (for no expense was spared to make me what is called accomplished) and at a very early age I was enabled to exhibit before my mother's visitors, whose silly praises would probably have injured me if I had not suffered so much in acquiring the means of obtaining them that they afforded me no pleasure. With this sort of education it is not extraordinary that I should have learnt a little of many things and nothing well. The society of my father's home was not calculated to improve my good qualities or correct my faults; and almost the only person of superior merit with whom I had been intimate in my early days was an enthusiastic female who was my governess from fourteen to fifteen years old, for whom I felt an unbounded admiration because her mind appeared more noble and her understanding more cultivated than any others I had known – from the time she left me my chief objects were to correct those faults she had pointed out and to cultivate my understanding as much as possible.

CLAIRE TOMALIN, *THE LIFE AND DEATH OF MARY WOLLSTONECRAFT*

(1974)

'So Much of a Woman'

By the end of the eighteenth century, girls were increasingly closely guarded. The issue of the desirability of respectable women moving freely about alone focused on concern over unmarried girls. Joseph Gibbins's youngest daughter Martha, who was born in 1798 and brought up in central Birmingham, was walking across the town to school by herself when she was nine years old. In a letter to her brother William she described the following incident:

I am become so much of a woman as to go to school by myself. One day, as I was returning from school, a boy was so rude as to offer to *kiss* me, and he called another boy to do the same, so I went into a reputable looking shop and asked the man if he would be so kind as to speak to those boys, for they had been behaving rude to me, and I told him I was Joseph Gibbins' little girl. He came out, sent them away, and I got home without being interrupted again.

I. DAVIDOFF, AND C. HALL, *FAMILY FORTUNES: MEN AND WOMEN OF THE ENGLISH MIDDLE CLASS* (1987)

A Loving Childhood

Mrs Oliphant (1828–97) grew up in a radical middle-class family. I include this extract from her Autobiography *both for the representation of a nineteenth-century family, and for its discourse, so similar to a letter. This suggests that experience in letter-writing gave women the confidence to use one of their few saleable skills. Mrs Oliphant, when widowed, not only supported her own children, but those of one of her brothers, by her skilful, popular novels.*

. . . I can see myself, a small creature seated on a stool by the fire, toasting a cake of dough which was brought for me by the baker with the prematurely early rolls, which were for Frank. (This dough was the special feature of the morning to me, and I suppose I had it only on these occasions.) And my mother, who never seemed to sit down in the strange, little, warm, bright picture, but to hover about the table pouring out tea, supplying everything he wanted to her boy (how proud, how fond of him –

her eyes liquid and bright with love as she hovered about); and Frank, the dearest of companions so long – then long separated, almost alienated, brought back again at the end to my care. How bright he was then, how good always to me, how fond of his little sister – impatient by moments, good always. And he was a kind of god to me – my Frank, as I always called him. I remember once weeping bitterly over a man singing in the street, a buttoned-up, shabby-genteel man, whom, on being questioned why I cried, I acknowledged I thought like my Frank. That was when he was absent, and my mother's anxiety reflected in a child's mind went, I suppose, the length of fancying that Frank too might have to sing in the street. (He would have come off very badly in that case, for he did not know one tune from another, much less could he sing a note!) How well I recollect the appearance of the man in his close-buttoned black coat, with his dismal song, and the acute anguish of the thought that Frank might have come to that for anything I knew. Frank, however, never gave very much anxiety: it was Willie, poor Willie, who was our sore and constant trouble – Willie, who lives still in Rome, as he has done for the last two- or three-and-twenty years – nearly a quarter of a century – among strangers who are kind to him, wanting nothing, I hope, yet also having outlived everything. I shrank from going to see him when I was in Italy, which was wrong; but how can I return to Rome, and how could he have come to me – poor Willie! the handsomest, brightest of us all, with eyes that ran over with fun and laughter – and the hair which we used to say he had to poll, like Absalom, – so many time a-year. Alas!

What I recollect in Lasswade besides the Monday morning aforesaid is not much. I remember standing at the smithy with brother Willie, on some occasion when the big boy was very unwillingly charged to take his little sister somewhere or other – standing in the dark, wondering at the sparks as they flew up and the dark figures of the smith and his men: and I remember playing on the road opposite the house, where there was a low wall over which the Esk and the country beyond could be seen (I think), playing with two little kittens, who were called Lord Brougham and Lord Grey. It must have been immediately after the passing of the Reform Bill, and I suppose this was why the kittens bore such names. We were all tremendously political and Radical, my mother especially and Frank. Likewise I recollect with the most vivid clearness on what must have been a warm still summer day, lying on my back in the grass, the little blue speedwells in which are very distinct before me, and looking up into the sky. The depths of it, the blueness of it, the way in which it seemed to move and fly and avoid the gaze which could not penetrate beyond that profound unfathomable.

ED. MRS H. COGHILL, *THE AUTOBIOGRAPHY AND LETTERS OF MRS M.O.W. OLIPHANT* (1899)

Emily Eden 'buys' Two Little Girls

Children in India might be as badly treated by drunken fathers as those in London. Emily Eden, sister of the Governor-General, went so far as to 'buy' two orphan girls, to help get them to a respectable orphanage.

Thursday, March 7 1839

I have made such a nice little purchase to-day – two little girls of seven years old, rather ugly, and one of them dumb. I gave three pounds for the pair – dirt cheap! as I think you will own. They are two little orphans. The natives constantly adopt orphans – either distant relations, or children that they buy – and generally they make no difference between them and their own children; but these little wretches were very unlucky. They belonged to a very bad man, who was serving as a substitute for a sick servant whom we sent back to Calcutta. This man turned out ill and got drunk, upon which all the other Mussulmauns refused to associate with him, and he lost caste altogether. Giles was very anxious to get rid of him, as a drunken Mussulmaun is something so shocking we are all quite *affected* by it. On Monday he gave us an opportunity to leave him at Kurnaul. I had tried to get hold of these children at Simla, hearing they were very ill-used, and that this man was just going to take them down to Delhi to sell them into the palace, where thousands of children are *swallowed up*. Luckily, his creditors would not let him go, and I told A. to watch that he did not carry off the little girls; so to-day he sent word I might have them if I would pay his debts, and the baboo has just walked in triumphantly with them. They have not a stitch of clothes on; and one of them is rather an object, the man has beat them so dreadfully, and she seems stupified. I hope to deposit them finally at Mrs Wilson's orphanage near Calcutta.

E. EDEN, *UP THE COUNTRY: LETTERS FROM INDIA* (1983)

George Eliot on Cupid the Enemy

George Eliot enjoyed learning, and read theology with real interest. At twenty she studied seriously, at home, but was sometimes attracted to young men. She wrote to a former teacher:

Spring 1840

To Miss Lewis

I feel that a sight of one being whom I have not beheld except passingly since the interview I last described to you would *probably* upset *all*; but as it is, the image now seldom arises in consequence of entire occupation and, I trust in some degree, desire and prayer to be free from rebelling against Him whose I am by right, whose I would be by adoption. I endeavoured to pray for the beloved object to whom I have alluded, I must still a little while say *beloved*, last night and felt soothingly melted in thinking that if mine be really prayers my acquaintance with him has probably caused the *first* to be offered up specially in his behalf. But all this I ought not to have permitted to slip from my pen.

ED. G. HAIGHT, *THE GEORGE ELIOT LETTERS* (1954)

At school she had already written to a friend, Patty Jackson:

Cupid listens to no entreaties; we must deal with him as an enemy, either boldy parry his shafts or flee. I find our language teacher, Joseph Brezzi anything but uninteresting, all external grace and mental power, but 'Cease ye from man' is engraven on my amulet. And to tell you the truth I begin to feel involuntarily isolated, and without being humble, to have such a consciousness that I am a negation of all that finds love and esteem as makes me anticipate for myself – no matter what; I shall have countless undeserved enemies if my life be prolonged, wherever my lot may be cast, and I need rigid discipline, which I have never yet had.

ED. G. HAIGHT (1954)

It was a prophetic remark. As time passed the prospect of a lover seemed more remote. In a letter to Patty, 20 October 1840, she said:

Every day's experience seems to deepen the voice of foreboding that has long been telling me, 'The bliss of reciprocated affection is not allotted to you under any form. Your heart must be widowed in this manner from the world, or you will never seek a better portion; a consciousness of possessing the fervent love of any human being would soon become your heaven, therefore it would be your curse.'

ED. G. HAIGHT (1954)

A Kansas Teacher on her Children

Mary Abell was a teacher, married to a farmer-preacher. Here she writes to her mother, 14 August 1872. This letter and the others that follow are all from Kansas. Nettie is six and going to school.

Nettie has commenced piecing a quilt. She sews very nicely – has finished six blocks – wants Grandma to send her a lot of pieces and the girls. Rob bought Robbie and Eddie each a little hatchet while at Manhattan – axe one side and hammer on the other – and Nettie a set of dolls' furniture, the smartest lot of little things I ever saw. There are four chairs, a bureau, table, sofa and bedstead, writing desk, stand, center table, footstool, and cradle, they are as perfectly made as any thing you ever saw – that is her present for taking care of baby. Robt. got her a drawing book for the slate a while ago – pages painted black and pictures white. She is learning to read also.

Mary Abell to her sister Kate, 7 March 1874; Nettie is now seven-and-a-half.

Robert and Nettie are digging a well – They have got eleven feet now. Shall I tell you how they manage. Robert has a box holding a bushel and a half with a string handle to it, to which is attached a long heavy well rope, which runs over pulleys. When he gets the box full of dirt he sings out to Nettie who leads off the horse, who draws up the dirt in fine style. Rob pulls out the pin that holds the box end of the rope – hitches another horse which is close by to a staple in the side of the box – and hauls off the dirt, comes back, changes riggings again and gets into the bucket and horse No. 1. lets him down into the well again. If you want this an idea of how they get along – I kept tally today, and they hauled up 22 boxes this a.m and 36 this p.m. Rob dug over three feet today. He has come to rock now but how solid he don't know. He had engaged men to help him, but when he went to see them they could not come. He gets along just as fast – as if he had a man and with only Nettie's help. One would hardly believe it. He says he can do 35 feet in that way. He has a long house ladder which he puts into the well to climb out with and will splice it and make it go that far. If we could only get water at that depth how little it would cost us. Nettie is quite tired out tonight she says it has kept her running all day. Eddie tends the baby for me in her place. Yesterday was a miserable day. Snow – rain – hail – mud – and a hard wind, but Nettie led the horse for Rob to work all day. I bundled her up good and warm, so she would not catch cold.

By the way John Abell's little girl May is dead. . . .

I have written a letter for Nettie to Nellie, that I shall mail at the same time I do this, but when that will be I do not know. This is a beautiful day. Eddie has led the horse today, so he relieves Nettie, and for both of them it will not be hard work – besides it makes it some easier for me, as Nettie can hold the baby some of the time – and Eddie can only rock him – cannot hold him.

ED. H. JORDAN, *LOVE LIES BLEEDING* (1979)

On a Son Growing Up

The Spanish novelist Emilia Pardo Bazán was born in 1851, in Galicia. She wrote many acclaimed novels, at a time when few women were able to publish in Spain. The best known are Los Pazos de Ulloa *and* La Madre Naturaleza. *Her aristocratic husband was less intellectual than she was, and she fell in love with a university professor, Linares. When he lost his job because he objected to the dominance of the Catholic Church, he had to move away. She wrote touching letters, ostensibly about her young son, in discourse suggesting a multiplicity of identities.*

Coruna, 24 December 1876

My friend,

I have left far too long a time since my last letter. I feel disappointed with myself whenever I recall the trivial circumstances which have prevented me. If I thought my silence upset you, it would be presumptious of

me, but that would decrease my low spirits somewhat. What can I write
to you about? the distance and different directions of our lives mean that I
don't know what your present preoccupations are, and mine can't interest
you. I believe that you are with your sister . . . What a life! The extent of
our affections depends on a few miles, more or less.

My son is growing, in body and mind. At two, his innocence is a
delight. At this moment I'm completely alone in the house, as the rest of
the family is out and he's on my lap. I've only got one free hand, so I can't
structure my ideas, or even write properly, because he keeps putting his
little hands on the pen, and distracting me.

When I close my eyes I can imagine him at 20. My friend, don't be surprised at my lyrical feeling for this child: it is so sweet to bring a person
into the world, and so necessary to love passionately when you lack
something you can never, never possess; and there are wounds which
bleed till your death and continue to hurt as much as the very day they
were inflicted. . . .

PRIVATE COLLECTION AND TRANS. OLGA KENYON

Edith Sitwell's Childhood

*Edith Sitwell's aunt, Aunt Florence, wrote of her, just before her brother
Osbert was born:*

November 1892

She is now five years old, a most interesting and dear little person . . . I
have been giving her tiny lessons after tea. Last Sunday, I began the life of
Our Lord with her. When the visit was ending, little Edith helped arrange
the flowers. I think she did four vases with her dear little hands, taking
great pains to make them pretty, and making quaint remarks, such as 'We
must make the best of things', 'We mustn't carol [quarrel] with what
we've got'.

She then complained about her nurserymaid, Martha, who she said
does 'nothing to amuse, and everything to displease me'. She is an unusually articulate small child, of the sort sometimes called 'old-fashioned',
and unusually retentive and intelligent.

It is wonderful the way in which the child is getting on with her reading
– really teaching herself – asking the meaning of unknown words, and

remembering them. Fairy tales have been her especial delight. She is very reflective and at the same time full of fun and mischief, delighting in a joke. . . .

Once she got one of her frightened fits, and clung to me. These unexplained attacks of terror are the only sign that anything is wrong at all for this dear little person. Dear little E has grown round one's heart, and it was sad parting with her.

V. GLENDINNING, *EDITH SITWELL: LION AMONG UNICORNS* (1981)

On the Birth of Baby Daughters

Millicent Fawcett worked unceasingly with her husband to further women's rights and education. They had a clever daughter, Philippa, of whom they were extremely fond and proud. Mrs Fawcett found no difficulty in combining her maternal feelings with her unremitting social work. In 1892 the Chicago Exhibition asked her to produce something to show the value of university education for women, and among other exhibits Millicent Fawcett decided to send 'a frame full of photographs of prize babies whose mothers are graduates'. The letters to students when a daughter was born reveal her delight. She wrote to Clotilda Marson, a Newnham graduate, when her baby Mary arrived that year:

1892

We were made very happy by the joyful telegram 'Strong daughter both well'. Strong daughter sounds so nice, it is what we all hope for her all through her life; it made us think of the beautiful bit in the Baptism service, 'Manfully to fight under His banner against sin, the world and the devil, and to continue Christ's faithful soldier and servant unto her life's end'. She will need to be a strong daughter for that, so well as for many other good and beautiful things.

RAY STRACHEY, *MILLICENT FAWCETT* (1931)

In July she wrote to her friend Mrs Merrifield, when her granddaughter Helen was born to May, whose Tripos Mrs Fawcett had secured for her. She uses public metaphor to celebrate this intimate event, to show that she saw daughters' roles to be as important in the public as in the private arena.

The 4th of July is a beautiful day for a birthday. I hope the baby's declaration of independence will date from it, and that she will be a worthy descendant of those who have gone before her.

RAY STRACHEY (1931)

A Daughter Analyses the Problems Caused by her Parents' Ill-matched Characters

The Tibetan expert and explorer, Alexandra David-Néel (1868–1969) here writes to her distant cousin Philippe, whom she married in 1905, to explain why she thinks they ought not to have children.

August 1905

I came into existence as a misconceived instrument of reconciliation between my parents. I blame my mother who felt things, rather than consciously analysing them. My greatest fear is that I may resemble her. When I look in the mirror I see those features and wrinkles which I hate.

I am the daughter of the man she did not love. I am his daughter alone in spite of the blood from which she made me and the milk with which she nourished me . . . See, my friend, that which sometimes awaits those imprudent women who look to maternity for consolation from an ill-matched union. I see myself as a wife being pulled inexorably into the self-annihilating role of my mother. If I had a child I would be as destructive toward it as my mother was to me.

My son and my daughter, in reliving what I was in earlier times, would be incomprehensible to you and *you* would not respect them. That would be the sad struggle amidst these children. Indifference would perhaps come on your part, but I am only too fully aware of the mother I would be to risk the terrible adventure. The child for me would be the god to whom would go all my adoration. He would be my unique hope and I would only live to see him live the life I did not live, to realize the ideal I did not attain. Without doubt he would not achieve this. But it could happen that I would become a person in whom lodged a spirit dissimilar to my present one . . . it would be the story of my mother, but intensified by all the superiority, sensitivity and intelligence that I have over that wretched woman in whom disappointments only changed into rancor and spitefulness against her unsuspecting child.

Ah, my poor dear, believe me, there is much wisdom, much foresight in my will not to be a mother. How support the terrible thought of not being able to expose all of one's life, sentiments and actions before the vigorous, implacable, severe judge which one's child would prove?

PRIVATE COLLECTION

Education

The second part of this chapter deals with education, defined both as a leading out of the child's innate abilities, or a putting in of knowledge. The Church tended to 'put in' many hours of theology, Greek and Latin, from which girls were excluded. Up to Virginia Woolf women have written of their frustration at not being allowed to learn this privileged discourse of men.

Hildegard of Bingen in the twelfth century, and Dame Julian of Norwich, like many aristocratic women, dictated their letters. It still remains a mystery how Hildegard learned Latin and theology; perhaps from listening to sermons very attentively, as so many girls had to do if they were to pick up an education. Hildegard's Latin is limited in its vocabulary, yet she deploys it with remarkable subtlety to describe her visions. She also wrote competently on science, herbal medicine and philosophy. Not to mention her brilliant composing of plain chant (which should no longer be called Gregorian!).

Héloïse, educated by a scholastic uncle, used arguments equal to her ambitious churchman-lover. She learned the ability to manipulate *their* language, as did Christine de Pisan two centuries later. By the late Middle Ages in England we have evidence of women writing skilfully, in collections such as the Stonor papers, and by Tudor times daughters of the rich were often well educated in arts and languages, as demonstrated by daughters of humanists and princes. Lady Jane Grey suffered 'nips and beatings' from her ambitious parents (who so nearly gained the throne through her). Henry VIII's sixth wife, Catherine Parr, chose one of the best tutors of the time for her stepchildren, in Roger Ascham. One can but admire the control of Elizabeth over language in persuading her father to accept a gift which will ingratiate her both in his eyes and those of her intelligent stepmother.

A Daughter to her Father in the House of her Step-grandmother

This letter was written in English, in about 1500, by Dorothy Plumpton to her father, Sir Robert Plumpton. On his remarriage he placed his daughter in the home of her stepmother's family. This was partly to improve her chances of meeting marriageable young men. However, she found life tough.

Let this be delivered in haste to my most honoured and wholly beloved, good, kind father, Sir Robert Plumpton, presently staying at Plumpton in Yorkshire.

Most Honoured father, in the humblest manner I know I send you my respects, and to my lady mother, and to all my brothers and sisters, whom I beseech Almighty God to maintain and preserve in health, prosperity, and increasing honour, asking of you only your daily blessing; this is to let you know that I sent a message to you, by Wryghame of Knaresborough, about me feelings, how he should ask you, in my name, to send for me to return home to you, and as yet I have had no answers, and my lady has obtained knowledge of my desire.

Because of this she has become a better lady towards me than she ever was before, and she has promised to be my good lady as long as she lives; and if you or she can find anything more suitable for me in this district or any other, she will help to further my interests to the limit of her power. So I humbly ask you, to be so good and kind a father to me as to let me know your pleasure, how you woud like me to be settled, as soon as you are pleased to.

And please write to my ladyship, thanking her good ladyship for the tender loving-kindness she has shown me, and asking her to continue it. Sir I beseech you to send a servant of yours to my lady and to me, and show by fatherly kindness that I am your child: for I have sent you various messages and letters, and have never had any answer. Because of this, it is believed in the district among those persons who would rather speak ill than good, that you have little feeling for me, an error which you can discredit, if it pleases you to be a good kind father to me.

And please send me a fine hat, and some good cloth to headscarfs.

And I pray to Jesus that he will be pleased to have you in His blessed keeping, and bring you happiness and your heart's desire.

Written at the Hirst, the thirteenth day of May,

By your loving daughter,

Dorothy Plumpton.

ED. C. MORIARTY, *THE VOICE OF THE MIDDLE AGES* (1989)

The Future Queen Elizabeth Sends the Present of a Translation to her Father

To the most glorious and mighty king Henry VIII, King of England, France and Ireland, Defender of the Faith, and Supreme Head under Christ of the Church of England and Ireland for whose every happiness His Majesty's most humble daughter Elizabeth every prays, and who she entreats to give her his blessing.

Inasmuch as the immortal mind excels the immortal body so every wise man will deem the works of the mind more highly to be esteemed and worthy of greater honour than any corporal act. As, therefore, your Majesty is of so high an excellence that none or few may be compared with you in royal and gracious attainments such that not only am I bound to you by the law of the land as my lord, by the law of nature as my lord and by divine law as my father, but as [you are] the most gracious of lords and my own matchless and most kind father so I would be bound to your Majesty by all laws and by all sorts of duties and by all means possible.

It seemed most appropriate to me that a work of such piety, a work compiled in English by the pious zeal and great industry of a glorious Queen and for that reason a work sought out by all, and by your Majesty highly esteemed, should be translated into other languages (this work which is its theme is truly worthy of a King and in its compilation worthy of a Queen) and it seemed fitting to me that this task should be undertaken by myself, your daughter and one who should be not only the imitator of your virtues but also heir to them. Whatever in this work is not mine, is worthy of the highest praise, inasmuch as the whole book is so pious in its argument, so skilful in its compilation and so well drawn up in the fittest order. But as to what is mine, if there by any error in it yet it may merit pardon on account of my ignorance, my youth, my short time of study and my goodwill, and if it be undistinguished, even though it merit no praise, yet if it be well received it will powerfully incite me to further efforts so that even as I advance in years so I shall advance also in learning and in the fear of God and so it shall come to pass that I shall worship Him ever more zealously and serve your Majesty ever more dutifully.

Wherefore I do not doubt but that your fatherly goodness and royal foresight will set no lower value on this private labour of my mind than on any other attainment and that you will feel that this holy work which is the more highly to be valued as having been compiled by the Queen your wife, may have its value ever so little enhanced by being translated by your daughter. May the King of Kings, in whose hands lie the hearts of all kings, so guide your mind and protect your life that under your Majesty's rule we may live long in true piety and religion.

From Hertford, the 30th day of December 1545.

MARIA PERRY, *THE WORD OF A PRINCE: A LIFE OF ELIZABETH I* (1990)

On the Education of Daughters

In this sensible letter to a prosperous tradesman recommends that girls be taught enough about business to manage their own and their husbands' money, and avoid 'ruin of soul and body'.

1739

'Tis the misfortune of this nation that the most part of our gentlemen and tradesmen bring up their daughters at a boarding school, where . . . time is, for the most part, employ'd in trifles, whilst the useful and becoming part of her education is wholly neglected, as her being taught to cut out and make up (her own and her family's) linen, and prudent management of household affairs, whereby she might become qualify'd for the government of a family, at her entrance into the married state.

But no sooner does the little creature leave school, furnish'd with all these trifling accomplishments, than the father and mother are for showing her off to get her a husband. This of course spoils the girl; for she now thinks of nothing but dress, receiving and returning visits, tea-drinking, and card-playing, which last is of the most fatal consequence . . . if this manner of life fails of getting her a husband, when young, and her parents are unable to give her a large fortune, she is obliged to live an old maid, and die useless to her generation. On the contrary, if her parents die, and leave her only a small fortune, she can't live upon the interest, and consequently must endeavour to marry for a livelihood; whence she becomes a prey to some designing mercenary fellow, or otherwise she spends her narrow income, and then what must she do for a support? Why she takes to ill courses; which makes so many women kept awhile, and then come upon the town, to the inevitable ruin both of soul and body.

. . . Let all gentlemen who have several daughters, and tradesmen, who can't give about 1000 or 1500 l. a piece to their daughters, and some who are able to give no more than two or three hundred pound . . . take care their daughters be taught the most useful part of needle-work, all the arts of economy, writing and book-keeping, with enough of dancing and French to give them a graceful easy freedom both of discourse and behaviour: And when they have acquir'd these necessary accomplishments in some degree of perfection, let them also at the age of fifteen or sixteen be put apprentices to genteel and easy trades, such as linen or woollen drapers, haberdashers of small wares, mercers, glovers, perfumers, grocers, confectioners, retailers of gold and silver lace, buttons, etc.

Why are not these as creditable trades for the daughters of gentlemen as they are for their sons?

. . . If women were train'd up to business from their early years, 'tis highly probable they would in general be more industrious, and get more money than men, and if so, what woman of spirit would submit to be a slave, and fling herself away, as many are forc'd to do, merely for a maintenance, because she cannot stoop to be a servant, and can find no reputable business to go into? . . .

As for tradesmen in particular, it would be much happier for them, if their wives and daughters knew how to keep their books, and be serviceable to them in their shops, than to have them walk through with that state and unconcernedness they usually do: They would then better know how to spend their husband's money, so as not to exceed his income . . .

. . . From the delicacy of their make, they are, indeed, unfit for certain laborious employments, which require considerable strength and robustness of body; but in all those were quickness of thought, activeness, dispatch, neatness, address, and a habit of pleasing are capital requisites, they would, I persuade myself, in no wise fall short of the men as are most remarkable for these qualifications.

GENTLEMAN'S MAGAZINE, VOL. 9, SEPTEMBER 1739

An Enlightened Woman Proposes Better Education for Girls

Lady Pennington, writing to her daughters, advocates a serious and sensible programme for women's education, with 'mornings wholly to improvement'. She realizes both the need for 'diversions' and sufficient knowledge to manage 'all domestic affairs'.

1770

It is an excellent method to appropriate the mornings wholly to improvement; – the afternoon may then be allow'd to diversions: – under the last head, I place company, books of the amusing kind, and entertaining productions of the needle, as well as plays, balls, cards, etc., which more commonly go by the name of diversions: . . . One half hour or more, either before or immediately after breakfast, I would have you constantly give to the attentive perusal of some rationally pious author, or to some part of the New Testament.

It is necessary for you to be perfect in the four first rules of Arithmetic – more you can never have occasion for, and the mind should not be burthen'd with needless application.

The management of all domestic affairs is certainly the proper business of woman – and, unfashionably rustic as such an assertion may be thought, it is not beneath the dignity of any lady, however high her rank, to know how to educate her children, to govern her servants . . . Make yourself, therefore, so thoroughly acquainted with the most proper method of conducting a family, and with the necessary expense of every article.

ED. B. HILL, *EIGHTEENTH CENTURY WOMEN* (1984)

The Right To Education

Maria Edgeworth (1768–1849) was the eldest daughter of a much-married Irish landlord. She felt responsible for the education of his many younger children and wrote Practical Education *with him in 1798. She designed enlightened reading schemes and here defends the right of women to education – by argument designed to appeal to men in power:*

You apprehend that knowledge must be hurtful to the sex, because it will be the means of their acquiring power. It seems to me impossible that women can acquire the species of direct power which you dread: the manners of society must totally change before women can mingle with men in the busy and public scenes of life. They must become amazons before they can affect this change; they must cease to be women before they can desire it. The happiness of neither sex could be increased by this metamorphosis.

MARIA EDGEWORTH, *LETTERS FOR LITERARY LADIES* (1795)

Senior Wrangler

Thanks to efforts of women such as Millicent Fawcett, Girton and Newnham College were founded, and the Tripos examinations finally opened for women. The student with the highest marks in the Finals Tripos is called Senior Wrangler. In 1890 it was Philippa, Millicent's daughter, who came top. Her affectionate father, old Mr Garrett came over from Aldeburgh with two of his other granddaughters, and one of these sent home to her mother a graphic description of the proceedings:

It was a most exciting scene in the Senate this morning. Christina and I got seats in the gallery, and Grandpapa remained below. The gallery was crowded with girls and a few men, and the floor of the building was thronged by undergraduates as tightly packed as they could be. The lists were read from the gallery and we heard splendidly. All the men's names were read first; the Senior Wrangler was much cheered. There was a good deal of shouting and cheering throughout; at last the man who had been reading shouted 'Women.' The undergraduates yelled 'Ladies,' and for some minutes there was a great uproar. A fearfully agitating moment for Philippa it must have been; the examiner, of course, could not attempt to read the names until there was a lull. Again and again he raised his cap, but would not say 'ladies' instead of 'women,' and quite right, I think. He signalled with his hands for the men to keep quiet, but he had to wait some time. At last he read Philippa's name, and announced that she was 'above the Senior Wrangler.' There was a great and prolonged cheering; many of the men turned towards Philippa, who was sitting in the gallery with Miss Clough, and waved their hats. When the examiner went on with the other names, there were cries of 'Read Miss Fawcett's name again,' but no attention was paid to this. I don't think any other women's names were heard, for the men were making such a tremendous noise. We made our way round to Philippa to congratulate her, and then I went over to Grandpapa. Miss Gladstone was with him. She was, of course, tremendously delighted. A great many people were there to cheer and congratulate Philippa when she came down into the hall.

RAY STRACHEY, *MILLICENT FAWCETT* (1931)

four

Love and Sexual Passion

Male writers have frequently declared that men feel greater sexual passion than women. And since Plato they have also claimed to experience greater spiritual love for other men. But the depth of women's responses can no longer be underestimated, as evidenced in these letters; intended for only one other person, they are both revealing and honest.

The letters range from apprehensive to passionate, from heterosexual to lesbian. Women show themselves as taking far greater initiative, and reacting in far more varied ways, than cultural role models usually acknowledged. The strikingly different discourses demonstrate abilities of assessing and judging a wide area of emotion, including lesbian.

The bold love letter from Héloïse to Abelard opens the book. She is worthy of this pre-eminence, with her passionate 'You alone have the power to make me sad, to bring me happiness or comfort'. Four centuries later Elizabeth I, fully aware of the real power of a husband, skilfully prevaricates, in order not to commit herself – or her country – to a foreigner (see Chapter Eleven).

Women in the French court of Louis XIV seemed to have more social influence in that they ruled over literary discussions in their salons. Yet the King's cousin, 'La Grande Mademoiselle,' was not allowed to marry the man of her choice, though a duke. I include three letters describing her unhappy, brief love affair because their author, Madame de Sévigné, transforms the account into a work of art. To continue this theme of the interlinking of fiction and reality, I include in Appendix I an extract from the first novel in English: *Love Letters Between a Nobleman and his Sister* (1676?). The passionate discourse of the Restoration both echoes and influences the ways in which the literate formed their ideas about sexual feelings. The *actual* letters of Lady Mary Wortley Montagu before she eloped with her future husband sound remarkably like the outpourings of a fictional heroine. They raise again the intriguing question of how far the concepts of the language we learn in a social context mould our psyche.

In the latter part of this chapter, letters analysing different approaches to courtship are compared to extracts which consider money settlements. A settlement on a Roman bride (the earliest letter we have in a woman's hand) and letters on French dowries in the nineteenth century show the continuing importance of a financial bond.

Royal Drama in the Making and Breaking of an Engagement

Mademoiselle, niece of Louis XIII, was a large, ungainly woman appreciated mainly because of her close relationship to Louis XIV. Madame de Sévigné recounts with dramatic suspense the amazed reaction of most courtiers when they heard that Mademoiselle had achieved a triumph, an engagement to the soldier-adventurer Duke of Lauzun. Coulanges to whom these letters were sent was cousin and lifelong friend of Madame de Sévigné.

Paris, Monday 15 December 1670

What I am about to communicate to you is the most astonishing thing, the most surprising, the most marvellous, the most miraculous, most triumphant, most baffling, most unheard of, most singular, most extraordinary, most unbelievable, most unforseen, biggest, tiniest, rarest, commonest, the most talked about, the most secret up to this day, the most brilliant, the most enviable, in fact a thing of which only one example can be found in past ages, and, moreover, that example is a false one; a thing nobody can believe in Paris (how could anyone believe it in Lyons?), a thing that makes everybody cry 'mercy on us', a thing that fills Mme de Rohan and Mme de Hauterive with joy, in short a thing that will be done on Sunday and those who see it will think they are seeing visions – a thing that will be done on Sunday and perhaps not done by Monday. I can't make up my mind to say it. Guess, I give you three tries. You give up? Very well, I shall have to tell you. M. de Lauzun is marrying on Sunday, in the Louvre – guess who? I give you four guesses, ten, a hundred. Mme de Coulanges will be saying: That's not so very hard to guess, it's Mlle de La Vallière. Not at all, Madame, Mlle de Retz, then? Not at all, you're very provincial. Of course, how silly we are, you say: It's Mlle Colbert. You're still further away. Then it must be Mlle de Créquy? You're nowhere near. I shall have to tell you in the end: he is marrying, on Sunday, in the Louvre, with the King's permission, Mademoiselle, Mademoiselle de . . . Mademoiselle . . . guess the name. He's marrying

Mademoiselle, of course! Honestly, on my honour, on my sworn oath! Mademoiselle, the great Mademoiselle, Mademoiselle, daughter of the late Monsieur, Mademoiselle, granddaughter of Henri IV, Mademoiselle d'Eu, first cousin of the King, destined for the throne, the only bride in France worthy of Monsieur [Louis XIV's brother]. If you shout aloud, if you say we have lied, that it is false, a fine old story, too feeble to imagine, you are perfectly right. We did as much ourselves.

Goodbye, letters coming by this post will show you whether we are telling the truth or not.

TRANS. L. TANCOCK, *MADAME DE SÉVIGNÉ: SELECTED LETTERS* (1982)

The following day Louis XIV decided that his cousin should not be allowed to marry a mere duke. Madame de Sévigné wrote again to her cousin.

Paris, Friday 19 December 1670

What you might call a bolt from the blue occurred yesterday evening at the Tuileries, but I must start the story further back. You have heard as far as the joy, transports, ecstasies of the Princess and her fortunate lover. Well, the matter was announced on Monday, as you were told. Tuesday was spent in talk, astonishment, compliments. On Wednesday Mademoiselle made a settlement on M. de Lauzun, with the object of bestowing on him the titles, names and honours needed for mention in the marriage contract, and that was enacted on the same day. So, to go on with, she bestowed on him four duchies: first the earldom of Eu, which is the highest peerage in France and gives him first precedence, the duchy of Montpensier, which name he bore all day yesterday, the duchy of Saint-Fargeau and that of Châtellerault, the whole estimated to be worth twenty-two millions. Then the contract was drawn up, in which he took the name of Montpensier. On Thursday morning, that is yesterday, Mademoiselle hoped that the King would sign the contract as he had promised, but by seven in the evening His Majesty, being persuaded by the Queen, Monsieur and divers greybeards that this business was harmful to his reputation, decided to break it off, and after summoning Mademoiselle and M. de Lauzun, declared to them, in the presence of Monsieur le Prince, that he forbade their thinking any more about this marriage. M. de Lauzun received this order with all the respect, all the submissiveness, all the stoicism and all the despair that such a great fall required. As for Mademoiselle, according to her mood she burst into tears, cries, violent outbursts of grief, exaggerated lamentations, and she remained in bed all day, taking nothing but broth. So much for a beautiful dream, a fine subject for a novel or a tragedy, but above all for arguing and talking for ever and ever. And that is what we are doing day and night, evening and morning, on and on without respite. We hope you will do the same. Upon which I most humbly kiss your hands.

Madame de Sévigné
TRANS. L. TANCOCK (1982)

The following letter, again to her cousin, shapes the real romance into a suitable fiction. Madame de Sévigné realized the potential of this drama for the stage, and with her vivid pen she has made the story into art.

Paris, Wednesday 24 December 1670
You now know the romantic story of Mademoiselle and M. de Lauzun. It is a real subject of tragedy according to all the rules of the theatre. The other day we were plotting out the acts and scenes, giving it four days instead of twenty-four hours, and it made a perfect play. Never have such changes been seen in so short a time, never have you seen such general emotion, never have you heard such extraordinary news. M. de Lauzun has played his part as to the manner born; he has endured this misfortune with a self-control, courage and yet grief mingled with profound respect which have earned him universal admiration. What he has lost is of inestimable value, but the goodwill of the King, which he has kept, is also beyond price, and his fortune seems by no means in a parlous state. Mademoiselle has behaved very well too. She has wept a lot, but today she returned to her duty calls at the Louvre, whence she had been receiving all the visitors. So that is that. Good-bye.

TRANS. L. TANCOCK (1982)

A Daughter Persuades her Father to Let her Marry

Lady Mary Wortley Montagu (1689–1762) was the eldest daughter of the 1st Duke of Kingston. She fell in love with a mere Member of Parliament, Wortley Montagu, and married him against her father's wishes. The marriage was not happy, as he proved cold and comparatively dull. However she was at first passionately attached to him, and her love letters are as dramatic as fiction. In this first one, dated 26 July 1712, she recounts what she has just written (notice the use of the letter here, though she was living in the same house) to her father, to persuade him to allow her to marry.

I said every thing in this Letter I thought proper to move him, and proffer'd in atonement for not marrying whom he would, never to marry at all. He did not think fit to answer this letter, but sent for me to him. He told me he was very much surpriz'd that I did not depend on his Judgement for my future happynesse, that he knew nothing I had to complain of etc., that he did not doubt I had some other fancy in my head which encourag'd me to this disobedience, but he assur'd me if I refus'd a settlement he has provided for me, he gave me his word, whatever proposals were made him, he would never so much as enter into a Treaty with any other; that if I founded any hopes upon his death, I should find my selfe mistaken. . . . I told my intention to all my nearest Relations; I was surpriz'd at their blameing it to the greatest degree. I was told they were sorry I would ruin my selfe, but if I was so unreasonable they could not blame my F[ather] whatever he inflicted on me. I objected I did not love him. They made answer they found no Necessity of Loveing; if I liv'd well with him, that was all was requir'd of me, and that if I consider'd this Town I should find very few women in love with their Husbands and yet a many happy. It was in vain to dispute with such prudent people; they look'd upon me as a little Romantic, and I found it impossible to persuade them that liveing in London at Liberty was not the height of happynesse. . . .

ED. R. HALSBAND, *THE COMPLETE LETTERS OF LADY MARY WORTLEY MONTAGU* (1965)

To Phillipa Mundy, August 1712:

For my part, I know not what I shall do; perhaps at last I shall do something to surprize everybody. Where ever I am, and wht ever becomes of me, I am ever yours. Limbo is better than Hell. My Adventures are very odd; I may go into Limbo if I please, but tis accompanny'd with such circumstances, my courage will hardly come up to it, yet perhaps it may. In short I know not what will become of me. You'l think me mad, but I know nothing certain but that I shall not dye an Old Maid, that's positive.

ED. R. HALSBAND (1965)

To Wortley, 17 August 1712:

Every thing I apprehended is come t[o p]asse. 'Tis with the utmost difficulty [and d]anger I write this. My father is in the house. . . . I am frighted
to death and know not what I say. I had yet more to suffer, for I have
been forced to promise to write no more to you.

ED. R. HALSBAND (1965)

Women's Views on Men's Love

*Anna Seward, who became a friend of the Ladies of Llangollen, wrote
many letters at the end of the eighteenth and the beginning of the
nineteenth centuries. She sometimes fell in love with women, but for years
felt a deep, chaste love for an unhappily married choirmaster at Lichfield.
In 1811 she wrote to a Mrs Hayley:*

Men are rarely capable of pure unmixed tenderness to any fellow creature except their children. In general even the best of them give their
friendship to their male acquaintances, and their fondness to their offspring. For their mistress, or wife, they feel, during a time, a tenderness
more ardent and more secret, a friendship softer and more animated.
But this inexplicable, this fascinating sentiment, which we understand
by the name of love, often proves an illusion of the imagination; – a
meteor that misleads her who trusts it, vanishing when she has followed
it into pools and quick sands where peace and liberty are swallowed up
and lost.

COLLECTED LETTERS OF ANNA SEWARD (1811)

Death of a Broken Heart

*Geraldine Jewsbury described the unhappy love affair of Mr —— and the
shabby way he treated the mistress who adored him. She died of cancer
'brought on by grief', but 'it now seems unreasonable to expect high-
pressure efforts except from a steam-engine'.*

[To Jane Carlyle]

April 19 1841

He did not come at all for some reason or another, and on the whole I was not sorry, for seeing him now is like the meeting of two ghosts on the other side Styx. Each has been connected so strangely with the history of so many feelings and incidents, which at the time seemed as if their memory could never pass away. And what has been the end of so much passionate suffering, so much love which all the parties thought would endure for ever? The woman he loved so madly – of whom he declared (to one he trusted) that he would rather obtain her friendship even, than have possession of her whole sex – died of a broken heart, or, rather, of a cancer, which Sir Astley Cooper said had been brought on by grief and anxiety of mind. She was a fine creature. I never saw her but once; but I heard of her from many quarters, and from those who knew her best. She was married to a man who did not care for her, and she, till she met ——, did not know what affection meant. His own testimony, and the way he spoke of love to me (that time we had our conversation), was enough to absolve her from all censure except the deepest commiseration. Her sister (who knew nothing of the matter) said, after her death, that she used to sit for hours gazing on the wall without seeing anything or speaking a word. When asked, 'What are you thinking about?' – 'Oh, many things; don't talk to me!' He, for whom she has risked everything – very soon after he had obtained everything – began to grow, not indifferent exactly, but satisfied. Unfortunately for her, she and her husband were obliged to leave this country: in absence she lost her influence over him. In a very short time he forced her to break with him: he married for expediency and is now the father of a family, is a respectable man, and in prosperous circumstances. Since her death he professes, to those who knew the facts, bitterly to regret the past; but it is somewhat dubious whether these brave sentiments are real, or assumed as a piece of his respectability.

I, who was a bystander, have the recollection of the faith I then had in his good qualities, and the strong feeling I had for him, and the firm belief in his chivalrous, honourable dealing towards her, and the undoubting trust in her submission to duty, honour, and so forth. I did believe, then, in many fine things, and even now I only doubt their durability, or rather it now seems unreasonable to expect high-pressure efforts except from a steam-engine, and even that wears out; and why should we regret that things are so constituted? The fact of all that is worth having, and even life itself, being precarious, gives it a value beyond its own, and those who have an eternity to trust to, little know the desperate tenacity of those who have to make the most of Time! I cannot explain to you the superstitious value I set on those I ever love, and the sort of religious feeling with which I try to guard every word or thought which might raise a shade between us.

No, my dear, you must first have no hope of anything beyond this world, before you can know how very precious is a friend we really love. This letter has been written *à plusieurs reprises*, for my eyes are rather worse, if anything, to-day than they were this day week, so that now I can hardly write, and what is to become of me I don't know!

I have more time for thinking than is at all agreeable. All this while I have never thanked you for your letter – it made me feel very sad. Those efforts after strength are weary things, and I doubt whether they do much good. They go to exhaust what strength we may possess. On the whole, I cannot help thinking it is the wisest to let ourselves be drifted along. Time brings quiet and strength naturally; in fact, the very change he works in us and in our feelings is equivalent to strength. There are two lines in Coleridge's translation of 'Wallenstein' that haunt me from morning to night, and have done so ever since I began to know what endurance meant. 'What pang is permanent with man? From the highest as from the vilest things he learns to wean himself, and the strong hours conquer him!'

If you will, from time to time, send me word how you go on, it will be a great favour. Just now I am especially anxious to hear from you; if you cannot guess why, I won't tell you. Do not plague yourself to write long letters, but say how you are in every way; patronise the pronoun 'I' as much as I do myself! Never mind telling me anything, except inasmuch as it affects or interests you! I have not said a tithe of what I have thought of when lying on the sofa. You little know the comfort it is to me to have you to think of, nor how much I think of you. If you take an interest in my friend ——, she is rather better, at least was last Tuesday. She had a scheme in her head which had quite roused her. Heaven only knows whether it will prove wise and feasible, but even the power of hoping is no small blessing to her!

ED. A. IRELAND, *SELECTIONS FROM THE LETTERS OF GERALDINE. E. JEWSBURY TO JANE WELSH CARLYLE* (1892)

In Love

Bertrand Russell edited the letters and diaries of his parents, which he called The Amberley Papers, *published in 1937. His mother, Kate Amberley, died when he was two, his father soon afterwards. Here she writes of her joy after their engagement.*

Dover Street

1/2 6. p.m. Friday

Oct 14 /64

My own dearest of darlings

I must just write you one line of goodnight, as I shall not be able to wish it to you to day. I feel quite lost, now I am come home & have not you to go to, or to look at. We have been shopping till this instant & it all appeared to me in another new light, when I was ordering very smart & elaborate toilettes, I could not fancy myself in them or think I should look the same Kätchen; as in the simple little blue gown.

My own great darling it does seem to me so delightful to be able to write & tell you how I love you; It is an old story I have told it you so often but I like writing it down & seeing it on paper. It makes me feel it a reality, to be able to write what I dream of for 6 months.

I do not like being away from you even now, it brings back to mind that awful feeling of when you last left me, & for an instant unconsciously the thought springs to my mind – 'I am alone again' – Do not think me very silly dearest Schatz but I am still feeling vexed with myself for my absurd & naughty irritation last night. It shall never happen again, at least I trust it will not. Is not one of the great objects of my life in future, to be; to keep that face, I love more than any earthly thing, free fr. all signs of vexation or care? So you can fancy how I shall blame myself if ever I am the cause of a little shade darkening its bonny brow. I am not going to tell you, that I do not wish you to look serious or to think, for I like you to do both, but there is a holy seriousness & a peaceful earnestness of expression which you have at times & which I like. The serious expression caused by thinking of man & men is so different fr. that caused by thinking of the way to be of *use* to them; you shall never be vexed my own darling if I can help it; those lines I sometimes see in your forehead shall be soothed away & may your's be the peace which passeth all understanding.

I am so glad I see you again to-morrow, about 3.30 I suppose; It will seem an age till then.

Once more my own & only darling goodnight.

From your own true love

KÄTCHEN.

I have forgotten all about commas etc but will not put them in at hazard. I daresay you will make out the drift of what I have said without their help.

ED. BERTRAND RUSSELL, *THE AMBERLEY PAPERS* (1937)

Admiration for George Eliot

Men admired George Eliot (Marian Evans). She also aroused tremendous admiration amounting to devotion in some women. A Dutch girl wrote her eighteen effusive pages beginning:

26 Dec 1874

Dear Miss Evans,

If I were a german girl I would add: 'much adored', but we Dutch are not *überschwänglich* in affectionate expressions, as we are too much fulfilled with respect for those who awake our best soul . . . since I finished with reading *Middlemarch* I could not resist something within me that draws me nearer to you. . . . You must have experienced much – you must much have felt. There are cries of the heart that awake an echo in every maiden's soul. . .

Jeanne Buskes

ED. G. HAIGHT, *THE GEORGE ELIOT LETTERS* (1954)

An American admirer, Melusina Fay Pierce, wrote to George Eliot for advice in 1866, and received a long thoughtful letter. In 1869 she wrote again.

Dearest ——

You will not be bored by another love letter – a little one? It is three whole years since I wrote to you before, and you sent me such a grave, kind, precious little answer. O how wise thou art! Where didst thou learn it all? . . . You wrote it for me, dearest, and often it has shamed me and spurred me on. . . .

Don't answer this, dearest. I don't require you to think of me as anything more than the evening breeze that sometimes kisses your cheek. I *love* you, you are so love-worthy. And once in a long time I *love* to say so to you. But I would not burden you with the weight of a rose leaf.

ED. G. HAIGHT (1954)

Marian Evans could not marry G.H. Lewes because his wife Agnes was living. Agnes had run away with another man and Evans offered devoted care to his three children. After his death she married a young admirer, John Cross. Her stepson, Charles Lewes, was so devoted to her that he forced himself to accept this unusual marriage. Here Charles's attitude is described by Annie Thackeray Ritchie.

23 May 1880

He gave her away, and looks upon Mr. Cross as an elder brother. . . . He is generous about the marriage. He says he owes everything to her, his Gertrude included, and that his father had no grain of jealousy in him, and only would have wished her happy, and that she was of such a delicate fastidious nature that she couldn't be satisfied with anything but an ideal tête-à-tête. George Eliot said to him if she hadn't been human with feelings and failings like other people, how could she have written her books?

He talked about his own mother in confidence, but his eyes all filled up with tears over George Eliot, and altogether it was the strangest page of life I ever skimmed over. She is an honest woman, and goes in with all her might for what she is about. She did not confide in Herbert Spencer.

ED. G. HAIGHT (1954)

Edith Wharton, American Novelist, Writes to her Lover W. Morton Fullerton

Sunday
[May 1908]

Oh, mon cher aimé, I don't think you can know what that little word of yours means to me today.

No, Dear, I don't mistake your silence. I am never so sure of you, I mean of your being happy with me, as when you don't feel it necessary to speak, because then I know that my nearness is no obstacle, no *interruption* to you; that I am part of the air you breathe.

I understand that, & I understand also what prompted you to write that little message just when you did. You knew I was sad at saying good-bye to you. You knew why sometimes I draw back from your least touch. I am so afraid – *so* afraid – of seeming to expect more than you can give, & of thus making my love for you less helpful to you, less what I wish it to be. And sometimes *mon corps ne peut pas oublier ton corps* [my body cannot forget your body], & then I am miserable.

I shouldn't say this if you hadn't shown me that you understood. I don't want to have any plan of conduct with you – to behave in this way or that way – but just to be natural, to be completely myself. And the completest expression of that self is in the desire to help you, to give you the chance to develop what is in you, & to live the best life you can. Nothing else counts for me now, Dear, except the wish to do some good work, & to have you see in it the reflection of all the beauty you have shown me.

Ton amie – E.

Believe me, a man of your intellectual value *has* a 'market value' when he brings such volonté to his task as you are capable of. This I never have doubted.

Tuesday
[May 17, 1908]

Alas, Dear – if you had felt as I felt, or a fraction of what I feel, you would not have 'wondered if I had a friend with me,' or if I should have been *surprised* at being surprised – you wouldn't have cared, because you wd have wanted so much to see me that nothing else would have counted. . . .

Sometimes I feel that I *can't* go on like this: from moments of such nearness, when the last shadow of separateness melts, back into a complete néant [nothingness] of silence, of not hearing, not knowing – being left to feel that I have been like a 'course' served & cleared away! . . .

Voilà ma dernière nouvelle. Et je me remets au travail –

[*c.* May 20, 1908]

I am mad about you Dear Heart and sick at the thought of our parting and the days of separation and longing that are to follow. It is a wonderful world that you have created for me, Morton dear, but how I am to adjust it to the *other* world is difficult to conceive. Perhaps when I am once more on land my mental vision may be clearer – at present, in the whole universe I see but one thing, am conscious of but one thing, you, and our love for each other.

EDS. R.W.B. AND NANCY LEWIS, *THE LETTERS OF EDITH WHARTON* (1988)

Vita Sackville-West to Virginia Woolf

Vita Sackville-West fell in love with Virginia Woolf in December 1926. This letter was written after her first stay at Rodmell, where Leonard and Virginia had bought a house, which can be visited today.

The Long Barn, Sevenoaks 17 June 1926

Dear Mrs Woolf

I must tell you how much I enjoyed my weekend.

Darling Virginia, you don't know how happy I was . . .

About prose and poetry, and the difference between them. I don't believe there is any, with all due respect to Coleridge. It is surely only a question of the different shape that words assume in the mind, not a question of drunkenness and sobriety. All too often the distinction leads people to think they may mumble inanities which would make them blush if written in good common English, but which they think fit to print if split up into lines. This alone shows that there isn't any real difference. None of the definitions fit. Matthew Arnold says that poetry describes the flowing, not the fixed; why should not prose?

A brilliant gathering at Sibyl's, – what you missed! The drawing room at Argyll House coruscated. Sibyl was, I thought, very stuffy about you; evidently cross at being cheated of a star in her firmament. 'If she could come up to London with *you*,' she snapped, 'she could have come here tonight.' I drew a touching picture of your frailty; she sniffed.

(London, Chelsea)

Now, having annoyed you (as I hoped) by telling you what you missed and what bad colour you are in with her ladyship, I'll tell you that I disenjoyed myself extremely; would have exchanged all the champagne in the cellar for a glass of Rodmell water; would have sent everybody flying with a kick.

I wish I were back at Rodmell. I wish you were coming here. Is it any good suggesting (you see that I am in a despondent mood,) that you should do so? It is very nice here, you know; but I expect you are busy. Only, it would be a nice refuge if you wanted to escape from London, and I would fetch you in the motor. In any case I shall see you on Friday? a damned long way off, too. Is this a dumb letter? You did spoil me so at Rodmell. I was terribly happy. *Tell me how you are.*

The following year:

Sevenoaks
Tuesday [31 May]
1927

My darling, I needn't tell you that it makes me wretched to know that you are ill. I feared the worst the moment I saw Leonard's writing on the envelope. Oh Virginia, I'd do anything to make you well. I wish to God that if you had got to be ill, it had happened here, and then you'd have been obliged to stay, and I could have looked after you. But that's selfish really, because I suppose you'd be miserable away from your own house.

Leonard says will I come and see you towards the end of the week, so you can't be *so* very bad. Of course I'll come any time you like. I shall be here all the week, so you have only to get Leonard to send me a postcard – or ring up.

I send you a few flowers. I fear they won't look as fresh when they reach you as when they leave me. Put ten grains of aspirin, powdered, in the water to revive them.

Are you in bed? yes, I suppose so. With an aching head. Able to read? Allowed to have letters? I am asking Leonard to let me know how you are. I do worry so about you, and above all can't bear the idea that you should be in pain.

Your

V.

EDS. L. DeSAHO AND M. LEASKA, *THE LETTERS OF VITA SACKVILLE-WEST TO VIRGINIA WOOLF* (1984)

Courting

Courtship, the wooing of women, is usually said to have begun with the troubadours in the Middle Ages. They had to praise the lady of the manor if they were to earn their daily bread. By Tudor times wooing is celebrated in courtly poetry, passionately exchanged by many of Shakespeare's lovers (half-mocked by Rosalind in *As You Like It*). Idyllic wooing was *not* the experience of most in the real court, as shown by the wives of Henry VIII.

Difficulties increased during the Civil War: Dorothy Osborne was forced to wait twelve years for her fiancé. He had espoused Cromwell's winning side, unlike her father, and she here deploys her witty, skilful, elegant, teasing pen to keep him interested. She was fortunate in finding a man whose love survived courtship, but many realized fully how short-lived wooing was, as shown in an anonymous seventeenth-century letter.

Jane Austen's novels analyse some of the follies, and occasional wisdom revealed by behaviour during courting. Her first novel, composed of seven brief letters written in early adolescence, suggested that courting could be ideally straightforward, and contrasts with her amused comments in later work.

In the nineteenth century there was a weakening of the external controls on courtship which brought greater personal autonomy, displayed in the letter from an American teacher, Bessie Huntting. The proposals here support feminists' contention that they offered women one of few moments of power. Yet it could scarcely be enjoyed, as it involved the disposing of a whole life. These answers reveal the thoughtful, unromantic approach of most to this irrevocable, irreversible decision.

'An Ideal Husband'

Dorothy Osborne (1628–98) was separated from her fiancé, Sir William Temple, both by the Civil War and her family's disapproval. During their long courtship she entertained him with witty, incisive letters which reveal gifts that would probably have made her a novelist today.

[No date; *c.* 1653]

There are a great many ingredients must go to the making me happy in a husband. My cousin F. says our humours must agree, and to do that he must have that kind of breeding that I have had, and used to that kind of company; that is, he must not be so much a country gentleman as to understand nothing but hawks and dogs, and be fonder of either than of his wife; nor of the next sort of them, whose time reaches no farther than to be justice of peace, and once in his life high sheriff, who reads no book but statutes, and studies nothing but how to make a speech interlarded with Latin, that may amaze his disagreeing poor neighbours, and fright them rather than persuade them into quietness. He must not be a thing that began the world in a free school, was sent from thence to the university, and is at his farthest when he reaches the inns of court; has no acquaintance but those of his form in those places; speaks the French he has picked out of old laws, and admires nothing but the stories he has heard of the revels that were kept there before his time. He must not be a town gallant neither, that lives in a tavern and an ordinary; that cannot imagine how an hour should be spent without company unless it be in sleeping; that makes court to all the women he sees, thinks they believe him, and laughs and is laughed at equally. Nor a travelled Monsieur whose head is feathered inside and outside, that can talk of nothing but of dances and duels, and has courage enough to wear slashes, when every body else dies with cold to see him. He must not be a fool of no sort, nor peevish, nor ill-natured, nor proud, nor courteous; and to all this must be added, that he must love me, and I him, as much as we are capable of loving. Without all this his fortune, though never so great, would not satisfy me, and with it a very moderate one would keep me from ever repenting my disposal. . . .

EDS. M. DUCKITT AND H. WRAGG, *SELECTED ENGLISH LETTERS* (1913)

The Views of a Real Woman on Male Wooing

To gentlemen:

If a woman falls into your snares, so cruel and unjust are you, that it is impossible she should ever retrieve her character, you can find an hundred excuses to extenuate the crimes of your own sex, you call them slips, tricks of youth, heat of young blood, or the like, and such an one has no more to do, than to take a trip into the country, or a voyage at most, and upon his return, put on a demure countenance, carry an air of gravity, and all's forgiven and forgotten; O he's become a mighty sober man! his wild oats are sown, and he'll make the better husband, now he has had his swing, and has seen his folly. But if a woman, decoy'd by the flattery and subtle arguments of treacherous men, steps the least awry, the whole world must ring with it, it's an indelible blot in her 'scutcheon, not to be wiped out by time, for it even pursues her after death, and contrary to all justice, the very children are upbraided with their mother's misfortune; no excuses are sought for her, no pity can be afforded to a ruin'd woman, but the fault is exaggerated with bitter expressions and railings against the whole sex, they are all immediately condemn'd of lewdness and wantonness . . .

ANON, WOMAN TRIUMPHANT (1721)

Weighing his Proposal

Helen Bourn (1797–1871) came from a distinguished middle-class family. She was wooed by Thomas, young brother of the writer Harriet Martineau. This letter displays the serious thought given to a proposal. Though she refuses him here, she married Thomas in 1822. The marriage was short, like many Victorian marriages, as he died of tuberculosis.

My dear Friend

I fully intended to have replied to your letter yesterday but our time is not always at our disposal when we are visiting our friends (& regret exceedingly that it was not in my power); I know too well what are yr feelings to keep you unnecessarily in suspense, & yr letter deserves to be answered with candour & sincerity – I was indeed deeply grieved some weeks ago to hear of such unfavorable accounts of yr health – the idea seized my mind that perhaps it might in fact be occasioned by the disappointment of yr hopes respecting me – & I felt that if yr. illness terminated as I then feared, from the accounts I heard, that I should never forgive myself; it was under this impression that I wrote to yr Sister Rachel being convinced that from her I should know the truth – her reply was long in coming & I anticipated the worst – when it did arrive it was the greatest possible relief to me to find that yr health was so much improved, but her account of the state of yr mind interested & affected me & per-haps prepared me to receive more favorably than I should otherwise have done renewal of yr former proposals which the conviction of the depth & steadiness of yr attachment has aided materially – If I know my own heart it is warm & affectionate & unwilling to give pain to anyone.

How much I was distressed at refusing a compliance with yr wishes on a former occasion, but I believed then that you would soon forget me & find that happiness in some other connection which I had it not in my power to bestow – I did feel at that time that I was hardly doing you justice in not permitting a correspondence, as a means of attaining a more thorough knowledge of yr character; but I had been taught to consider it in the same light as an engagement, & I thought that if I consented to it & after some time perceived no change in my own feelings towards you, that it would be trifling with yr. best affections, & using you ill – as I before told you I consider those feelings of too sacred a nature to be trifled with.

Esteem for your virtues & a deep admiration of your mental qualities is all that I can now give you.

Believe me, my dear friend

Yours with great sincerity

H.B.

EDS. E.O. HELLERSTEIN *ET AL, VICTORIAN WOMEN* (1981)

Her First Proposal

Marriage was the most important social step in a woman's life, since her status depended on her husband – as did her happiness. By the nineteenth century girls attempt a little more control over this decision. Stéphanie Jullien was twenty-one when she wrote these two letters. She had just received her first proposal, six months after losing her beloved mother (and confidante). She could not decide whether to accept the young man.

[To her older brother, Auguste]

6 March 1833

Mon Dieu! Such indecision! Such perplexity! What should I do? The stronger the emotion, the more fleeting it is. And if I, cold and calm, if I refuse his entreaties and little by little I become attached to him, and then, he grows weary of me and draws away from me, then in two years I'll almost be an old maid, and he'll still be so young that he'll scarcely be of an age to marry. Is that reasonable? And what guarantees me that he'll succeed at getting a position? It may take him ten years to assure it; he might not even be able to present himself in two years. I'll wait, watching as the beautiful years of my youth slip away, losing little by little the hope

94

and the means of being advantageously established. Then the situation that I will put myself in by promising to wait will be even more uncomfortable. There will be cause for fear, for jealousy.

But it is necessary to answer him. We can't leave him in this incertitude for two years. I believe it is great madness to accept and I don't have the heart to refuse. I'm telling you everything, Auguste, everything. You asked me to take you completely into my confidence; you seem to have some ulterior motive. But now you know everything that's going on inside me, maybe better than I. My aunt is dissuading me, dissuading me as much as she can. All of her reasons seem so cold. Calculation! Always calculation! As if wealth were happiness. No, but it does help. I feel that and must take it into account. *En voilà*! Enough! My indecision is probably tiring you out. Oh this indecision is a torment, a frightful torment.

[Stéphanie Jullien to her father, 6 April 1833, Dieppe]
M. Forester came to the house and asked me if I would become angry if he offered to marry me. . . . I was quite embarrassed by the question and told him to talk to you about it. . . .

The three great obstacles against him are his extreme youth (he is only six months older than me) and his lack of fortune (he can only bring 20,000 francs to the marriage). If I marry, I want to be sure that, if I don't marry a very rich man, at least I'll marry a man who has enough wealth to keep me from the brink of want, from worries and cares. Finally the third objection, on which my aunt lays great stress, is that he hasn't made a position for himself; that it will take him many years to do so; that his extreme youth [does not inspire?] confidence; that no one knows if he has talent, if he has a capacity to succeed in his chosen profession. . . .

However, I must confess that I have some distaste for refusing. M. Forester is the first man to present himself to me. It seems, according to what I am told, that he has some fondness for me. Then, too, in the situation that I find myself – without my mother – will frankly confess to you that I want to get settled one way or another, to have a position, a future. When I was with my good *maman*, I did not want anything but to stay as long as possible. But now that I am deprived of her, I find myself in a false, awkward, troublesome position; I want to break away. Moreover, if I want to get married it's time I started thinking about it. Time flies and I have come to an age when, if I put it off too long, I'll lose the hope and the means of getting established. On the other hand, it would cost me a lot to marry an unknown. It is very difficult to get to know the character of a man, particularly now that I am alone and cannot get out much in society. I tremble to think of all the chances one takes in getting married. . . .

EDS. E.O. HELLERSTEIN ET AL, VICTORIAN WOMEN (1981)

Charlotte Brontë Turns Down an Offer of Marriage

Charlotte Brontë, though she considered herself unattractive, received quite a few proposals from her father's indigent curates. Here she turns down the brother of her great friend Ellen Nussey. The author of Jane Eyre *and creator of Mr Rochester recognized that this young man was not passionate enough for her. It is generally believed that she knew he had proposed to another girl not long before.*

12 March 1839

. . . You ask me, my dear Ellen, whether I have received a letter from Henry. I have, about a week since. The contents, I confess, did a little surprise me, but I kept them to myself, and unless you had questioned me on the subject, I would never have adverted to it. Henry says he is comfortably settled at Donnington, that his health is much improved, and that it is his intention to take pupils after Easter. . . . [Easter fell on 31 March that year.]

He then intimates that in due time he should want a wife to take care of his pupils, and frankly asks me to be that wife. Altogether the letter is written without cant or flattery, and in a common-sense style, which does credit to his judgement. . . .

Now, my dear Ellen, there were in this proposal some things which might have proved a strong temptation. I thought if I were to marry Henry Nussey, his sister could live with me, and how happy I should be. But again I asked myself two questions: Do I love him as much as a woman ought to love the man she marries? Am I the person best qualified to make him happy? Alas! Ellen, my conscience answered *no* to both these questions. I felt that though I esteemed, though I had a kindly leaning towards him, because he is an amiable and well-disposed man, yet I had not, and could not have, that intense attachment which would make me

96

willing to die for him; and, if ever I marry, it must be in that light of adoration that I will regard my husband. . . .

. . . I was aware that Henry knew so little of me, he could hardly be
conscious to whom he was writing. Why, it would startle him to see me
in my natural home character; he would think I was a wild, romantic
enthusiast indeed. I could not sit all day long making a grave face before
my husband. I would laugh, and satirise, and say whatever came into
my head first. And if he were a clever man, and loved me, the whole
world weighed in the balance against his smallest wish should be light
as air. Could I, knowing my mind to be such as that, conscientiously say
that I would take a grave, quiet, young man like Henry? No, it would
have been deceiving him, and deception of that sort is beneath me. So I
wrote a long letter back, in which I expressed my refusal as gently as I
could. . . .

W. GERIN, *CHARLOTTE BRONTË* (1967)

An American Woman to her Fiancé

*American women enjoyed more freedom than their European
counterparts. In this letter a young teacher, Bessie Huntting (1831–62)
writes to her fiancé, who worked at a publishing firm in New York. We
see both the importance of her family and her degree of choice.*

Sept 26–7, 1858

Monday night 11 O'clock. I wrote you a long letter, *kind friend* at yes-
terdays twilight hour, for my thoughts rested on the memories of the
Sabbath previous, but I laid it aside to join the loved circle. Sister Mary
was playing & singing those good old hymns; sister Hattie assisting her
while little brother & I were listeners with the most intense interest. It
never seems like the Sabbath, unles we have sacred music after tea. My
dear father loved it so – and I know you love it, and join us in its rich
notes of praise. . . . I welcomed your pennings by *to-day's mail* – the
outgushings of *your thoughts* which *time* will sober, into deeper realities, for I know, you have not yet awoke from the *reverie* into which
you have plunged for the last week. Will you therefore strive to be
calm? for do you know how excited you were, when you jumped off the
cars before we went into the tunnel? Look out, or your friends will

accuse you of abstractedness when you are least aware of it. Remember, when the excitement wears away, you will see matters in *their real light* and as such, I wish you to see then – and would have you see them so now. The eye may not always be bright; nor the voice sweet & musical – better to know how it really is, than to imagine it different from its reality. You do not know yourself, though you think you do; I can read you better than you can read yourself. Therefore think deeply, and study your feelings. Do not feel hurt, that I speak thus *plainly*. But you know I told you a week was too short a time to *learn much*, of any person's character. A correspondence sometimes brings out more of the inner soul than long converse together. May ours prove such a communion. It is far better to find new beauties, at every unfolding of the flower, than to find it a single rose, that blasts with the early frost. Yet I appreciate every kind sentiment of your letter, and time shall reveal thoughts & feeling, as we know each other better. You saw enough of me to know, & I told you not to be too hasty. You must know my family and have an insight into the home-circle. . . . I have not yet mentioned your name to my dear mother. There has been no opportunity for me to do so . . .

Today I have begun my school duties. I hope I may not find them disagreeable although rather confining – *You know I told you, you might dislike your name associated with a teacher*. Think of these matters and if a change comes over your dream, I shall quickly discover it in the tones of your letters. Your generous, noble and impulsive nature, will soon give token, should such a feeling take possession of your mind – Now only one day has elapsed and the *dream* (if such it be) is *still* there – but your feelings and the test of *time* & trial yet – I appreciate the noble gift you *lay* at *my disposal*, and while I would be its 'guardian angel' I would see every affection of that loving heart, called forth. I have seen you, as the strong man, bowed down, and I bless you for the offering – were you satisfied with what you received in return? Do you remember what I told you Friday night that you had not asked for? . . . It was 11 oclock before our friends left and then I began this long epistle! may you not tire of it! but reply to it soon, and now I must say Good-night wishing you every blessing – prosperity in your daily cares and toils – 'blessings in your basket and in your store,' but do not forget to take care of *yourself*, for you say 'I have brought back to my house another true heart.' *Then I have a right to claim a care over it* – you are not 'quite certain of its happiness depending upon me' – for you may find it happier to be as you have been – I do want you to try yourself and you must not call this letter exacting or formal, I write as I talked with you *calmly* & *plainly*. Know thyself, fully & truly – and while I pray for thee, think kindly of your true friend.

Bessie H

HUNTTING-RUDD, FAMILY PAPERS, RADCLIFFE COLLEGE, U.S.A.

A Rejected Wife Rejects her Lover, to Prevent his Wife Suffering

Mariama Bâ was born in 1929 in Senegal; she died tragically in 1981, just after the publication of her now famous novel So Long a Letter *(Virago, 1982). Orphaned young, she was brought up a Muslim by her grandparents. She worked as a primary schoolteacher until she married the Minister of Information. She gave him nine children after which he divorced her, an experience central to her novel; this work, in letter form, is an outcry against polygamy, against the suffering of the rejected wife. Here she writes to a friend who has proposed marriage in her loneliness.*

Daouda,

You are chasing after a woman who has remained the same, Daouda, despite the intense ravages of suffering.

You who have loved me, who love me still – I don't doubt it – try to understand me. My conscience is not accommodating enough to enable me to marry you, when only esteem, justified by your many qualities, pulls me towards you. I can offer you nothing else, even though you deserve everything. Esteem is not enough for marriage, whose snares I know from experience. And then the existence of your wife and children further complicates the situation. Abandoned yesterday because of a woman, I cannot lightly bring myself between you and your family.

You think the problem of polygamy is a simple one. Those who are involved in it know the constraints, the lies, the injustices that weigh down their consciences in return for the ephemeral joys of change. I am sure you are motivated by love, a love that existed well before your marriage and that fate has not been able to satisfy. It is with infinite sadness and tear-filled eyes that I offer you my friendship. Dear Daouda, please accept it. It is with great pleasure that I shall continue to welcome you to my house.

Shall I hope to see you again?

Ramatoulaye

TRANS. M. BODÉ-THOMAS, MARIAMA BÂ, *SO LONG A LETTER* (1982)

Daouda replied: 'All or nothing. Adieu.' He never came back again.

Dowries

The earliest records of marriages in the West mention dowries. From ancient Greece to France today the financial arrangements of two families uniting their son and daughter were frequently central. One of the first women's letters which historians have found, in Alexandria, concerns problems over a dowry. There is mention of 'dowrie and gift' in Genesis XXIV v. 12 which indicates its social importance and the financial value – or cost – of a wife.

In Europe the dowry could pose real barriers to girls wishing to get married. From the Middle Ages in France there are records of girls saving for dowries: a French maid in the late Middle Ages stated that she saved for her own dowry (to escape remaining single and despised) – 'Jeanne Valence, a farm labourer's daughter, provided, out of her domestic labour the sum of £30 and a blanket and wooden chest.'

A Woman Takes Back her Dowry

The first letter about a dowry dates from the first century before Christ. It is from a woman with financial problems, faced with harsh physical restraints.

To Protarchus, from Dionysarion, the daughter of Protarchus, with her brother Protarchus as guardian, and from Hermione, daughter of Hermias, a citizen, on the authority of her *brother's son, Hermias*:

Dionysarion agrees that the contract is invalidated which the son of Hermione, Hermias, made with her, with Hermione serving as bondsman ... It is agreed, on behalf of her deceased husband, that Dionysarion take from Hermione's house by hand the dowry which she brought to

Hermias, with Hermione serving as bondsman: a dowry of clothes to the value of 240 silver pieces, earrings, and a ring. . . . The contract is invalidated with all documents sealed by her. Dionysarion is not to enter suit against Hermione, nor is any man acting on her behalf, not for any of the deceased Hermias' possessions nor concerning the dowry or support nor about any other written or unwritten agreement made in the past up the present day. Since Dionysarion has become pregnant, she is not to sue for childbirth, because she is more persuasive on that account; she is permitted to expose her baby or to join herself in marriage to another husband. She agrees that if she breaks this authorized agreement she is subject to damages and the established fine. . . .

EDS. MARY R. LEFKOWITZ, AND M.B. FANT, *WOMEN'S LIFE IN GREECE AND ROME* (1982)

In France dowries contined to be more important than in England. There is evidence from the silk manufacturing mills in Lyons in the 1830s that girls from peasant families came 'to accumulate savings for their dowries.' Financial arrangements were even more important for the bourgeoisie. In this letter the mother seems more interested in money than in her daughter's feelings towards a young suitor, la Roche.

[Céline Gouever to her uncle]

17 Dec 1890

Now let us talk about la Roche. You ask me how Mama handled it. First she spoke about their wealth, saying that theirs was greatly superior to ours. They replied to her that they weren't concerned with money. That it was the young girl they were asking for and not anything else. Mama decided that the young man should come and he came to make an offer fifteen days ago. Friday Mama saw her sister again. She told her that I hadn't yet made up my mind. She said that we would see a little later, that there was no hurry, that they should give me some time, and shouldn't give up hope.

My ears are still ringing from all the advice. Everybody who knows them tells me they are decent people and I couldn't find anyone better than this boy on every count, so that I am very confused. Even more confused than I was, what should I do? I haven't the faintest idea. O my poor uncle, there is nothing worse than being a *demoiselle* of marriageable age.

EDS. E.O. HELLERSTEIN *ET AL*, *VICTORIAN WOMEN* (1983)

five

Marriage and Childbirth

Marriage was usually an economic and social bond, though based on an individual relationship. After marriage, the church and state granted men jurisdiction over their wives, and expected offspring. For women marriage seemed to offer adult status, though it could mean subjection to house, and loneliness, as with Pepys's wife; his diaries give unwitting evidence.

Men and women were both expected to contribute. In labouring homes this meant equal labour at work, while the wife also had to undertake most home chores. In middle- and upper-class families, male and female spheres were increasingly differentiated. The church presented women with the ideal of helpmate; St Paul opined that if men must 'sin', they should channel this into the respectability of marriage. The wife bore the burden of 'honour', of upholding cultural concepts of 'virtue'.

Prior to the seventeenth century some sections of society considered a man would do well to marry an older woman with experience and skills. In France and Ireland, peasant women often waited to marry till their late twenties. Yet by the end of the eighteenth century a young dependent wife is represented as the ideal in fiction. In 1780, according to local records in England, 73 per cent of husbands were older than their wives. This situation made it more difficult for young women to assert their rights. They were sexually and economically vulnerable, since divorce was seldom possible, except for the very rich, and even separation rare – above all, it was socially reprehensible.

Courtship and marriage were serious steps for both men and women, particularly the middle-class. Men were expected to have begun in business or a profession, and often waited till their late twenties or thirties. No stigma was attached to the bachelor during this time, whereas the unmarried woman, who had previously fed herself by spinning, became a ridiculed 'spinster'. A girl might be persuaded into marriage merely to avoid the single state.

Wives found contradictions between the cultural ideal of the 'angel in the house' and the reality of hard household work, with almost yearly childbearing. English society remained ignorant of the many ways of limiting families practised in Africa and Japan. There are few letters on such intimate topics, but I have included an attempt at abortion by an aristocrat, two letters on confinements, and the Empress Eugénie of France on her wretched pregnancy. As motherhood is a topic on which a great deal has been published, I offer only Madame de Sévigné, on an aspect overlooked till recently: the searing sense of loss when an adult daughter leaves home.

Elizabeth I's Honour

Elizabeth I exploited her unviolated status as Virgin in a skilful propagandistic aim to replace some of the worship of the Virgin Mary. However, her ministers urged her to marry throughout her reign, mainly to produce an heir. She may have guessed that her father's syphilis would make her sterile, like her unhappy sister, Mary Tudor. On 30 September 1566, Parliament met yet again, to beg her to reconsider an Austrian pretender. Here she expresses her anger to Parliament:

Was I not born in the realm? Were my parents born in any foreign country? Is not my kingdom here? Whom have I oppressed? Whom have I enriched to other's harm? What turmoil have I made in this commonwealth that I should be suspected to have no regard to the same? How have I governed since my reign? I will be tried by envy itself. I need not to use many words, for my deeds do try me.

Well, the matter whereof they would have made their petition (as I am informed) consisteth in two points: in my marriage and in the limitations of the succession of the crown, wherein my marriage was first placed, as for manners' sake. I did send them answer by my council, I would marry (although of mine own disposition I was not inclined thereunto) but that was not accepted nor credited, although spoken by their Prince.

I will never break the word of a prince spoken in a public place, for my honour's sake. And therefore I say again, I will marry as soon as I can conveniently, if God take not him away with whom I mind to marry, or myself, or else some other great let happen. I can say no more.

ED. G. HARRISON, *LETTERS OF QUEEN ELIZABETH I, 1558–1570* (1935)

However, Elizabeth I sometimes needed the support of a loving man. Once Leicester, her beloved Robin, had married, she encouraged the overtures of Monsieur, the heir to the French throne, from 1572 for nine years. Writing to Monsieur began as a diplomatic ploy, but it was also an outlet for her tangled emotions. Two themes dominate the letters: her deep appreciation of his constancy, which she said was un clair rocher [a clear rock] amid life's storms and tempests, and her concern over the delays in the marriage negotiations, which she always blamed on the French. He sent her a golden flower with a frog perched on its petals, and with his miniature inside; she sent him constant assurances that their souls were meant to be united, but she was not sure when.

Nevertheless, she did not trust the French. When she heard Monsieur was thinking of taking over the Low Countries from Spain, she wisely feared another war. She wrote, in the summer of 1580, warning him that she would not marry for the perpetual harm of England:

Let him never procure her harm whose love he seeks to win. My mortal foe can wish me no greater loss than England's hate. Neither should death be less welcome unto me than such a mishap betide me. You see how nearly this matter wringeth me. Use it accordingly. If it please him the deputies may have the charge of this matter joined with the other two that were aforementioned. I dare not assure Monsieur how this great matter will end until I be assured what way he will take with the Low Countries for rather will I never meddle with marriage that have such a bad covenant added to my part. Shall it be ever found true that Queen Elizabeth hath solemnised the perpetual harm of England under the glorious title of marriage with Francis, heir of France? No, it shall never be.

ED. H. ELLIS, *ORIGINAL LETTERS: ILLUSTRATIVE OF ENGLISH HISTORY*
(1924)

After an undistinguished campaign in the Netherlands, Monsieur died in 1584.

On the Marriage of a Daughter

Madame de Sévigné adored her daughter, but began to feel a little worried about her prospects after four years of unsuitable suitors. Mme de Sévigné had married at seventeen; now her daughter was already twenty-two.

The matter was settled at last. Mlle de Sévigné was to marry a man who was neither handsome nor young (he was then about forty) and who had had two wives already. But François Adhémar, Count of Grignan, had other

*qualifications. He belonged to one of the oldest and best families in France.
One of his ancestors had been mentioned by Tasso, and the Adhémars had
held the comté of Grignan, in Provence, for more than a century.*
Here she writes to her cousin for his consent:

Paris, 4th December, 1668

I must tell you some news I am sure you will be delighted to hear. 'The pret-
tiest girl in France' is to be married, not to the handsomest young fellow,
but to one of the most worthy men in the kingdom – to M. de Grignan,
whom you have known for a long time. All his wives have died to give place
to your cousin; and, with extraordinary kindness, his father and son have
died too, so that he is richer than he has ever been before. And since by his
birth, his establishments and his own good qualities he is all that we could
wish, we have not bargained with him in the usual way, but have relied on
the two families that have preceded us. He seems very pleased at the
thought of being allied with us; and as we expect to hear from his uncle, the
Archbishop of Arles (his other uncle, the Bishop of Uzès, is here), the affair
will no doubt be concluded before the end of this year.

As I like to do what is usual on all occasions, I now ask for your advice
and approval. People outside our family seem to be satisfied, which is a
good thing; for we are foolish enough to be influenced by other people's
opinions.

TRANS. L. TANCOCK, *MADAME DE SÉVIGNÉ: SELECTED LETTERS* (1982)

A Mother Mourns her Daughter
Leaving Home

*Madame de Sévigné adored her only daughter, who stayed with her in
Paris for months after her wedding, and felt at a loss when her daughter
finally left. Here she writes to her daughter to comfort her and share the
grief they both feel after their first separation.*

To Madame de Grignan

[Paris, Wednesday 18 February 1671]

I do urge you, dear heart, to look after your eyes – as to mine, you know
they must be used up in your service. You must realize, my love, that
because of the way you write to me I have to cry when I read your letters.

To understand something of the state I am in over you, add to the tenderness and natural feeling I have for you this little circumstance that I am quite sure you love me, and then consider my overwhelming emotion. Naughty girl! Why do you sometimes hide such precious treasures from me? Are you afraid I might die of joy? But aren't you also afraid that I should die of sorrow at believing I see the opposite? I call d'Hacqueville as witness to the state he saw me in once before. But let's leave these gloomy memories and let me enjoy a blessing without which life is hard and unpleasant; and these are not mere words, they are truths. Mme de Guénégaud has told me of the state she saw you in on my account. Do please keep the reason, but let us have no more tears, I beg you – they are not so healthy for you as for me. At the moment I am fairly reasonable. I can control myself if need be, and sometimes I go for four or five hours just like anyone else, but the slightest thing throws me back into my first condition. A memory, a place, a word, a thought if a little too clear, above all your letters (and even my own as I am writing them), someone talking about you, these things are rocks on which my constancy founders, and these breakers are often met with.

I have often seen Raymond at the Comtesse du Lude's. She sang me a new solo from the ballet – quite admirable. But if you want someone to sing it, do it yourself. I see Mme de Villars and enjoy seeing her because she enters into my sentiments. She sends you her kindest regards. Mme de La Fayette [the gifted novelist] also appreciates fully the affection I feel for you and is touched by the affection you show me. I am most often in my family circle, sometimes here in the evening out of weariness, though not often.

So far I have only felt like going to see Mme de La Fayette. People are very eager to look me up and take me out, and that frightens me to death.

I do urge you, my dear child, to look after your health. Look after it for my sake, and don't give yourself up to that cruel self-neglect from which it seems to me one cannot recover. I embrace you with a love that can have no possible equal, with due respect to everybody else's.

TRANS. L. TANCOCK, *MADAME DE SÉVIGNÉ: SELECTED LETTERS* (1982)

A Blue Stocking's Son's Marriage

Elizabeth Montagu was called 'Queen of the Bluestockings'. Here she discusses financial arrangements of her son's marriage in a letter to Mrs Robinson, 15 March 1785.

. . . I know my brother and you and your daughters will be glad to hear Montagu is going to be married, in a manner which is agreeable to himself and to me. The young lady is so form'd and qualified to please both the fancy and the judgement, and her fortune such as to content any reasonable wishes. She has 45,000 l. in present; 3,000 l. more is to remain in the funds to secure an annuity to a very old person during his life, and who has been sometime bedridden; so it will soon come into Miss Charlton. She has also an annuity of 300 l. a year on the life of a young prodigal; but the regular payment of this is not to be depended upon. She has also some other little contingencies; so that her fortune is not estimated at less than fifty thousand pounds, by her guardians.

DR DORAN, *A LADY OF THE LAST CENTURY: MRS ELIZABETH MONTAGU*
(1873)

Fanny Burney On Her Marriage

Fanny Burney wrote to a friend about her marriage to the impoverished Général d'Arblay, who left Paris soon after the French Revolution. Though middle-aged, and a respected writer, she was worried about her father's reactions. He was Dr Burney, the eminent musicologist.

1793

My father's apprehensions from the smallness of our income have made him cold and averse; and though he granted his consent, I could not even solicit his presence. I feel satisfied, however, that time will convince him I have not been so imprudent as he now thinks me. Happiness is the great end of all our worldly views and proceedings, and no one can judge for another in what will produce it. To me, wealth and ambition would always be unavailing; I have always seen that the happiness of the richest and the greatest has been the moment of retiring from riches and from power. Domestic comfort and social affection have invariably been the sole as well as ultimate objects of my choice, and I have always been a stranger to any other species of felicity.

M. d'Arblay has a taste for literature, and a passion for reading and writing, as marked as my own; this is a sympathy to rob retirement of all superfluous leisure, and insure to us both occupation, constantly edifying or entertaining. He has seen so much of life, and has suffered so severely from its disappointments, that retreat, with a chosen companion, is become his final desire.

Mr Locke has given M. d'Arblay a piece of ground in his beautiful park, upon which we shall build a little neat and plain habitation. We shall continue, meanwhile, in his neighbourhood, to superintend the little edifice, and enjoy the society of his exquisite house, and that of my beloved sister Phillips. We are now within two miles of both, at a farmhouse, where we have what apartments we require, and no more, in a most beautiful and healthy situation, a mile and a half from any town. The nearest is Bookham; but I beg that my letters may be directed to me at Captain Phillips's, Mickleham, as the post does not come this way, and I may else miss them for a week.

Whatever may be the general wonder, and perhaps blame, of general people, at this connexion, equally indiscreet in pecuniary points for us both, I feel sure that the truly liberal and truly intellectual judgment of the most venerated character would have accorded its sanction, when acquainted with the worthiness of the object who would wish it.

Adieu, my sweet friend. Give my best compliments to Mr ——, and give me your kind wishes, your kind prayers, my ever dear M ——.

F.D'A

ED. A. DOBSON, *THE DIARY AND LETTERS OF MME D'ARBLAY* (1904)

Charlotte Brontë Advises a Friend

Charlotte Brontë writes to Ellen Nussey, her close friend, on Willie Weightman, whom her sister Anne probably loved.

15th May 1840

I am fully convinced, Ellen, that he is a thorough maleflirt, his sighs are deeper than ever and his treading on toes more assiduous. – I find he has scattered his impressions far and wide – Keighley has yielded him a fruitful field of conquest, Sarah Sugden is quite smitten so is Caroline Dury – she however has left – and his Reverence has not yet ceased to idolise her memory – I find he is perfectly conscious of his irresistibleness and is as vain as a peacock on the subject – I am not at all surprised at this – it is perfectly natural – a handsome – clean – prepossessing – good-humoured young man – will never want troops of victims amongst young ladies – So long as you are not among the number it is all right – He has not mentioned you to me, and I have not mentioned you to him – I believe we fully understand each other on the subject. I have seen little of him lately and talked precious little to him – now that he has got his spirits up and found plenty of acquaintances I don't care and he does not care either.

There is no doubt he will get nobly through his examination, he is a *clever* lad.

EDS. T.J. WISE AND J.A. SYMINGTON, THE BRONTËS: THEIR LIVES, FRIENDSHIPS AND CORRESPONDENCE IN FOUR VOLUMES (1932)

'A Grandmother's Advice' to Ellen Nussey concerning a young man was later provided by Charlotte (the Brontës' biographer, Winifred Gerin, suggests that the man in the letter is Branwell Brontë).

20th November 1840

. . . no young lady should fall in love, till the offer has been made, accepted – the marriage ceremony performed and the first half year of wedded life has passed away – a woman may then begin to love, but with great precaution – very coolly – very moderately – very rationally – if she ever love so much that a harsh word or cold look from her husband cuts her to the heart – she is a fool . . .

. . . Did I not once tell you of an instance of a Relative of mine who cared for a young lady till he began to suspect that she cared more for him and then instantly conceived a sort of contempt for her? You know to what I allude – never as you value your ears mention the circumstance – but I have two studies – *you* are my study for the success the credit, and the respectability of a quiet, tranquil character. Mary is my study – for the contempt, the remorse – the misconstruction which follow the development of feelings in themselves noble, warm – generous – devoted and profound – but which being too freely revealed – too frankly bestowed – are not estimated at their real value.

EDS. T.J. WISE AND J.A. SYMINGTON (1932)

A Great Happiness

Elizabeth Barrett writes to her sisters describing the great happiness she experiences with Robert Browning once married.

Feb 1847

He loves me more every day . . . If all married people lived as happily as we do how many good jokes it would spoil! . . . Flush [her dog] has grown from being simply insolent, a complete tyrant now . . . I was saying to Robert (who spoils him) the other day that soon we shd. have to engage a page for his sole use – a brown livery turned up with white. . . . I write like a racehorse 'scouring the plain' . . . the haste drives the words before me.

On 9 March 1847, from Pisa, she wrote a long letter, 'treating,' as she says, 'of Heaven, cash and the kitchen,' and many other topics.

[After referring to the departure of her brother 'Stormie' (Charles) for Jamaica and Mr Barrett's leave taking] . . . How much better it would be if Papa had spoken before, openly, calmly, kindly . . . and not kept for the hours of parting, confidences which would have brightened and softened the years of actual association. I know by myself his influence over me, how one is powerless . . . how I should have dropped . . . not the sense of a right . . . but the power of claiming a right . . . As to prayer, I really do *not* understand the principle he goes upon . . . I love him and grieve for him – he cannot be happy. I think, in the depths of his heart, when he can give no sympathy, extend no pardon, make no allowances – it must be a continual wrestling against those natural feelings, which he HAS, let him heap the stones over them ever so . . . and if he cast if from us, what remains? [Goes on to speak of publishing matters and money received from Moxon.]

. . . I assure you we shall make our way by poetry yet . . . [Thanks her for mittens she is sending and describes the clothes she is wearing.] . . . The green gown like yours [which] Robert likes so much [&c.] . . . [Sends news of Wilson (her maid) and Flush.] . . . Robert is very anxious for me to be free of the morphine . . . I gradually diminish to seventeen days for twenty-two doses which I used to take in eight days . . . [Gives an amusing description of their 'plate and china'] . . . two silver spoons which have to put the sugar into the cups, then, stir the coffee, and then help the eggs. If I forget to stir my coffee before I break my egg, I turn to supplicate Robert for the use of his spoon . . . [Italian cookery] Robert: 'Really Ba you are so prejudiced! Now this seems as good as possible': 'Well dear, I am delighted that you like it . . . I only hope it won't poison you' – 'Very good indeed! only rather rich . . . here, Flush, you shall have it!' [but pigeon pies were better] . . . Was I ever chronological in my life before, I wonder? Perhaps some of it is Robert's fault, who began by keeping the anniversary of our marriage once a week, and who now, three days in every month, as I assure him, says 'Another month is gone, Ba!' He is fond of telling me that I have not 'the least idea' of the depth of the love he feels for me and that by the time we have been married 'ten years' I may guess at it perhaps . . .

Private Collection, O. Kenyon and M. Foster

April, 1847, Pisa.

. . . Robert's goodness and tenderness are past speaking of . . . He reads to me, talks and jests to make me laugh, tells me stories, improvises verses in all sorts of languages . . . Sings songs, explains the difference between Mendelssohn and Spohr by playing on the table, and when he has thoroughly amused me accepts it as a triumph . . . Of course *I am spoilt to the uttermost* – who could escape – I think sometimes of your opinion on the demoralizing effects of 'a long courtship.' and then I admit that 'the courtship,' with me, was by no means the most dangerous thing. There has been a hundred times as much attention, tenderness, nay, *flattery* even, ever since – and isn't this the close of the seventh month Arabel? Isn't it? We never *do* 'quarrel'!

Private Collection, O. Kenyon and M. Foster

George Eliot's Second Marriage

Reactions differed to George Eliot's marriage to John Cross after the death of her great love Lewes. Some radical friends were shocked. Jowett wrote 'You know that you are a very celebrated person and therefore the world will talk a little about you, but they will not talk long, and what they say does not much signify. It would be foolish to give up affection for the sake of what people say.' On 17 May, 1880, her brother wrote at last, after so many years of silence over Lewes, 'to break the long silence which has existed between us, by offering our united and sincere congratulations to you and Mr Cross . . . My wife joins me in sincerely hoping it will afford you much happiness and comfort. She and the younger branches unite with me in kind love and every good wish.' Marian replied from Milan, 26 May:

112

My dear Brother

Your letter was forwarded to me here, and it was a great joy to me to have your kind words of sympathy, for our long silence has never broken the affection for you which began when we were little ones. My Husband too was much pleased to read your letter. I have known his family for nine years, and they have received me amongst them very lovingly. He is of a most solid, well tried character and has had a great deal of experience. The only point to be regretted in our marriage is that I am much older than he, but his affection has made him chose this lot of caring for me rather than any other of the various lots open to him.

Always your affectionate sister

Mary Ann Cross

ED. G. HAIGHT, *SELECTED LETTERS OF GEORGE ELIOT* (1968)

Her good friend, the writer Barbara Bodichon wrote:

My dear

I hope and I think you will be happy. Tell Johnny Cross I should have done exactly what he has done if you would have let me and I had been a man.

You see I know all love is so different that I do not see it unnatural to love in new ways – not to be unfaithful to any memory. If I knew Mr Lewes he would be glad as I am that you have a new friend.

I was glad to hear you were going to Italy but I did not guess this. My love to your friend if you will.

Your loving

Barbara

ED. G. HAIGHT (1968)

Two Contrasting Victorian Views on Marriage

Many men felt, as did this male letter-writer to the Daily Telegraph *in 1888, that*

> monogamous marriage was instituted for the protection of women, and
> as a means of raising our own more debased ideas of love, and that any
> woman is a fool, and any man a criminal, who tries to tamper with an

institution which has always been held sacred in the great and noble ages of the world. (Quoted in Harry Quilter ed., Is Marriage a Failure (1888).)

Annie Besant, the social reformer, took a quite different view as she writes in 1882. She was to lead the match-girls' strike, to help the exploited underpaid women workers.

Looking at a woman's position both as wife and mother, it is impossible not to recognise the fact that marriage is a direct disadvantage to her. In an unlegalised union the woman retains possession of all her natural rights; she is mistress of her own actions, of her body, of her property; she is able to legally defend herself against attack; all the Courts are open to protect her; she forfeits none of her rights as an Englishwoman; she keeps intact her liberty and her independence; she has no master; she owes obedience to the laws alone.

Anne Besant

A. BESANT, *AN AUTOBIOGRAPHY* (1893)

A Public Quarrel

The New Zealand writer Katherine Mansfield married Middleton Murry, a friend of D.H. Lawrence. During the First World War they lived fairly near each other for a time. Here she describes one of the famous, public marital quarrels. Note her reporting of details, her building up of effects based on observation.

[1916?]

Let me tell you what happened on Friday. I went across to them for tea. Frieda said Shelley's *Ode to a Skylark* was false. Lawrence said: 'You are showing off; you don't know anything about it.' Then she began. '*Now* I have had enough. Out of my house – you little God Almighty you. Ive had enough of you. Are you going to keep your mouth shut or aren't you.' Said Lawrence: 'I'll give you a dab on the cheek to quiet you, you dirty hussy.' Etc. Etc. So I left the house. At dinner time Frieda appeared. 'I have finally done with him. It is all over for ever.' She then went out of the kitchen & began to walk round and round the house in the dark. Suddenly Lawrence appeared and made a kind of horrible blind rush at her and they began to scream and scuffle. He beat her – he beat her to death – her head and face and breast and pulled out her hair. All the while she screamed for Murry to help her. Finally they dashed into the kitchen and round and round the table. I shall never forget how L. looked. He was so white – almost green and he just hit – thumped the big soft woman. Then he fell into one chair and she into another. No one said a word. A silence fell except for Frieda's sobs and sniffs. In a way I felt almost glad that the tension between them was over for ever – and that they had made an end of the 'intimacy'. L. sat staring at the floor, biting his nails. Frieda sobbed. Suddenly, after a long time – about quarter of an hour – L. looked up and asked Murry a question about French literature. Murry replied. Little by little, the three drew up to the table. Then F. poured herself out some coffee. Then she and L. glided into talk, began to discuss some 'very rich but very good macaroni cheese.' And next day, L. whipped himself, and far more thoroughly then he had ever beaten Frieda; he was running about taking her up her breakfast to her bed and trimming her a hat.

CLAIRE TOMALIN, *KATHERINE MANSFIELD: A SECRET LIFE* (1987)

Edith Wharton (1862–1937) Writes Reasonably to her Husband

The American novelist's husband was not her intellectual equal and refused to value her writing, or her friends. To put an end to his verbal aggression, she offered him a generous monthly allowance.

The Mount
Monday
July 24, 1911

Dear Teddy,

I am much obliged to you for writing to H. Edgar that you will resign the trust; & I wish to repeat here that I asked you to do so, after having tried every other expedient to distract you from your endless worrying about money, in the hope that, once you were relieved of a duty you were not well enough to discharge, you would cease to worry about it.

I wish you had taken my request in the spirit in which I made it to you three months ago, giving you the reasons I have just named. Instead of this, on your arrival here, you met me with a scene of such violent and unjustified abuse that, as you know, my first impulse was to leave you at once.

You implored me not to do this, & I agreed to stay on here for the next few weeks, provided such scenes were not repeated, & to join you here again next summer. You then asked to come to Paris in March & stay with me there till our return. I agreed to this also, & I furthermore offered, of my own accord, to give you back the full management of this place & of the household, & to deposit a sum of money in the bank here in your name for that purpose.

As this was what you have always attached more importance to than anything else, I hoped you would be satisfied, & that I should be spared the recurrence of scenes which made a peaceful & dignified life impossible between us; & you gave me your promise to that effect.

Regardless of this, the scenes have been renewed more than once in the last week. – Finally, the day before yesterday, you came to me, asked me to forgive you, said that you were perfectly happy in the arrangement proposed, & renewed your promise to control your nerves & your temper.

Within two hours from this you had reopened the question of the trust, accusing me of seeking to humiliate & wound you by my request, abusing me for my treatment of you during the last few years, & saying that, rather than live with me here or elsewhere after you had resigned the trust, you preferred an immediate break.

You had said this many times before, & I had disregarded it, hoping that on your return here, & with the resumption of your old interests & occupations, you would regain a normal view of life.

But your behaviour since your return has done nothing to encourage this hope, & as nothing I have done seems to satisfy you for more than a few hours, I now think it is best to accede to your often repeated suggestion that we should live apart.

I am sorry indeed, but I have done all I can to help your recovery & make you contented, & I am tired out, & unwilling to go through any more scenes like those of the last fortnight.

I have written this to Billy, as I wish him to know that I have done all I could.

Yrs.

E.W.

H. Edgar will deposit $500 a month in your Boston bank, beginning with this month.

EDS. R.W.B. AND NANCY LEWIS, *THE LETTERS OF EDITH WHARTON*

(1988)

Childbirth and Confinement

Most women had their children at home – or wherever they happened to be when labour pains began. Not many workers could afford a midwife, even skilled artisans had to save for some time if they wished to help their wives – and offspring. Up to the late nineteenth century the survival rate was low – about a third died in early infancy. Until this century many mothers died of puerperal fever because little was understood about post-natal hygiene.

A few fortunate aristocratic women were able to benefit from the money and loving care of family, as shown by Madame de Sévigné. She kept her daughter protected in her house in Paris during her pregnancy. A century later, Lady Mary Wortley Montagu studied the good sense of Turkish women, rose from her bed soon after the birth of her son, and found she felt better. Jane Austen observes the difference in looks of relatives during 'lying-in'.

Madame de Sévigné on her Daughter's Confinement

[To M. de Grignan (her son-in-law)]

Paris, 6 August 1620

You cannot conceive what worries she has gone through about your health, and I am delighted that you are better, both for love of you and love of her. I beseech you, if you still have any squalls to expect from your inside, to ask it to wait until my daughter has had her baby. She still grumbles every day about being kept here, and says in all seriousness that it is very cruel to have been separated from you. It is just as though we have kept you two hundred leagues from her for fun. I urge you to reassure her about this and let her know what joy you feel in hoping she will have a happy confinement here. Nothing was more out of the question than to move her in her condition, and nothing will be better for her health, and even for her reputation, than to have her confinement here, where the greatest skill is available, and to have stayed here, given her way of life.

TRANS. L. TANCOCK, *MADAME DE SÉVIGNÉ: SELECTED LETTERS* (1982)

Jane Austen on 'Lying-In'

The dishevelled Mary was James's wife; the better arranged Elizabeth was Edward's. Cassandra was her sister.

My dear Cassandra

Mary does not manage matters in such a way as to make me want to lay in myself. She is not tidy enough in her appearance; she has no dressing-gown to sit up in; her curtains are all too thin, and things are not in that comfort and style about her which are necessary to make such a situation an enviable one. Elizabeth was really a pretty object with her nice clean cap put on so tidily and her dress so uniformly white and orderly. We live entirely in the dressing room now . . .

We are very much disposed to like our new maid: she knows nothing of a dairy, to be sure, which, in our family, is rather against her, but she is to be taught it all. In short, we have felt the inconvenience of being without a maid so long, that we are determined to like her, and she will find it a hard matter to displease us.

Affectionately yours, J.A.

ED. R.W. CHAPMAN, *JANE AUSTEN: LETTERS* (1952)

Termination of a Pregnancy

Unwanted pregnancies were a frequent experience of women. As there was no reliable birth control until the pill, women with too many pregnancies suffered early deaths. Those who wanted to terminate yet another pregnancy underwent back street attempts at abortion, tried folk recipes, and even died from badly performed abortions. Obviously, there are few letters on the topic. In this rare extract Lady Henrietta Stanley (1807–95) who had already produced nine children in seventeen years, writes to her husband about a termination they both wanted.

[Edward to Henrietta, 9 November 1847]

My dearest love:

This your last misfortune is indeed most grievous & puts all others in the shade. What can you have been doing to account for so juvenile a proceeding, it comes very opportunely to disturb all your family arrangements

& revives the nursery & Williams in full vigour. I only hope it is not the beginning of another flock for what to do with them I am sure I know not. I am afraid however it is too late to mend & you must make the best of it tho' bad is best. . . .

[Henrietta to Edward, 9 November 1847]
A hot bath, a tremendous walk & a great dose have succeeded but it is a warning. . . . I feel not too well which makes me idle.

[Edward to Henrietta, 10 November 1847]
I hope you are not going to do yourself any harm by your violent proceedings, for though it would be a great bore it is not worth while playing tricks to escape its consequences. If however you are none the worse the great result is all the better.

[Henrietta to Edward, 10 November 1847]
I was sure you would feel the same horror I did at an increase of family but I am reassured for the future by the efficacy of the means.
EDS. E.O. HELLERSTEIN *ET AL, VICTORIAN WOMEN* (1981)

A Difficult Pregnancy

Even women who were extremely carefully nursed could undergo difficult pregnancies. These letters are from Empress Eugénie (1826–1920) who married Louis Napoleon of France. She writes to her sister in Spain.

May 1, 1853. – Today I have been in bed for fourteen days without moving and God only knows how much longer I will be here. I was very ill for 17 hours. The pains gave me a cold sweat. Finally. M. Dubois told me that I now know what it is like to give birth. The sharp pains stopped and at the very moment I had begun to have some hope, I had the misfortune of learning that I had suffered much in vain. I had been delighted at the idea of having a beautiful baby like yours. And I was in despair, but I thank God that this accident did not occur later. I would have had even more trouble. On the other hand, maybe it is better for my health for me not to recover too quickly. But I can assure you, I already lack the patience to stay in bed. *Adieu.* Your sister who loves you.

May 3, 1853, – They tell me that the Medinaceli will come this year. Since they love to dance so much, I will give a few little dances if they come. God willing, you will be in a state to dance too; I was so sick that it scares me to know you are pregnant. However, I would be very happy to be so again; when I say that I don't like children, I suppose it's due to jealousy. Especially to have some like yours, I would cut off my arm.

May 9, 1853 – I admit that your stories of last year made me laugh; I also look back very often and I don't laugh during those moments, for I see all that I have given up forever. . . . In exchange I have won a crown, but what does that mean except that I am the first slave of my kingdom, isolated in the midst of everyone, without a woman friend, and needless to say without a male friend, never alone for an instant; an unbearable life if I didn't have, as compensation, a man near me who loves me madly, but who is a slave like me, who has no other motive, no other ambition than the good of his country, and God only knows how he will be rewarded; at this moment, my sister, I thank God for not fulfilling a hope that filled me with joy, for I think with terror of the poor Dauphin Louis XVII, of Charles I, of Marie Stuart, and Marie-Antoinette. Who knows what will be the sad destiny of my child! I would a thousand times prefer for my sons a crown less resplendent but more secure. Do not believe, dear sister, that I lack courage. . . . You see that my thoughts are not very gay, but remember that I have been in bed for 22 days, for being in the *chaise-longue* is not exactly what you would call getting up. Moreover, I just got into that yesterday for the first time. I am beginning to ache in all my bones. Today I wanted to stand up, but could not, so great is my weakness, resulting no doubt from loss of blood. You asked me about the cause of my accident. I swear to you that I don't know, nor does anybody else. It is true that I took a warm bath (not hot) but according to the two doctors, the misfortune had occurred earlier, for the child had already 'come loose.' I suppose you understand, for I can't give you any more explanation. As for myself I don't attribute it to anything because I don't know. Some time back I fell, but I didn't feel anything. Another day, my squire's horse ran away at Saint-Cloud, and I thought this man was going to kill himself by falling down an embankment onto the railroad track, but fortunately he steered the horse in another direction and only skinned his face in falling, but I had a dreadful fright. You see that I don't know what caused it. It is useless to look for reasons, so I will say, like the Moors: 'It was written.' Mama thinks it wouldn't have happened if she had been here. As if it were possible – I have been cared for as you can imagine and, besides, I have had a model midwife who has satisfied me perfectly by her diligence and devotion.

July 1855. – You know already that I will go to Biarritz toward the 27th of July. I really need that, although I am somewhat better, though far from being recovered. Would you believe that the doctors told the Emperor that, happily, they got there on time, but if I had neglected it much longer, I would never have any children. Jobert will cauterize me again tomorrow. Truly, I spend my life being sick. Who would have predicted this when I was sixteen?

LETTRES FAMILIÈRES DE L'IMPERATRICE EUGÉNIE, CONSERVÉES DANS LES ARCHIVES DU PALAIS DE LIVIA ET PUBLIÉES PAR LES SOINS DU DUC D'ALBE
(1935)

six

Housekeeping and Daily Life

Housekeeping has always involved organizational skills, in the ordering and making of provisions for groups of people. Poorer housewives had to eke out meagre supplies of vegetables from the tiny patches they cultivated, find kindling for fires on which to cook, and heat any water, often to be brought from a distance. (In Wales until the end of the nineteenth century, some crofters could not afford peat for necessary fires in winter, and so had to dig pieces of turf, which produced even more smoke than the central medieval hearth.)

The few records available from the Middle Ages indicate that wives were extremely competent managers. The largest groupings of people were in the lord's manor – or monastery and convent. Not only was everybody fed, washed, bedded and organized, the estates had to be run efficiently to provide wool for clothes, firewood, and drink in every season. Accounts were kept, which indicate that women were not only numerate, but skilled in many areas, such as herbal medicine and gardening. Accounts from monasteries show that women were employed regularly, planting or spinning flax, etc. The propagating of the first seeds in the Stone Age and the developing of medieval fruit and flower gardens was often skilled female work.

We are fortunate in having medieval records in the family archives of the *Paston Letters* and the *Lisle Letters*. The letters of Margaret Paston show her ordering provisions from London, knowing precise prices, and supervising the entire work of the estate while her lawyer husband was at his practice. The letter included here indicates that she also managed the collection of money from tenants and competently used her employees to protect the house when under siege during the Wars of the Roses.

The letter to Lady Lisle describes the many areas which women had to supervise, from unlawful fishing of the estate, to immoral behaviour of the local vicar with his 'harlot'. Twenty years later a housewife's work was prescribed in detail in the (ironically) named *A Boke of Husbandrye* by Sir Anthony Fitzherbert:

First set all things in good order within thine house, milk thine kine, suckle calves, strain the milk . . . Get corn and melt ready, bake and brew [women usually made the beer, as we know from the word 'brewster']. Make butter and cheese, serve thy swine both morning and evening. Every month there are especiall chores: In March sow flax and hemp, to be weeded, pulled, watered, washed, spun and woven. . . .

Obviously such husbands obeyed the church dictate that idleness was a source of evil.

This chapter offers a comparison between late medieval and nineteenth-century housework. Medieval wives of important men often wielded great power in the absence of their husbands, yet the tone of the letters suggest that they saw (or presented) themselves as understudies. Nevertheless these were powerful women, though their remit remained narrow.

Hildegard of Bingen, in the twelfth century, proved an extremely competent manager, setting up her own convent in order to be free of the dictates of male churchmen. Saint Teresa of Avila, in the sixteenth century, travelled around Spain setting up convents. She saw to many aspects of the running of the large household constituted by a convent, stating 'God walks among the cooking pots'. Nuns demonstrate the capacity to take patriarchal roles.

At the end of the eighteenth century Wollstonecraft wrote of the need for greater equality and respect. Unfortunately the backlash after the French Revolution led to a consolidating of middle-class division of the world into public and private spheres which had not been expressed in this way in the Middle Ages. The influential Hannah More considered that women occupied separate spheres by nature as well as by custom. It is now women who were keeping women in their place by accepting the male division of men into 'occupations' while women supported male status by the well-regulated ordering of their households. The instructions given to women are detailed, both in letters and in new journals such as *The Magazine of Domestic Economy*, begun in 1835. They suggest God-given authority and knowledge in their epistolary advice to fellow women on 'women's mission'.

Women from the provincial middle class wrote increasingly on the place of women, which was dignified by the 'secret influence' of the moral 'angel in the house'. Only in private letters do we read of the tension between subordination and influence, moral power and political impotence. The country house, and town home, is now organized around sexual difference, unlike the medieval manor.

Women had no property rights in the seventeenth, eighteenth and nineteenth centuries, though they had possessed some in Anglo-Saxon Britain. The ownership of property produced the concept of the 'heavenly home'. This trapped women because their relegation as home-makers was underscored by religious preaching, just at the time when some middle-class women might have been able to make more fulfilling use of their leisure. Mrs Gaskell, wife of a Unitarian minister, agreed with this view, despite her important, successful work as a writer, as she wrote to her friend Eliza Fox in 1850: 'Women must give up living an artist's life, if home duties are to be paramount.' She respected her husband, and did not object that her royalties went to him. Others, however, were torn between motherhood, felt as both drudgery and religious vocation, and the desire to write.

A Mrs Taylor wrote prolifically on running a household, managing a business and bringing up children. In books such as *Correspondence between a Mother and Daughter* (1817) and *Practical Hints on the Duties of a Wife, a Mother and a Mistress of a Family* (1815) she preached: 'A house is only well conducted where there is a strict attention paid to order and regularity. To do everything in its proper time, to keep everything in its right place, is the very essence of good management'. Her example inspired her daughters to take up writing. Though both prolific when young, they changed once they produced large families. With eight children, Ann voiced the tensions which make creative writing at home so very tough for mothers:

every hour I devote to writing now is almost against my conscience, as I have not the time to spare. My mind is never in that composed careful state which I have always found necessary for writing; my ear is waking perpetually to the voice or cry of a dear child, and I am continually obliged to break off at a moment's notice to attend to him.

She envied her sister Jane who had no children and was able to concentrate. This letter of 1817 expresses the contradictory longings of many creative mothers:

Dear Jane,

If your fame, and leisure for the improvement of your mind, could be combined with the comfort and pleasures of a larger domestic circle; and if, with a husband and children, I could share a glimmer of your fame, and a portion of your reading, we should both perhaps be happier than it is the usual lot . . .

Alice Walker took these longings into the epistolary *The Color Purple* and allowed her protagonist to build a cottage industry, sewing, while waiting for her children to be restored to her, offering a symbolic possibility to mothers outside the capitalist system.

Hard work was a necessity for the lower middle class unable to afford much help. The three letters from Mary Abell in 1870s America reveal the difficulties of a mother forced to turn her hand to every household task, from emptying the excrement, and nursing a sick husband while trying to entertain children, to cooking in a tiny room. She was an educated woman married to a preacher (who was also a farmer) but she expresses the difficulties of many working-class mothers.

The poet Marina Tsvetayeva in twentieth-century Russia describes the painful attempts of a mother to find enough food for her two small daughters. Her husband was 'missing', she was their sole support, a situation undergone by so many mothers in war-time.

The really hard labour of domestic servants has rarely been communicated in letters. It was Arthur Munby who asked the servant he loved to describe her working life to him, with its dirt and small joys.

Women's lives have been unnecessarily restricted for centuries. Yet, in the last section of this chapter, we have much evidence of their making the most of their limited existence. A letter from Mrs Delany, a friend of Fanny Burney, recounts her enjoyment of aristocratic entertainments, attitudes and dress. Burney expresses the pleasures of everyday occupations during a visit to friends in the country. Lady Mary Wortley Montagu goes much further and builds an almost ideal garden for herself in Italy. She had gone there hoping to live with her lover. When he let her down, she decided to remake her life beside the beautiful river Oglio. She plans fulfilling days, supervising her smallholding, reading in her retreat, 'where I enjoy every moment that solitude can afford'. Her positive approach to apparent limitations is also echoed in the more recent final letter in this section.

Margaret Paston Manages her Husband's Estate

While her husband was away, Margaret Paston forced to take power, appealed to male authority, though she showed herself resourceful and courageous in the war, demanding crossbows to defend her home against rebels, during the Wars of the Roses.

Right worshipful husband, I commend myself to you. This is to let you know I sent you a letter by Berney's man from Witchingham, which was written on St Thomas's day at Christmas, and I have had no news or letter from you since the week before Christmas, which surprises me very much. I am afraid that all is not well with you, because you have not come home or sent news up to now. I had indeed hoped that you would be home by Twelfth Night at the latest. I beg you with all my heart to be so kind as to send me word how you are as quickly as you can, because my mind will never be easy until I have news from you.

The people in this part of the world are beginning to grow wild, and it is said here that my lord Clarence and the duke of Suffolk, and certain judges with them, shall come down and try such people as are reputed to be causing riots around here. And it is also said that a new release has been made cancelling what was done at the last shire court. I expect that such talk comes from evil men who want to start a rumour in the country. People here say that they would rather all go up to the king together and complain of the evildoers who have wronged them, than be complained against without good reason and hanged outside their own doors. Indeed, men are very afraid here of a rising of the common people, unless a better way is quickly found of calming the people, and men are sent down to settle matters whom the people like and who will be impartial. They do not in the least like the duke of Suffolk or his mother. They say that all the traitors and extortioners in this country are maintained by them and by those whose support they buy in order to maintain the kind of extortion that their underlings have practised before. Men think that if the duke of Suffolk comes, things will go badly unless others come with him who are more popular than him. People are much more afraid of being hurt because you and my cousin Berney have not come home. They say they are sure that all is not well with you, and if things are not well with you, they are sure that the men who want to harm you, will soon do them some harm, and that makes them furious. God in his holy mercy give grace that a good and sober government is soon set up in these parts, because I never heard of so much robbery and manslaughter here as there has been recently.

As for gathering money, I never saw a worse season, for Richard Calle says he can get little of the substance of what is owing, either on your estates or Fastolf's. And John Paston [III] says that those who are best able to pay, pay worst. They behaved as though they hoped to have a new world.

The blessed Trinity have you in their keeping and send us good news of you. Yelverton is a good friend in hard times for you and others in these parts, so I am told.

Written in haste on Thursday after Twelfth Night.

By your Margaret Paston
ED. ALICE D. GREENWOOD, *SELECTIONS FROM THE PASTON LETTERS*
(1920)

Work for the Lady of the Manor

Margery Paston, daughter-in-law of the indefatigable Margaret, not only supervised the large estate in Norfolk, for which she needed 'gold' to be sent from her lawyer husband in London, but also superintended his growing fleet and kept accounts for him. Like many wives she seems to be blamed when a piece of clothing is mislaid, here a 'tippet of velvet'. Note her postscript: they often tell us more than the letter, according to Fanny Burney.

1486

To my master, John Paston, be this delivered

Right reverend and worshipful sir, in my most humble wise I recommend me to you, desiring to hear of your welfare, the which I beseech God to preserve to His pleasure and to your heart's desire. Sir, I thank you for the venison that ye sent me; and your ship is sailed out of the haven as this day.

Sir, I send you by my brother William your stomacher of damask. As for your tippet of velvet, it is not here; Anne saith that ye put it in your casket at London.

Sir, your children be in good health, blessed be God.

Sir, I pray you send me the gold, that I spake to you of, by the next man that cometh to Norwich.

Sir, your mast that lay at Yarmouth is letten to a ship of Hull, 13s. and 4d., and if there fall any hurt thereto, ye shall have a new mast therefor.

No more to you at this time, but Almighty God have you in His keeping. Written at Caister Hall, the 21st day of January, in the first year of King Henry VII.

By your servant,

Margery Paston

I pray God no ladies no more overcome you, that you give no longer respite in your matters.

ED. ALICE D. GREENWOOD (1920)

Difficulties in Managing a Tudor Household

Lord and Lady Lisle moved to Calais in 1533. Their unmarried step-daughter kept an eye on their property. Here she complains to Lady Lisle of Sir John Bonde, vicar of the parish, who was responsible for overseeing the estate and the accounts. He had brought a lady of reprehensible reputation into the family manor house. Jane Basset had only a tiny income to live on, so earns her place in the household by overseeing its management – and morals.

13 September 1535

I pray you heartily, good Madam, have me heartily recommended unto my special good lord as a poor maiden may be. . . .

And also it may please you to be advertised, that through the counsel of Mr Vicar, and divers others, that my sister Thomasine is gone from me unto my brother Marys, without any manner knowledge given unto me, in the morning early before my rising, and, to say the very truth, asleep; and so there did ride with her the Smith, a little boy, and Mistress Thomasyne, sometime Thomas Seller his harlot, and now God's holy vicar here in earth, as he may be, without devotion, as all the whole country says; and here the said Thomasyne is covered underneath John Bremelcomb, the which men think her well near as unthrifty as the other.

Wherefore they have rid away my sister in hope and trust to rid me also, because they might the bolder keep forth their bawdy and unthrifty rule without any further trouble. And sithens my sister's departing she hath sent for part of her clothing, the which she left behind her, the which I do retain in my keeping, and will do, until such time that I may know your further pleasure herein.

And also the vicar shewed me that your ladyship had written unto him that she should depart, and go from me whither that she would; and also he says, that I have written many and divers letters unto your ladyship, the which you shall never have knowledge thereof, or else I shall never have answer again: the which I never had indeed, as he hath said. And also he will not suffer me to have the looking upon none of your stuff, the which putrefieth for lack of good governance. And, further, he says that I do covet to have my brother's evidence, and none thing else regarding your profit.

. . . And as for your fishing, he hath utterly dispraised it unto your ladyship and divers others, and Bremelcum also, to this intent that none body should offer for it. And now that they perceive that men will offer for it, they say that your ladyship's mind is turned, and will not sell. Wherefore, if it be your pleasure to sell it, I pray you, madam, to call to your remembrance what ye promised me, that ye willed me divers times to desire one thing of you when I should espy my time; and you of your own goodness promised me that I should obtain therein. Wherefore I heartily pray you, madam, that I may be your farmer thereunto, as there is or shall be offered for with reason, so that I may be somewhat the better therefore, as my special trust is in you. For I ensure you it is very necessary for me, dwelling here under your goodness, towards the augmentation and amendment of my poor living, as in apparelling and welcoming your Ladyship's friends whensoever they come, for your sake and honour, the which is chargeable unto me in buying all things, as corn, flesh and fish.

And I pray you send me word whether I shall maintain your taper in the chapel of our Lady of Alston, the which hitherto I have done; and as for the cleanly keeping of your house, the which is very uncleanly. I pray you, good madam, send me some good works.

By your daughter, Jane Basset

ED. M. ST CLARE BYRNE, *THE LISLE LETTERS* (1985)

Help to Found a Convent

Saint Teresa of Avila, in the sixteenth century, displayed spiritual and entrepreneurial qualities. Here she writes to her brother in the Indies, where he prospered, about help he sent to found a convent.

Avila 23 December 1561

Sir,

May the Holy Spirit be ever with you. Amen. And may He repay you for the trouble you have taken in helping us all and the great diligence you have shown about it. I hope in God's Majesty that it will profit you much in His sight, for it is certain that all those to whom you are sending money have received it just at the right moment, and personally I found it a very great comfort. And I believe it was an inspiration from God that moved you to send me so much.

I have written to you already, at great length, about something which, for many reasons and causes, I have been unable to avoid doing, because the inspiration came from God. I ought not to write about such things in a letter; I will only say that, in the opinion of holy and learned persons, I must not be cowardly, but put all I can into this task, which is the foundation of a convent. There are to be only fifteen nuns in it, and this number is never to be added to; they will live in the strictest enclosure, never going out, and seeing no one without having veils over their faces, and the foundation of their lives will be prayer and mortification.

I am being helped by that lady, Doña Guiomar, who is writing to you. She is the wife of Francisco Dávila, of Salobralejo, if you remember. Her husband died nine years ago, leaving a million maravedís a year. She has a family estate of her own, as well as her husband's, and, although she was only twenty-five when left a widow, she has not married again but has given herself devotedly to God's service. She is an extremely spiritual person. For over four years we have been closer friends than if we were sisters; but, although she is helping me a great deal by giving me a large part of the income for the convent, she has no money available just now, so the purchase of the house and everything that needs to be done to it has to be seen to by me. By the goodness of God I have been given two dowries in advance, so I have bought the house, keeping the purchase secret, but I can find no way of getting the necessary work done on it. However, as God wants it done, He will provide for me, so I have put all my trust in Him and am engaging the workmen. It seemed a foolish thing to do – but now His

Majesty comes and moves you to provide the money; and what amazed me most was that you added those forty pesos, of which I had the very greatest need. I think St Joseph, whose name the house is to bear, was not going to let me want for them: I know he will repay you. Poor and small though the house is, it has lovely views and grounds. So that settles the matter of money.

Your servant

Teresa

TRANS. ALLISON PEERS, *COMPLETE WORKS OF SAINT TERESA OF AVILA*
(1946)

France in the Intellectual Middle Class, at the End of the Eighteenth Century

Mary Wollstonecraft went to live in France at the time of the Revolution. She met the revolutionary Madame Roland, who told her of the qualities and attractions of life up to 1789, especially for women. We can hear the enthusiasm in this feminist's voice in this letter.

It is a mistake to suppose that there was no such thing as domestic happiness in France, or even in Paris. For many French families, on the contrary, exhibited an affectionate urbanity of behaviour to each other, seldom to be met with where a certain easy gaiety does not soften the difference of age and condition. The husband and wife, if not lovers, were the civilest friends and tenderest parents in the world; the only parents, perhaps, who really treated their children like friends; and the most affable masters and mistresses. Mothers were also to be found, who after suckling their children, paid a degree of attention to their education, not thought compatible with the levity of character attributed to them; whilst they acquired a portion of taste and knowledge rarely to be found in the women of other countries. Their hospitable boards were constantly open to relations and acquaintances, who, without the formality of an invitation, enjoyed their cheerfulness free from restraint; whilst more select circles closed the evening, by discussing literary subjects. In the summer, when they retired to their mansion houses, they spread gladness around, and partook of the amusements of the peasantry, whom they visited with paternal solicitude. These were, it is true, the rational few, not numerous in any country – and where is led a more useful or rational life?

. . . Besides, in France, the women have not those factitious supercilious manners, common to the English; and acting more freely, they have more decision of character, and even more generosity. Rousseau has taught them also a scrupulous attention to their personal cleanliness, not generally to be seen elsewhere: their coquetry is not only more agreeable, but more natural: and not left a prey to unsatisfied sensations, they were less romantic indeed than the English; yet many of them possessed delicacy of sentiment.

CLAIRE TOMALIN, *THE LIFE AND DEATH OF MARY WOLLSTONECRAFT*
(1974)

A Well-to-do Family at the Beginning of the Nineteenth Century

After her widowed mother's death, Nellie Weeton found she could not make a living by running their small school, so looked for a job as a governess, at 30 guineas a year. Here she writes to her friend Bessy Winkley, 28 December 1809, describing her first evening at her new employers, the Pedders' Home, Dove's Nest.

Mr and Mrs Pedder were seated at their wine after dinner, Mrs P. dressed in a pink muslin, with a very becoming head dress of the same. At supper we had two servants in livery attending, and some display of plate, silver nutcrackers, &c., and some things of which poor ignorant I knew not the use. I felt a little awkward, but as you may suppose, strove not to let it appear. I now feel much more at home, and quite comfortable. For more than a week I was far otherwise, not knowing exactly what was expected of me. I am now better acquainted with the task I have undertaken, and find it both an easy and agreeable one. Mr and Mrs Pedder treat me in a most pleasing, flattering manner. So far from making me feel any dependance, I am treated with so much deference, that I must endeavour to be cautious lest I thoughtlessly assume too much. Mr P. is very good tempered in general, a little passionate sometimes. Mrs P. is a most sweet tempered woman, and of a disposition upright and amiable in the extreme. I have had some instances of it that have delighted and astonished me. I am fortunate to have such an one under my care, for she is my pupil as well as Miss Pedder. The latter is not a pleasing child; far otherwise. Her fits, I think, have an effect upon her disposition. She has them very frequently, sometimes five in a day; seldom a whole day without. I don't feel so much alarmed with them as I expected. I have frequently to hold her in them. They seldom last five minutes.

I have to attend to the direction of the House, the table, &c., as well as literary studies; to assist in entertaining company in the parlour; and give directions to the servants. I am studying the art of carving, and learning, as far as books will teach me, as well as giving instructions. Mr P. has a most excellent library.

Mrs Pedder was a dairy maid at Darwen-Bank, Mr P's house near Preston, when he fell in love with her. Her father heard of the connexion and fearing his daughter might be seduced, sent for her home. He lives near-by here. Mr P. followed her, took her off to Gretna Green and married her. They lived some time at Darwen-Bank, and then took this house, where he intends to live retired until his wife (every way worthy her present rank, in my opinion), is fit to appear in the presence of his relations; and her improvement is so rapid, her application so close, and her disposition and understanding so superior, that a little time will make her all he wishes. He is a lucky fellow to have hit upon such an one. She is not eighteen yet. She expresses herself as much pleased with me, and satisfied with my attentions; and Mr Barton told me, Mr Pedder did the same. – How gratifying!

ED. E. HALL, MISS WEETON: JOURNAL OF A GOVERNESS (1936)

Housekeeping at Buckingham Palace

Difficulties in housekeeping at Buckingham Palace were greater than we might imagine. Queen Victoria often complained that her windows were never clean enough, because one department was responsible for washing windows inside, and never co-ordinated its work with the government department responsible for the cleaning of the exterior. Here she writes to the Prime Minister, Sir Robert Peel.

Pavilion, 10th February 1845

Though the Queen knows that Sir Robert Peel has already turned his attention to the urgent necessity of doing something to Buckingham Palace, the Queen thinks it right to recommend this subject herself to his serious consideration. Sir Robert is acquainted with the state of the Palace and the total want of accommodation for our little family, which is fast growing up. Any building must necessarily take some years before it can be safely inhabited. If it were to be begun this autumn, it could hardly be occupied before the spring of 1848, when the Prince of Wales would be nearly seven, and the Princess Royal nearly eight years old, and they cannot possibly be kept in the nursery any longer. A provision for this purpose ought, therefore, to be made this year. Independent of this, most parts of the Palace are in a sad state, and will ere long require a further outlay to render them *decent* for the occupation of the Royal Family or any visitors the Queen may have to receive. A room, capable of containing a large number of those persons whom the Queen has to invite in the course of the season to balls, concerts, etc., than any of the present apartments can at once hold, is much wanted. Equally so, improved offices and servants' rooms, the want of which puts the departments of the household to great expense yearly. It will be for Sir Robert to consider whether it would not be best to remedy all these deficiencies at once, and to make use of this opportunity to render the exterior of the Palace such as no longer to be a *disgrace* to the country, which it certainly now is. The Queen thinks the country would be better pleased to have the question of the Sovereign's residence in London so finally disposed of, than to have it so repeatedly brought before it.

ED. A.C. BENSON, LETTERS OF QUEEN VICTORIA (1907)

House Duties Versus the Individual Life

Mrs Gaskell here writes to a friend, Eliza Fox, on the difficult balance between household duties and the development of the individual.

Feb 1850

One thing is pretty clear, *Women* must give up living an artist's life, if home duties are to be paramount. It is different with men, whose home duties are so small a part of their life. However we are talking of women. I am sure it is healthy for them to have the refuge of the hidden world of Art to shelter themselves in when too much pressed upon by daily small Lilliputian arrows of peddling cares; it keeps them from being morbid as you say; and takes them into the land where King Arthur lies hidden, and soothes them with its peace. I have felt this in writing, I see others feel it in music, you in painting, so assuredly a blending of the two is desirable. (Home duties and the development of the Individual I mean), which you will say it takes no Solomon to tell you but the difficulty is where and when to make one set of duties subserve and give place to the other. I have no doubt that the cultivation of each tends to keep the other in a healthy state, – my grammar is all at sixes and sevens I have no doubt but never mind if you can pick out my meaning. I think a great deal of what you have said.

Thursday – I've been reading over yr note, and believe I've only been repeating in different language what you said. If Self is to be the end of exertions, those exertions are unholy, there is no doubt of *that* – and that is part of the danger in cultivating the Individual Life; but I do believe we have all some appointed work to do, which no one else can do so well; Wh. is *our* work; what *we* have to do in advancing the Kingdom of God; and that first we must find out what we are sent into the world to do, and define it and make it clear to ourselves, (that's *the* hard part) and then forget ourselves in our work, and our work in the End we ought to strive to bring about. I never can either talk or write clearly so I'll ee'n leave it alone.

ED. J.A.V. CHAPPLE, *LETTERS OF ELIZABETH GASKELL* (1967)

A Mother's Work is Never Done

In 1865 a young schoolteacher, Mary, married a farmer who was also a preacher. She moved with him from a relatively prosperous home to a tough homesteading. She had five children in nine years, and had to do virtually all the work single-handed. Even so, she hoped to earn a living teaching the melodeon. She died young.

[Mary Abell to her mother, 12 November 1871]
The rain is falling out of doors and has been all day – but we are snug and warm in comfortable quarters. We never thought of having such a good home for this winter; we are indeed thankful you may be sure. I have commenced giving Alice Fullington music lessons, am going to give her three lessons a week. She is an only child, and they (her parents) are very anxious she should learn music as she has never learned much at school, she is seventeen years old and quite diffident – her father is wealthy, they are all pleased with the idea of my teaching her. I think she is going to do first rate. I could have a large class if I could manage any way to leave home and give lessons or have them come here. I can do nothing till I get my melodeon here. . . .

I had to lug all the water, and do most of the chores for several days. Carrying the water up the hill was the hardest work for me, but Rob is now able to attend to his wonted work himself – though his leg troubles him – pains

135

him a good deal of the time, he is lame in both knees now. He has picked corn two half days – was intending to work a good deal this fall, but he will be able to do scarcely anything. His school commences the first of Dec. . . .

I expect to earn money to get some things after a little. I get all our provisions now by my sewing – Mother Abell sent us two lbs. of tea which will last us at least all winter – so the most we have to get in the grocery line will be sugar. We have soda to last six months at least, the children have got to have new every day aprons, dresses – and must have doublegowns – they have worn their old duds patched and repatched all summer till they are good for nothing but paper rags. Indeed I cannot let them go looking so any longer. You see I have a good winter's work before me – with the 'little sewing' I have to do. I shall take all the sewing I can get aside from Mrs H's [Humphrey]. . . .

The calico you sent, I am very much obliged for. I needed it so much for the children, shall have to get twice as much to make up besides, for I must do my sewing for some months to come – I can not do much in that line after another 'little stranger' comes, even if I could my eyes are always so weak, my limbs swell badly, but have not felt as bad for a few days. I've not been on my feet as much.

[Mary Abell to her mother, 31 December 1871]
This is the last day of 1871. The 1st I spent in Attica [her parents' home] and I remember it quite well – I wish I were there this year, but it will be perhaps many years before I shall see you again – my cares increase instead of diminish. No sooner are the children a little out of the way than another comes – and so they come along. I have been quite nervous for a couple of weeks. More so than before this winter. The children worry me completely out by night – and none of them sleep any through the day, and it is a continual worry – when I am sewing as hard as I can all the time.

H. JORDAN, *LOVE LIES BLEEDING* (1979)

Settlers in America in the Nineteenth Century

Isabella Bird trekked through the Rocky Mountains, on horseback, mainly alone. Her letters home give an informative picture of the life of the new settlers in America in 1873.

Great Platte Canyon Oct 23

Denver is busy, a distributing-point for an immense district, with good shops, some factories, fair hotels, and the usual deformities and refinements of civilisation. A shooting affray in the street is as rare as in Liverpool, while asthmatic people form a veritable convention of patients cured and benefitted.

Numbers of invalids who cannot bear the rough life of the mountains fill its hotels and boarding-houses, and others who have been partially restored by a summer of camping out, go into the city in the winter to complete the cure. It stands at a height of 5000 feet, on an enormous plain, and has a most glorious view of the Rocky Range. I should hate even to spend a week there. The sight of those glories so near and yet out of reach would make me nearly crazy. Denver is at present the terminus of the Kansas Pacific Railroad.

The number of 'saloons' in the streets impresses one, and everywhere one meets the characteristic loafers of a frontier town, who find it hard even for a few days or hours to submit to the restraints of civilisation, as hard as I did to ride sidewise to ex-Governor Hunt's office. To Denver men go to spend the savings of months of hard work in the maddest dissipation, and there such characters as 'Comanche Bill,' 'Buffalo Bill,' 'Wild Bill,' and 'Mountain Jim,' go on the spree, and find the kind of notoriety they seek. A large number of Indians added to the harlequin appearance of the Denver streets the day I was there. They belonged to the Ute tribe, through which I had to pass, and ex-Governor Hunt introduced me to a fine-looking young chief, very well dressed in beaded hide, and bespoke his courtesy for me if I needed it. The Indian stores and fur stores and fur depôts interested me most. The crowds in the streets, perhaps owing to the snow on the ground, were almost solely masculine. I only saw five women the whole day. There were men in every rig: hunters and trappers in buckskin clothing; men of the Plains with belts and revolvers, in great blue cloaks, relics of the war; teamsters in leathern suits; horsemen in fur coats and caps and buffalo-hide boots with the hair outside, and camping blankets behind their huge Mexican saddles; Broadway dandies in light kid gloves; rich English sporting tourists, clean, comely, and supercilious-looking; and hundreds of Indians on their small ponies, the men wearing buckskin suits sewn with beads, and red blankets, with faces painted vermilion, and hair hanging lank and straight, and squaws much bundled up, riding astride with furs over their saddles.

I. BIRD, *A LADY'S LIFE IN THE ROCKY MOUNTAINS* (1982)

A Servant's View of Housework

Hannah Cullwick (1833–1909) was the daughter of a servant. She began 'service' at the age of eight, and moved to London in her teens when her parents died. She met the writer Arthur Munby, who was so interested in the details of dirt and drudgery that he asked her to write about her work. This extract was written in 1864 when she was a servant in a boarding-house:

I often thought of Myself & them, all they ladies sitting up stairs & talking & sewing & playing games & pleasing themselves, all so smart & delicate to what i am, though they was not real ladies the missis told me – & then *me* by myself in that kitchen, drudging all day in my dirt, & ready to do any thing for 'em whenever they rung for me – it seems like been a different kind o creature to them, but it's always so with ladies & servants & of course there is a difference cause their bringing up is so different – servants may feel it sharply & do sometimes i believe, but it's best not to be delicate, nor mind what work we do so as it's honest. i mean it's best to be really strong in body & ready for any sort o rough work that's useful: but keeping a soft & tender heart all while & capable o *feeling*. How shamed ladies'd be to have hands & arms like mine, & how weak they'd be to do my work, & how shock'd to touch the dirty things even, what i black my whole hands with every day – yet such things must be done, & the lady's'd be the first to cry out if they was to find nobody to do for 'em – so the lowest work i think is honourable in itself & the poor drudge is honourable too providing her mind isn't as coarse & low as her work is, & yet loving her dirty work too – both cause it's useful & for been content wi the station she is placed in. But how often poor servants have to bear the scorn & harsh words & proud looks from them above her which to my mind is very wicked & unkind & certainly most disheartening to a young wench. A good hard day's work of cleaning with a pleasant work & look from the Missis is to my mind the greatest pleasure of a servants life. There was two Miss Knights, & one was always in bed, & couldn't bear a bit o noise, so it was tiresome often to be stopp'd doing a job when i was doing it as quiet as ever i could, but i bore it patient knowing she was ill & that it vex'd the Missis so to have her disturb'd, & Miss Julia (the Missis) was the first real lady that ever talk'd to me, & she doing all the light part o cooking was a good deal wi me in the kitchen – she lent me a very nice book (The Footsteps o St. Paul), & said she was sure i shd not dirty it & I read it through wi a bit of paper under my thumb & give it her back as clean as when she give it me. She used to tell me things too about the moon & stars & fire & earth & about history that I knew not of & it surprised me, & she advised me to read the Bible now i was got older for that i may understand better than when i was younger – But she said it was difficult in some parts even to her & she'd study'd a great deal having bin a governess – And so I enjoy'd Miss Knight's company in the Kitchen & she sat one day ever so long seen me clean the paint, & she said she could watch me all day, there was something so very interesting in cleaning & that i seem'd to do it so hearty & i said i was really fond of it. But the poor thing couldn't wash a plate or a saucepan or peel a tato, nor even draw a cork of a bottle, which was unlucky for her, been so poor in pocket – & she *did* wish she could afford to give me more wages.

ARTHUR J. MUNBY: *LIFE AND DIARIES* (1972)

Housekeeping in Russia soon after the Revolution

The poet Marina Tsvetayeva was at first enthusiastic about the Russian revolution, but underwent great hardships. In July 1919 she was invited to read her poems in the Palace of Arts and chose as her theme 'the three-fold lie of freedom, equality and brotherhood'. This letter to her sister, Anastasia, was written later in 1919. Seryozha, her young husband, whom she adored at first, was 'missing'.

I live with Alya and Irina (Alya is six, Irina two) in our same flat opposite two trees in the attic room which used to be Seryozha's. We have no flour and no bread. Under my writing desk there are about twelve pounds of potatoes which is all that is left from the food 'lent' by my neighbours. These are the only provisions we have. I walk all over Moscow looking for bread. If Alya comes with me, I have to tie Irina to a chair, for safety. I feed Irina, then put her to bed. She sleeps in the blue armchair. There is a bed but it won't go through the door. I boil up some old coffee, and drink it, and have a smoke. I write. Alya writes or reads. There is silence for two hours; then Irina wakes up. We heat up what remains of the mashed goo. With Alya's help, I fish out the potatoes which remain, or rather have become clogged in the bottom of the samovar. Either Alya or myself puts Irina back to bed. Then Alya goes to bed. At 10 pm the day is over.

ELAINE FEINSTEIN, *MARINA TSVETAYEVA* (1989)

Just over a year later, in December 1920, she wrote again to her sister, Anastasia.

Forgive me if I keep writing the same things – I'm afraid of letters not getting through. In February of this year Irina died – of hunger – in an orphanage outside Moscow . . . Irina was almost three. She could hardly speak all the time rocking and singing. Her ear and her voice were astonishing – if you should find any trace of Seryozha, write him that it was from pneumonia.

ELAINE FEINSTEIN (1989)

However, by spring the worst of the famine was over and the government allocated her a ration of food, which led her to encourage her sister:

Asya! . . . Come to Moscow. You have a miserable life. Here things are returning to normal. We have bread! there are frequent distributions for children; and since you insist on having a job I could arrange for a grand position for you, with rations and firewood. I hate Moscow, but I cannot travel, so I must wait for S. I love only him and you. I'm very lonely. . . .

ELAINE FEINSTEIN (1989)

Appalachian Mountains Life

Daily life in the Appalachian mountains was tough at the turn of this century, as testified by this letter taken from Lee Smith's novel.

Dear Mister Castle,

You do not know me, I am your grand-daughter, Ivy Rowe. The daughter of your girl Maude who left Rich Valley to come to Blue Star Mountain with my daddy John Arthur Rowe. My daddy is sick now Momma is not pretty no more but crys all the time now I thoght you migt want to know this I thoght you migt want to help out some iffen you knowed it and send some money to us at the P.O. at Majestic, Va., you can send it to me, Ivy Rowe. I am hopen you will send us some money. I am hopen you will get this letter I will send it to you at Rich Valley, Va. by Curtis Bostick he comes up here courting Beulah who has not been bleeding for a while now, we do not know iffen she will marry Curtis Bostick or not his momma is pitching a fit agin it so they say. It is one more thing to contend with, Momma says. Beulah says she wuldnt have him on a stick but she wuld I bet, nevermind what she says. We have not got hardly a thing up here now but meal and taters and shucky beans. Danny has a rising like a pone on the side of his neck and Daddy breths awful. Please if you are alive now send us money, tell no one I am writting you this letter they wuld kill me for axing but I know you are a rich man I will bet you are a good man too. I remane your devoted granddaghter, Ivy Rowe

LEE SMITH, *FAIR AND TENDER LADIES* (1989)

Transforming Limitations into a Beautiful Lifestyle

Mary Delany corresponded with many well-known women writers in the eighteenth century. She was a member of the ancient Granville family. Her letters are not distinguished, but describe the manners and attitudes of her circle. Her almost daily letters to Ann, her younger sister, form an epistolary diary, rather like Fanny Burney's to her sister.

22ND JAN. 1739

After such a day of confusion and fatigue as yesterday, my dearest sister I am sure is too reasonable to expect my head should be composed enough to write a folio, so I very prudently, knowing my own strength, undertake but a quarto.

Lady Dysart, Miss Dashwood and I went together. My clothes you know. I was curled, powdered, and decked with silver ribbon, and was told by critics in the art of dress that I was well dressed. Lady Dysart was in scarlet damask gown, facings, and robings embroidered with gold and colours, her petticoat white satin, all covered with embroidery of the same sort, very fine and handsome, but her gaiety was all external, for at her heart she is the *most wretched virtuous woman that I know*! The gentle Dash was in blue damask, the picture of modesty, and looked excessively pretty. She danced, and was only just so much out of countenance as to show she had *no opinion* of her own performance, but courage enough to *dance very well*. The Princess's clothes were white satin, the petticoat, crowned with jewels; and her behaviour (as it always is) affable and obliging to everybody. The Prince was in old clothes and not well; he was obliged to go away very early. The Duchess of Bedford's clothes were the most remarkably fine, though finery was so common it was hardly distinguished, and my little pretension to it, you may imagine, was easily eclipsed by such superior brightness. The Duchess of Bedford's petticoat was green paduasoy, embroidered very richly with gold and silver and a few colours; the pattern was festoons of shells, coral, corn, corn-flowers, and sea-weeds; everything in different works of gold and silver except the flowers and coral, the body of the gown white satin, with a mosaic pattern of gold facings, robings and train the same as the petticoat; there was abundance of embroidery, and many people in gowns and petticoats of different colours. The men were as fine as the ladies, but we had no Lord Clanricard. My Lord Baltimore was in light brown and silver, his coat lined *quite throughout* with ermine. His lady looked like a *frightened owl*, her locks strutted out and most furiously greased, or rather gummed and powdered. The Duchess of Queensbury was remarkably fine *for her*, had powder, and certainly shewed she had *still a right* to be called '*beautiful.*' My Lord Carlisle, his lady, son, and two daughters, were all excessively fine. But I grow sick of the word '*fine*' and all its appurtenances, and I am sure you have enough of it. The ball began at nine.

ED. A. DAY, *LETTERS FROM GEORGIAN IRELAND* (1992)

Housekeeping in the Bath Home of Jane Austen

Here Jane Austen writes to her sister Cassandra.

STEVENTON: SATURDAY JANRY 3d [1801]

My dear Cassandra

As you have by this time received my last letter, it is fit that I should begin another . . .

My mother looks forward with as much certainly as you can do, to our keeping two maids – my father is the only one not in the secret. We plan having a steady cook, and a young giddy housemaid, with a sedate, middle-aged man, who is to undertake the double office of husband to the former and sweetheart to the latter. No children of course to be allowed on either side . . .

I have now attained the true art of letter-writing, which we are always told, is to express on paper exactly what one would say to the same person by word of mouth: I have been talking to you almost as fast as I could the whole of this letter . . .

My mother bargains for having no trouble at all in furnishing our house in Bath – and I have engaged for your willingly undertaking to do it all. I get more and more reconciled to the idea of our removal. We have lived long enough in this neighbourhood, the Basingstoke Balls are certainly on the decline, there is something interesting in the bustle of going away, and the prospect of spending future summers by the sea or in Wales is very delightful . . . It must not be generally known however that I am not sacrificing a great deal in quitting the country – or I can expect to inspire no tenderness, no interest in those we leave behind.

My father is doing all in his power to increase his income by raising his tithes etc., and I do not despair of getting very nearly six hundred a year. In what part of Bath do you mean to place your *bees*? We are afraid of the South Parade's being too hot . . .

Yours affectly J.A.

ED. R.W. CHAPMAN, *JANE AUSTEN: LETTERS* (1932)

Running a Household in India

Emily Eden (1797–1869) longed for a home in England, yet went to live in India. She was one of fourteen children born to the affectionate Baron Auckland. She and her brother George were devoted to each other, and as neither married she agreed to accompany him to India when he was made Governor-General in 1835. She wrote numerous letters back to her family, which she later published as Up The Country: Letters from India (1872), *from which these extracts are taken.*

Oct 1835

You cannot think what a whirl and entanglement buying and measuring and trying-on makes in your brain. Nightdresses with short sleeves, and net night-caps because muslin is too hot. Then such anomalies – quantities of flannel which I never wear at all in a cool climate, but which we are to wear at night because the creatures who are pulling all night at the punkahs sometimes fall asleep. Then you wake from the extreme heat and call to them, they wake and begin pulling away with such vigour that you catch your death with a sudden chill . . . Indeed it is so very HOT I do not know how to spell it large enough . . .

I get up at eight, and with the assistance of three maids, contrive to have a bath and be dressed for breakfast at nine. When I leave my room I find my two tailors sitting cross-legged in the passage making my gowns, a sweeper plying his broom, two bearers pulling the punkahs and a sentry to mind that none of these steal anything. I am followed downstairs by my Jemdar or head servant, four couriers who are my particular attendants, and by Chance, by spaniel, carried under his own servant's arm. At the bottom of the stairs I find two more bearers with a sedan chair in case I feel too exhausted to walk to the immense marble hall where we dine. All these people are dressed in white muslin with red and gold turbans and sashes, so picturesque that when I can find no other employment for them I make them sit for their pictures.

E. EDEN, *UP THE COUNTRY: LETTERS FROM INDIA* (1872)

But by December 1837, she was writing,

We are a very limited group and have lost all semblance of cultivation. We are very nearly savages – not the least ferocious, not even mischievous – but simply good natured, unsophisticated savages, fond of finery, precious stones and tobacco, quite uninformed, very indolent and rather stupid. We are all dying of fever brought on by the rainy season. The only way I'll survive is by embarking on an interminable course of sketching.

E. EDEN (1872)

Old Age in Italy

Lady Mary Wortley Montagu describes to her daughter, the Countess of Bute, the beautiful life she made in her old age in Italy.

LOUVERE, JULY 10, N.S., 1753

Dear Child, – I received yours of May the 12th but yesterday, July the 9th. I am surprised you complain of my silence. I have never failed answering yours the post after I received them; but I fear, being directed to Twickenham (having no other direction from you), your servants there may have neglected them.

I have been these six weeks, and still am, at my dairy-house, which joins to my garden. I believe I have already told you it is a long mile from the castle, which is situate in the midst of a very large village, once a considerable town, part of the walls still remaining, and has not vacant ground enough about it to make a garden, which is my greatest amusement, it being now troublesome to walk, or even go in the chaise till the evening. I have fitted up in this farm-house a room for myself, that is to say, strewed the floor with rushes, covered the chimney with moss and branches, and adorned the room with basons of earthen ware (which is made here to great perfection).

This spot of ground is so beautiful, I am afraid you will scarce credit the description, which, however, I can assure you, shall be very literal, without any embellishment from imagination. It is on a bank, forming a kind of peninsula, raised from the river Oglio fifty feet, to which you may descend by easy stairs cut in the turf, and either take the air on the river, which is as large as the Thames at Richmond, or by walking an avenue two hundred yards on the side of it, you find a wood of a hundred acres, which was all ready cut into walls and ridings when I took it. I have only added fifteen bowers in different views, with seats of turf. They were easily made, here being a large quantity of underwood, and a great number of wild vines, which twist to the top of the highest trees, and from which they make a very good sort of wine they call *brusco*. I am now writing to you in one of these arbours, which is so thick shaded, the sun is not troublesome, even at noon. Another is on the side of the river, where I have made a camp kitchen, that I may take the fish, dress it, and eat it immediately, and at the same time see the barks, which ascend or descend every day to or from Mantua, Guastalla, or Pont de Via, all considerable towns. This little wood is carpeted, in their succeeding seasons, with violets and strawberries, inhabited by a nation of nightingales, and filled with game of all kinds, excepting deer and wild boar, the first being unknown here, and not being large enough for the other.

My garden was a plain vineyard when it came into my hands not two years ago, and it is, with a small expense, turned into a garden that (apart from the advantage of the climate) I like better than that of Kensington. The Italian vineyards are not planted like those in France, but in clumps, fastened to trees planted in equal ranks (commonly fruit trees), and continued in festoons from one to another, which I have turned into covered galleries of shade, that I can walk in the heat without being incommoded by it. I have made a dining room of verdure . . .

I am afraid you will think this a very insignificant letter. I hope the kindness of the design will excuse it, being willing to give you every proof in my power that I am,

Your most affectionate mother,

M. Wortley

ED. R. HALSBAND, *THE COMPLETE LETTERS OF LADY MARY WORTLEY MONTAGU* (1965)

The Middle Class in the Late Eighteenth Century

Fanny Burney gained almost immediate fame for her novel Evelina. *However, she was exceedingly shy, and avoided praise, preferring the company of her adored sister Susan. When they were separated she wrote to her regularly. After turning her letters into a diary for the sister, Fanny had the idea of publishing it, thanks to which we learn about the details, trials and joys of the daughters of the musicologist Dr Burney.*

Friday 8 October 1784

For Susan,

I set off with my dear father for Chessington where we spent 5 days very comfortably. Father was all humour, all himself, such as you and I mean by that.

Thursday, Oct. 14, I arrived at dear Norbury Park, at about seven o'clock, after a pleasant ride in the dark. Mr Locke most kindly and cordially welcomed me; he came out upon the steps to receive me, and his beloved Fredy [Mrs Locke] waited for me in the vestibule. Oh, with what tenderness did she take me to her bosom! I felt melted with her kindness, but I could not express a joy like hers, for my heart was very full – full of my dearest Susan, whose image seemed before me upon the spot where we had so lately been together.

Next morning I went up stairs as usual, to treat myself with a solo of impatience for the post, and at about twelve o'clock I heard Mrs Locke stepping along the passage. I was sure of good news, for I knew, if there was bad, poor Mr Locke would have brought it. She came in, with three letters in her hand, and three thousand dimples in her cheeks and chin! Oh, my dear Susy, what a sight to me was your hand! I hardly cared for the letter; I hardly desired to open it; the direction alone almost satisfied me sufficiently. How did Mrs Locke embrace me! I half kissed her to death. Then came dear Mr Locke, his eyes brighter than ever – Well, how does she do?

Nothing can be more truly pleasant than our present lives. I bury all disquietudes in immediate enjoyment; an enjoyment more fitted to my secret mind than any I had ever hoped to attain. We are so perfectly tranquil, that not a particle of our whole frames seems ruffled or discomposed. Mr Locke is gayer and more sportive than I ever have seen him; his Fredy seems made up of happiness; and the two dear little girls are in spirits almost ecstatic; and all from that internal contentment which Norbury Park seems to have gathered from all corners of the world into its own sphere.

Our mornings, if fine, are to ourselves, as Mr Locke rides out; if bad, we assemble in the picture room. We have two books in public reading, Madame de Sévigné's 'Letters,' and Cook's last 'Voyage.' Mrs Locke reads the French, myself the English.

Our conversations, too, are such as I could almost wish to last for ever. Mr Locke has been all himself – all instruction, information, and intelligence – since we have been left alone; and the invariable sweetness, as well as judgment, of all he says, leaves, indeed, nothing to wish.

ED. A. DOBSON, *THE DIARY AND LETTERS OF MME D'ARBLAY* (1904)

Simple Life on a Boat in the 1990s

This is a recent letter from a Buddhist friend. When her husband lost money in business and the bank threatened to foreclose on their jointly owned house, she went to live on a tiny boat near her work. She soon realized that simplicity and calm are more important than having a large income.

21 June 91

Dear Olga,

It's three weeks now since I've been living on my small boat, alone for virtually the first time in my life. Trying to enjoy it, and succeeding – most of the time. I still feel so torn about my work, about whether to stay working here or go back to London.

On a more positive side, by living here on my own, I'm learning to become less attached to the house, other than physical comfort; and towards the family, I've become more open and less dependent.

It is sometimes a bit too lonely, but by writing letters to people like you and just knowing that friendship is always with me in thought, is very comforting. That weekend we Buddhist women all spent together was inspiring. With which other group of people could one discuss so openly, so trustingly?

I usually write part of a letter each evening and the rest of time I listen to the radio, but more often read Buddhist books. I enjoy the peace and the slow pace of life. The local canoe club often come by and swans and ducks make very welcome visitors. A few people from work have come for meals and trips up the canal too. But just observing nature and having the time to listen to its sounds is one of the best things.

The setting is quite lovely. Where I'm moored there is a bank of willow trees inhabited by several birds. Their dawn chorus is a delightful advent to the day. Buttercups and daisies are my back garden together with a sloping bank of grass. When the weather is good it is the ideal place for me to practice my Tai Chi. I go once a week, on Mondays, to my Tai Chi class, which gives me a focus for the week. It is a difficult discipline and very exacting of mindfulness but it is also extremely energizing. Unfortunately I have disturbed my equanimity by fancying the instructor! It's all pure fantasy and obviously something I will have to work at.

Living on the boat itself is an extreme exercise in mindfulness as well as control of energy. The above fantasy has made me realize how important it is to use one's energy in positive and useful ways rather than dissipating it on ephemeral dreams. My mind is continually considering how to make a reasonable living without all the hassles which intrude into our equanimity in a normal working day. Living here in a simple way has made me aware of how little money I need to make life pleasurable. That's an incredibly comforting lesson. Come soon and try it – any weekend. Write!

Love, Barbara

O. KENYON (1992)

seven

Work

'Women's work' has a pejorative ring in our male-dominated culture. Yet women have always worked, continuously and continually, in every culture and country. These letters show women involved in a wide variety of tasks. Work was often a shared experience in field and household before the nineteenth century, for poor and for powerful. The previous chapter showed medieval Margaret Paston and Honor Lisle dealing with financial and estate matters competently. In this chapter, Elizabeth I shrewdly assesses the needs of a Protestant monarchy.

Hildegard Bingen and St Teresa worked hard for others: they set up convents, proving that nuns could be remarkable businesswomen, running large households, overseeing self-sustaining estates. Both achieved fame in their lifetime for their mysticism, and their advice was sought by men in power. And Hildegard found time, like many women, to study medicine, publishing a comprehensive study in the twelfth century. Her advice is admirable, particularly on herbal remedies, and respecting the body's needs:

> If the stomach is irritated through different harmful foods and the bladder weakened through miscellaneous detrimental drinks, then they both will bring bad juices to the intestines and send a foul smoke to the spleen.

The death of a husband frequently precipitated a widow into his business, or job-hunting. After the deaths caused by the Great Plague in 1665, widows like the playwright Aphra Behn accepted any remunerative work. As she spoke Dutch, she agreed to spy for the English government, at war with Holland; dangerous work for which she was briefly imprisoned – but not paid!

Though women were more vulnerable financially than men, they complained little about money. The Ladies of Llangollen, for example, though from wealthy aristocratic families, were given only £100 a year – because they refused to marry. But they turned their penury into a model of subsistence living, sharing work in kitchen and garden, and studying daily together.

More typical of the nineteenth century is the real misery of the Brontës exploited and undervalued as governesses. I also include one of the very few letters available from an American factory girl.

Social work became a lifelong mission for Harriet Martineau and Florence Nightingale. Their Victorian seriousness is echoed in what George Sand and George Eliot say about their work as writers.

Work on the Pastons' Estate

Margaret Paston writes to her eldest son, Sir John Paston, about work she is carrying out on the estate. She allows herself to express irritability at her son for leaving her so much to oversee financially.

[Norwich]

15 July 1470

I greet you well and send you God's blessing and mine, letting you know that your farmers have brought me a great bill for repairs, which I send you, together with 60s. in money. I would have the rest of the money from them but they said that it was in your agreement that these repairs should be done and allowed for in this payment, and so I could get no more money from them. And they say that the parson [Thomas Howes] was aware of the repairs. If you were thus agreed and will have the repairs examined you may send word, but I wish you would settle your affairs as hastily as you may, and come home and take heed to your own [property], and mine as well, otherwise than you have done before this, both for my profit and yours. Or else I shall arrange otherwise for myself in haste, in a way that, I trust, shall be more to my ease and profit and no ease nor profit to you in time to come. I have yet little help nor comfort from any of you, God give me grace to have more hereafter. I would that you should consider whether it would not be more profitable to serve me than to serve such masters as you have served before this . . . I pray God we may be in quiet and rest with our own property from henceforth. My power is not as great as I would wish it for your own sake and for others, and if it were, we should not for long be in danger. God bring us out of it, who have you in His keeping.

Written without ease of heart the Monday next after Relic Sunday.

By your mother.

ED. ALICE D. GREENWOOD, *SELECTIONS FROM THE PASTON LETTERS*
(1920)

Eviction by a Rapacious Clergyman

Margery Clerke, a well-born woman, wrote to Thomas Cranmer to protect herself and her five children, after they had been evicted.

1526

To Thomas, Archbishop of York and Chancellor of England
It is the humble complaint of your beadswoman Margery Clerke of Cheshire, once the wife of William Clerke that, although her late husband and his ancestors had for many years enjoyed undisturbed tenancy of a property in the parish of St Werberga, at the discretion of the Abbot of St Werberga in Westchester, according to immemorial tradition, at an annual rent of forty shillings, John, the late abbot, although there had been nothing done to forfeit the tenancy and though there was no other reason, in the eighth year of the current reign sent certain of his servants to the said property and evicted from it your present petitioner, her late husband, and five small children, this being the coldest part of the winter. They were forced by necessity to go to their parish church for relief and remained there three weeks, as they had no house to stay in, until the abbot, out of his yet further malice, ordered the vicar of the church to evict them from there as well.

The same servants took all the farm stock, and they took all the furniture and household effects and threw it into a deep pond. As a result of brooding about this her husband fell into depression and shortly died.

Your petitioner has complained about this to your highness on various occasions, and your grace has appointed certain gentlemen to examine her case, and bring it to a conclusion, as their commissions direct; but the said abbot has delayed and extended the investigation by improper means, so that the said commissioners were unable to conclude it. And now the said abbot has recently resigned from his post, and another has been elected. Your petitioner has made representations to him, but he refuses redress unless ordered to make it by the King's writ, which your beadswoman has not the ability or power to deploy against him, she being an poor woman and he a great lord in these parts, high in both rank and office.

ED. C. MORIARTY, *THE VOICE OF THE MIDDLE AGES* (1989)

From Elizabeth I to Henry IV of France

Henry IV was an able man, who reunited France after civil war. Though a Protestant, he decided to become a Catholic in order to gain, and retain, the loyalty of leading French families. It is believed he said 'Paris vaut bien une messe' (It's worth saying a Mass to gain Paris). Elizabeth I, now more isolated in her Protestant faith, complained to him:

1593

My God! Is it possible that worldly considerations can so erase the fear of God which threatens us? Can we in reason expect any good result from an act so impious? He who has supported and preserved you through the years, can you imagine that he will forsake you in time of greatest need? Ah! It is dangerous to do evil, even for a good end. I hope that you will return to your senses. In the meantime I shall not cease to put you foremost in my prayers, that the hands of Esau do not snatch away the blessing of Jacob. And as for promising me all amity and faithfulness, I have merited it dearly; I have not tried to change my allegiance to my father. For I prefer the natural to the adopted parent, as God well knows. May He guide you back to the right way. Your most assured sister, if it is after the old manner, for with the new, I have nothing to do.

E.R.

MARIA PERRY, *THE WORD OF A PRINCE: A LIFE OF ELIZABETH I* (1990)

Despite his defection, Elizabeth remained in firm alliance with Henry IV. Although she had worked to dissuade him, she was skilful enough to accept defeat in that area. She then turned her pen to support her religion. In the autumn of 1593 she translated De Consolatione Philosophiae *(The Consolations of Philosophy) by Boethius. Half in prose, half in verse, partly in her own erratic hand and partly dictated, she succeeded in only seventeen days in rendering the Latin into 'antique English' to widen the reading available to her subjects.*

Working Women's Demands before the French Revolution

Working women petitioned to improve their situation at the beginning of the French Revolution. Notable are the dignified tone and unpretentious demands, in spite of their proclamation of women's suffering in so many areas, from education to old age. This letter is addressed to Louis XVI of France in 1789, in a Petition from the Women of the Third Estate to the King:

Sire,

All women of the Third Estate are born poor. Their education is either neglected or misconceived. At the age of fifteen or sixteen, girls can earn five or six sous a day . . . They get married, without a dowry, to unfortunate artisans and drag out a gruelling existence . . . producing children whom they are unable to bring up . . . If old age overtakes unmarried women, they spend it in tears and as objects of contempt for their nearest relatives. To counter such misfortunes, Sire, we ask that men be excluded from those crafts and practising work that are women's prerogative.

We ask, Sire, to be instructed and given jobs, not that we may usurp men's authority, but so that we might have a means of livelihood.

This was a mild request, since they were suffering from invasion of their traditional crafts by men already earning an average of 30 sous, for jobs which paid women only 14 or 15 sous a day.

Nineteenth-century Factory Life

There is little information about the attitudes of women to work in the first half of the nineteenth century. This letter, to a former co-worker, H. Robinson, is valuable, as it gives insights into reactions to work in a factory.

Sept. 7, 1846, Lowell, Mass.

Dear Harriet,

With a feeling which you can better imagine than I can describe do I announce to you the horrible tidings that I am *once more a factory girl*!

yes; once more a factory girl, seated in the short attic of a Lowell boarding house with a half dozen of girls seated around me talking and reading and myself in the midst, trying to write to you, with the thoughts of so many different persons flying around me that I can hardly tell which are my own. . . . My friends and my mother had almost persuaded me to stay at home during the fall and winter but when I reached home I found a letter which informed me that Mr Saunders was keeping my place for me and sent for me to come back as soon as I could and after reading it my Lowell fever returned and, come I would, and come I did, but now, 'Ah! me. I rue the day' although I am not so homesick as I was a fortnight ago and just begin to feel more resigned to my fate. I have been here four weeks but have not had to work very hard for there are six girls of us and we have fine times doing nothing. I should like to see you in Lowell once more but cannot wish you to exchange your pleasant home in the country for a factory life in the 'great city of spindles.' I hope you will learn to perform all necessary domestic duties while you have an opportunity for perhaps you may have an invitation from a certain dark eyed gentleman whom you mentioned in your letter to be mistress of his house his hand and heart and supposing such an event should take place then I will just take a ride some pleasant day and make you a visit when I will tell you more news than I can write – but I will not – anticipate.

I almost envy your happy sundays at home. A feeling of loneliness comes over me when I think of *my home*, now far away; you remember perhaps how I used to tell you I spent my hours in the mill – in imagining myself rich and that the rattle of machinery was the rumbling of my chariot wheels but now alas that happy tact [?] has fled from me and my mind no longer takes such airy and visionary flights for the wings of my imagination have folded themselves to rest; in vain do I try to soar in fancy and imagination above the dull reality around me but beyond the roof of the factory I can not rise. . . .

I have no more that you would be interested in, to write. When you receive this letter I shall expect that *long* one you promised me do write it wont you.

Your friend H.E. Back
H. Robinson Papers, A. & E. Schlesinger Library, Radcliffe College, U.S.A.

A Writer in Nineteenth-century Rural Spain

Work in the north of Spain, in Galicia, in the nineteenth century, was frequently tough, often left to overburdened women. The poet Rosalía de Castro (1837–85) loved her region and its language so much that she seldom went to Madrid, though life among Madrid intellectuals would have helped to sell her work. In this open, prefatory letter, she describes why she writes about peasant women.

1880

In my new book I gave preference to those poems which tried to express the misfortunes of those I saw suffering, over those poems which could be called personal.

And there is so much suffering in our beloved Galician land! Entire books could be written about the eternal misfortune that afflicts our villagers and sailors, the only true workers in our country. I saw and felt their sorrows as if they were mine. But what has always moved me, and consequently finds an echo in my poetry, are the innumerable sufferings of our women. They are creatures who are loving to their family and to strangers, full of feeling, strong of body but soft of heart, and unfortunate because it seems they were born only to bear all the troubles that afflict the weaker and more naive half of humanity. In the fields they do the same share of heavy work as their men and, at home, they valiantly endure the worries of motherhood, housework, and the barrenness of poverty. Alone most of the time, having to work from sunrise to sunset, without help to support their children and perhaps a sickly father, they seem condemned to find rest only in their grave.

Immigration and the King are forever claiming their lovers, brothers, or husbands – the main support of families that are always large. Left behind to cry helplessly, women spend a bitter life amidst uncertain hope, dark loneliness, and the worries that constant misery brings. The greatest heartbreak for them is that all their men leave: some by force, some by need, some by greed. They leave mothers of numerous children, too small to fathom the unhappiness of the orphanage to which they are being condemned.

EDS. AND TRANS. ALDAZ, GANTT, *POEMS OF ROSALÍA DE CASTRO* (1991)

Work as a Governess

The first mention of a governess is in the letters of St Jerome. He recommends that a Christian Lady Laeta, in Rome, should educate her daughter for a religious life with an 'honest woman of sad age'. She should be grave and pale, like the despondent looking governesses in Brontë novels so many centuries later. There were a few 'maistresses', as Chaucer called them, in lively Plantagenet and troubadour courts. By the end of the fifteenth century more aristocratic girls were being educated, including Lady Jane Grey, and Henry VIII was enthusiastic about education both for himself and his daughters. The Court's example was followed in many a new manor house, where girls might share the classical education of their brothers and all could learn music. A Tudor governess may have been a poor relation, but would have been paid and respected for her learning or her devotion.

A Glorious Employment

One of the best-known governesses is Elizabeth Elstob (1683–1756). Brought up by a narrow-minded uncle, but with an aunt who fortunately encouraged her love of languages, she wrote an English Saxon Grammar which brought her fame and the nickname 'Saxon Lady'. She went to live for a happy thirteen years with her beloved brother, Vicar of St Swithin in London, but after his death, like so many single women, she was destitute. She founded a village school in Evesham where she charged only one groat per pupil and suffered from 'Nervous Fefer from which I despair of ever being free'. Friends tried to help, but she wrote 'it is as Glorious an Employment to instruct Poor Children as to teach the Greatest Monarch'.

In 1739 the Duchess of Portland was persuaded to employ her, to teach her four children 'in the principles of religion, and cultivate their minds as far as their capacity will allow, to keep them company in the house, and when her strength and health permit to take the Air with them.' As Elstob loved teaching, she was happy with the children, but like many governesses, allowed very little of the adults' company, as she relates in this letter:

I want nothing here to make my happiness complete as this world can make it, but the pleasure of seeing Mrs Delany oftener, who is entirely engrossed by Her Grace. I can send you nothing new from hence; Mrs Delaney can do it better, who hears and sees more than I do . . . We begin to talk of going to Bulstrode, where I long to be because I hope to have the honour of more of her Grace's company – for it is impossible to have any of it here.

However, she soon wrote happily to her friend George Balland:

My charming little Ladies take up my time so entirely that I have not the least leisure to do anything from the time they rise till they go to bed, they are so constantly with me, except when they are with her Grace, which is not long at a time.

B. HOWE, A GALAXY OF GOVERNESSES (1954)

The Governess as Gentlewoman

It was considered bad manners to be rude to the governess during the eighteenth century; nor was she slighted in public by her pupils unlike the Victorian governess. Maria Edgeworth informed readers in her letters on education, how 'in her time, the Governess was no longer treated as an Upper Servant but as a Gentlewoman'. In the recently published Heber Letters *(1782–1832) the Reverend Reginald Heber, Rector of Malpas and Parson of Hodnet, was told by his sister in a letter dated 1798:*

We will make all the enquiries we can after a governess for little Mary, but such as are in every respect eligible are difficult to be met with and their terms very high. There are plenty of emigrant ladies, some of the rank of Viscountess, to be had, but I think you would not prefer a Frenchwoman, and I am sure would not take a Roman Catholic into your House. We have just hired a governess for Mary Ann, her wages or salary is to be forty guineas a year, her washing is done at home or paid for, and she is to eat at their own table. She undertakes to instruct her pupil in English, French, Geography, Music, Writing & Arithmetic. The wages are now, it seems, thought low, fifty or sixty pounds or guineas being frequently given.

HEBER LETTERS (1950)

A Better Position

The rising middle class offered employment to educated young women as governesses. Some were well treated, but most overworked and ill-appreciated, even publicly humiliated, as here, and in Jane Eyre.

Nellie Weeton (1776–1844) lost her father at five. Her asthmatic mother opened a small school where Nellie had to help with all the teaching and all the housework. Yet both overburdened sickly women supported the fortunate son Tom in his law studies. He helped to find her a position considered better by society, after the mother's early death. She was paid 30 guineas a year.

Jan. 26, 1810

Dear Brother,

The comforts of which I have deprived myself in coming here, and the vexations that occur sometimes during the hours of instruction with a child of such a strange temper to instruct, would almost induce me to give up my present situation, did not the consideration which brought me here, still retain me. O Brother! Sometime thou wilt know perhaps the deprivations I have undergone for thy sake, and that thy attentions have not been such as to conpensate them. For thy sake I have wanted food and fire, and have gone about in rags; have spent the flower of my youth in obscurity, deserted, and neglected; and now, when God has blessed me with a competence, have given up its comforts to promote thy interest in the world. Should I fail in this desire, should I not succeed – what will recompense me? – God perhaps will bless me for the thought that was in my heart; and if I am rewarded in heaven – I am rewarded indeed! I will be patient – I will be resigned, and – with the help of the Power around me, I will persevere.

ED. E. HALL, *MISS WEETON: JOURNAL OF A GOVERNESS* (1936)

Nellie Weeton to her brother, 15 September 1810. Mr Pedder's child was killed in a fire, but Weeton was asked to stay on as companion to Mrs Pedder. The situation soon became intolerable, owing to Mr Pedder's ungovernable temper.

I am scarely permitted either to speak or stir in his presence; nor ever to maintain any opinion different to his own. When in a violent passion (which is but too frequent), on the most trifling occasions he will sometimes beat and turn his wife out of doors. Twice she has run away to her father's – oh! brother, and then, such a house! Mr P. roaring drunk and swearing horridly, and making all the men about the house drunk. I have thought at such times, I really could not bear to stay any longer, particularly when he has been in his violent passions with me, which has occurred six or seven times. As he at one time found fault with almost everything I did, I have ceased to do anything I am not asked to do. The consequence is, I have almost all my time to myself, as I do little else than sew for Mr and Mrs P. Mr P. will have Mrs P. take such an active part in the house, that she has little time for my instruction; and as my assistance in domestic concerns has not been required for 3 or 4 months back, I sit a great deal alone, chiefly employed at my needle. Whether Mr P. means to keep me thus idle, or to dismiss me, I know not. Mrs P's gentle and kind treatment of me makes me very comfortable, for in general, I see little of Mr P. except at dinner.

ED. E. HALL (1936)

Nellie Weeton to her brother, 28 December 1810

How often do I wish that I could see you for a few weeks. I could tell you much that would exceed the limits of a letter – perhaps when Mr and Mrs P. go to Preston in the Spring, I may get a seat with them as far as there, if they go in a chaise – not that I think there is any chance of it either, for they always take such a load of luggage with them, when they go from home – perhaps I may come soon enough, for Mr P. when he is in one of his violent fits of passion, often threatens to turn me out, so he does with his wife, or the servants. I am not worse treated than others; often better, but still feel very uncomfortable.

If I listen in a kind of submissive silence, he will attack me in high style for disrespect. These humours often hold for a week – till visitors arrive; then he is exactly the opposite and treats me with too much deference. . . .

ED. E. HALL (1936)

Later she took a post as governess to the many small children of a wealthy industrialist, Joseph Armitage, near Huddersfield. She writes to a friend, Bessy Price, in July 1812.

He and his wife are young people, not 30 yet. He has a handsome fortune and four women servants. There has been a good deal of company since I came; but though I dine or drink tea with them, I am obliged to leave the room so immediately after I swallowed it, that truly I see little of them.

My time is totally taken up with the children; from 7 o'clock in the morning till half past 7, or 8 at night. I cannot lie longer than 6 o'clock in a morning; and, if I have anything to do for myself, in sewing, writing, and etc, I must rise sooner. At 7, I go into the nursery to hear the children say their prayers, and to remain with them till after they have breakfasted, when I go out with them whilst they play; and am often so cold that I join in their sports to keep warm myself. About half past 8, I breakfast with Mr and Mrs Armitage, and then return again to the children till 9, when we go into the schoolroom till 12. We then bustle on our bonnets, etc, for play or for a short walk. At one, we bustle them off again, to dress for dinner, to which we all sit down at quarter past; the children always dine with their parents. By the time dinner is well over, it is 2 o'clock, when we go in to school, and remain till 5.

Whilst I am at tea in the parlour, the children eat their suppers in the nursery. I then go with them till 7, either walking out of doors, or playing within, as the weather may permit. I then hear their prayers and see them washed; at half past 7 they are generally in bed. All their children, though well-ordered by their parents, when out of sight are as unruly, noisy, insolent, quarrelsome and ill-tempered, etc, as I ever met with. I am beginning to get them to pay some respect to my mandates, and perhaps by & bye, I may to my requests . . .

Mr and Mrs A. are pleasant and easy, make my situation as comfortable as such a one can be; for it is rather awkward for a female of any reflection or feeling. A governess is almost shut out of society; she must possess some fortitude and strength of mind to render herself tranquil or happy.

ED. E. HALL (1936)

In 1814 her brother persuaded her to marry a friend of his, Aaron Stock, who soon began ill-treating her. She was beaten and bullied, and not even allowed her only child Mary, when she was forced to leave him.

Four Hours Wasted in Transit

In the nineteenth century some governesses were treated as respected companions, but more commonly they were thought too 'lowly' to be appreciated by the parents, too educated to be allowed to consort with servants. Even after the wide sales of Jane Eyre, *governesses were still often publicly humiliated and their wages remained painfully low. Claire Claremont, a friend of Mary Shelley wrote to her in 1863:*

I am so worried I fear I shall go out of my mind – this is now my life – I go by nine to Mrs Kitchener's house where I give lessons until one – then I rush to the top of Wilton Place and get a Richmond omnibus and go to Richmond to the Cohens – their daughter is going to marry a Genoese and must have an Italian lesson every day . . . that vile omnibus takes two hours to get to Richmond and the same to come back and so with every giving my lesson I am never back before seven. Four hours wasted in transit. Four precious hours of earning capacity!

B. HOWE, *A GALAXY OF GOVERNESSES* (1954)

Governesses rarely earned as much as £80. Misery in abandoned old age became a public scandal, and led to the founding of the Governess Benevolent Institution by the end of the nineteenth century.

Setting Up a School

Setting up small schools offered a respectable if not prosperous living for a few middle-class daughters. Charlotte and Emily Brontë begged their aunt for their small inheritance to pay for a stay in Brussels which would improve their French and so enable them to advertise among the rising industrialist middle class. Kind fathers, particularly in the upper middle class, sometimes supported their daughters' philanthropic efforts. In the 1840s, the daughters of a Birmingham banker set up a Sunday School at the back of their house. When the family moved to Leamington on the father's retirement from active business, the Sunday School became a day school, partly in the interest of the daughter, Adele, who was a semi-invalid, as described in this letter.

My father allowed us to have a little school for poor children, chiefly for Adele's pleasure, as she could enter into so few amusements. He built a room for it next door to our stables, and we took forty little girls. . . . We taught reading, writing and arithmetic, sewing, mending, marking and cutting out. We also taught them to plait straw and make their own bonnets. When old enough to go into service, my Mother allowed us to have the girls in the house for a fortnight, to learn under our maids, who took great pride in their pupils and turned them out tidy little servants.

I. DAVIDOFF AND C. HALL, *FAMILY FORTUNES: MEN AND WOMEN OF THE ENGLISH MIDDLE CLASS 1780–1850* (1987)

A Boarding School

Teaching offered a career for a few determined unmarried well-educated women from the seventeenth century onwards. By the nineteenth there were dame schools, ragged schools and a few boarding schools – more in America than Britain. Mary Lyon (1797–1849) pioneered academies for young ladies in Londonderry, New Hampshire. She seems to have had sole responsibility for teaching and boarding her pupils.

[Mary Lyon to her friend and fellow teacher Hannah Chickering, 21 February 1825. Buckland, Mass.]

My school here consists of twenty-five young ladies. After so large a number had been admitted, I had some anxiety respecting it. I feared that I might attempt more uniformity about books than, considering the circumstances, would be expedient. I expected, also, a cold winter, and my design was to have the scholars study in school. And as I possess not much natural dignity, I could foresee my scholars crowding around the fire, some whispering, some idle, &c. I remembered that, several years ago, I had a school of young ladies in this town, in which there was more whispering than in all the schools in which I had been engaged for the last three or four years. The fault then was mine, and I knew not but that the effects might be felt even now. . . .

At the commencement, I thought it best to assume as much artificial dignity as possible; so, to begin, I borrowed Miss Grant's plan to prevent whispering. All, with one exception, strictly complied; and that was one of the first young ladies in age and improvement. It appeared altogether probable that the termination of this affair would be a matter of considerable importance in relation to her, her father's family, and perhaps to the school generally. But after I had passed a few almost sleepless nights about it, a kind Providence directed the result in a manner that seemed best calculated to promote the interests of the school; for at length she came cheerfully to the arrangement.

A circumstance in relation to the first set of compositions was somewhat trying. One pupil refused entirely to write: but I was assisted in leading her to comply with the requirement. Some other things I *could* mention. Suffice it to say, that I have had just enough of such things to give me continual anxiety: but God in his providence has been very kind to me. Many events have terminated as I desired, when it seemed not at all in my power to control them. Perhaps I have generally been able to accomplish about what I have undertaken.

My school in many respects is very pleasant. I have but two or three pupils under sixteen years of age. With the exception of two or three, they are very studious. On the whole, I think it the best school I have ever had; the best, because the most profitable to its members; I do not mean the best in which I have been engaged. I have an opportunity this winter to see the value of what I gained at Derry [Londonderry].

EDS. E.O. HELLERSTEIN ET AL, VICTORIAN WOMEN (1981)

Mary Lyon to Zilpah Grant, 26 December 1825, Buckland, Mass.

My school is larger than I expected, having about fifty scholars. . . . My heart is pained to see so much important unaccomplished labor accumulating on my hands, and I have engaged an assistant. . . .

Fourteen of my scholars board in the family with me. Before I came here, and for the first week after, I had much anxiety about the arrangements for these young ladies. We have finally become settled, so that everything seems to go on well. The members of the school in the family have a table by themselves. As I was well aware that it would require more than an ordinary share of dignity to prevent too much, if not improper, conversation at meals. I thought it the safest to introduce some entertaining exercise. This requires an effort on my part which I had scarcely realized. I frequently think, 'How *could* Miss G. take care of so many last summer?' But I recollect hearing you say that your first schools were as much your all as your one hundred pupils at Derry.

My spirits have been unusually uniform for four weeks. I do not recollect an hour of depression. I consider this a blessing for which I ought to be thankful. . . .

EDS. E.O.HELLERSTEIN ET AL (1981)

A Respectable Employment

Teaching offered respectable employment to adolescent girls and young women once primary education became compulsory. Towards the end of The Rainbow *D.H. Lawrence depicts the difficulties with large classes, the long hours on low pay. Conditions in isolated French villages could be unenviable too, as recounted in* Lettres d'institutrices rurales d'autrefois: rédigées à la suite de l'enquête de Francisque Sarcey en 1897. *This account is from a vulnerable young teacher in 1892.*

When I arrived at Selles-Saint-Denis – it was past ten at night – the mayor had not yet gone to bed; he was waiting for me in order to give me the keys, and welcomed me with 'good night.' – The first driver took me to his place; he kept an inn. I had to sleep there until my furniture arrived. . . .

Finally I was at home. The house belonged to a rich farmer, and was ill-equipped to be a school. There was a little garden where the teacher who preceded me had taken care to destroy the half-grown crops so that I would not be able to enjoy them. . . .

Because I had no kitchen, I could not cook for myself. Therefore I arranged with the mistress of the big hotel to provide my meals for forty-five francs a month. In the morning they bring me breakfast at home; I am going to the hotel for the other two meals. There I sometimes enjoy the distraction of other dining companions. I am not too bored. . . .

Sept. 18, 1892. – It seems that I shock my colleagues more and more; they have never seen a teacher take her meals at an inn. The hostess . . . has asked me to eat at home.

It has cost me a great deal to go back to cooking and washing up. I have no vegetables and have to pay the mailman to bring me some from Salbris, or to do my shopping at Romorautin on market days. I don't want to patronize the other inns, which are real dumps.

Jan. 4. 1893. – Solitude, bitter cold, frosted walls in my rooms – nothing to read. . . . The class is distraction for me, but how hard. Oh! that little Ch——, a true alcoholic's daughter. One could call her half-cracked. How she makes me suffer!

February 1893 – No courage to live. . . .

[No date, but after April 15] – This winter the mayor has received all the benedictions of Bacchus. Suddenly he has begun to speak to me in rather spicy language. And because I have kept silent out of respect for his office, he probably believes that I go along with his talk, and he continues his idiotic declarations, all in order to attract me to him, to make me fall into his arms. My gesture to him expressed my complete disgust. . . .

And now my innocent walks [in the neighbouring woods] have become suspect. Madame L—— has been spreading absurd rumours: that I go there for trysts.

Sept. 7. 1893. – Before shaking the dust of this rotten town off my feet forever, I want to go over the sufferings I have endured. I have not had the energy to write for a long time. These last three months have been hell. I wanted to die! Today I await my reassignment and the world begins to brighten.

Money

Women depended on male relatives financially, despite continual hard work in field and house. A few aristocratic women might own land, but as property grew more important in the eighteenth century, women lost rights both to land and to a personal income. Even earnings from books went to husbands. Interestingly, letters about money worries are more often to help other women rather than pleas for the writers themselves. Margery Clerke in 1526 wrote to Cranmer to protect her five children (see p. 152); Lady Lisle in 1538 attempted to protect her husband's land for him. Anna King, in the nineteenth century, wrote to prevent her husband's bankruptcy. Florence Nightingale complains to her mother about her tiny allowance, which she needed to educate four orphan boys.

When women managed money they could be extremely efficient, as shown by one medieval woman who exported goods to Gascony, and imported wine in those same ships. Aphra Behn supported not only herself but her lover, in spite of not always being paid for work (see p. 173). Louisa May Alcott's account demonstrates the writer coping well with a complicated budget and virtually two full-time jobs.

Surprisingly, the frequent money worries of dependent women are seldom mentioned in their letters. Jane Austen occasionally refers to her mother's income, and her own need to economize on clothes. Eleanor Butler, one of the Ladies of Llangollen, reveals the very real difficulties of even well-born women when they displeased their families.

One Hundred Pounds a Year

At a time when the economical Dr Johnson complained that he could not manage on £400 a year, Eleanor Butler and Sarah Ponsonby were ekeing out £100 for their joint household. They wisely kept a cow in their garden, in order to crop the grass and receive fresh milk. The annoyed relations refused to pay more than a paltry allowance. When her wealthy mother, reputed to enjoy £16,000 a year, died, the distraught Butler received almost nothing. Eleanor requested a copy of the will from her sister-in-law:

Dear Lady Ormonde,

Your silence to the recent application I troubled you with the first of this month (an instance of disregard to yourself and me for which I was totally unprepared) will influence my abridging (much as is possible) the present intrusion on your attention.

Last Thursday's post brought a Duplicate of the Will accompanied by your promise of letting me know 'when' I may be permitted to draw for the One Hundred Pounds my Mother had the goodness to bequeath me. In Seven Weeks from the Event which added so considerably to your already Princely Resources could nothing be afforded except a promise of future information when I might apply for such a sum?

I shall only lead your Observation to the evident, the unmerited cruelty of this treatment! It may indeed be pronounced so unexampled, that with difficulty will it obtain belief. Equally incredible must it appear that my remonstrance to *Your Friendship* and my *Brother's justice* experienced no other return than a *Silent* Contempt. But now (impelled by many powerful motives, independent of my own particular interests) I once more conjure you to bestow even a momentary consideration on the *Moderate Object* of that remonstrance, and the claims I have upon those to whom it was addressed. Let me also remind you that though for near sixteen Years the constant Inhabitant of 'so remote a dwelling' yet when the Title of Ormande is pronounced at St James this ensuing Birthday the recollections of a Daughter and Sister of that House will consequently be awakened to the minds of some distinguished Characters in the circle, many of whom, as your Ladyship cannot be ignorant, I have the happiness to count in the list of acquaintance and not a few in that of my *real* friends. If the eyes of these persons should unanimously turn towards you on your first introduction to their majesties, let it be I entreat with that degree of approbation which it shall prove my immediate business to convince them you are entitled to from all who feel an interest in my welfare, if by obtaining me the slender addition of One hundred a year you at once fulfill my utmost ambition and Secure to yourself my liveliest Gratitude. I have only one additional favour to solicit, it is the Obligation of not being kept in a state of painful suspense, but that whatever may be your determination, you will without delay communicate it to, dear Lady Ormonde,

Your Most faithful and most Obedient Humble Servant,

Eleanor Butler

E. MAVOR, *THE LADIES OF LLANGOLLEN: A STUDY IN ROMANTIC FRIENDSHIP* (1971)

A Wife Writes to Save her Husband from Bankruptcy

Waverley, 3d March 1842

My dear Sir

It cannot be unknown to you that the unfavorable seasons for some years past, and the almost annual ravages of the Caterpillar have cut short the crop of Sea Island cotton on the coast of Georgia, and in some locations almost destroyed it. My husband has probably been one of the greatest sufferers from these successive disasters. At a time when negroes were selling from five to six hundred dollars round in gangs – he unfortunately purchased largely; relying on the proceeds of his cotton crops to enable him to make payment, but the almost total failure in some years, short crops and low prices in others have prevented him from realizing the means to meet his engagements. The result is that his creditors have seized and taken from him all his property which in the condition of the country and at present Prices will probably not pay his debts: This may render it necessary for me to call on your friendly aid as one of my Trustees, to protect the property bequeathed in my Fathers will for the benefit of myself and children.

I do not impute any blame, or mismanagement to my husband, nor has his misfortunes, in the slightest degree impaired my confidence in his integrity, or his ability to manage property. Nor is it my desire to give you unnecessary trouble. I simply ask that you will stand the friend of my fathers child in case my husbands creditors shall after taking all his property attempt to seize that upon which I can alone rely for the support of a family of nine children most of them small and at that peculiar age when instruction and parental support are essential and necessary. I do not know that my husbands creditors will disturb me but in case they attempt it I desire permission to call on you and Mr Joseph Jones – my other trustee – to protect my property – as my husband cannot act and I can rely alone upon my Trustees.

It is my desire that my husband be left as your or my agent, in the management of my plantations and business generally.

If my memory serves me a copy of my Fathers will was sent to you soon after his decease. If you cannot lay your hand upon it I will send you another immediately.

I send you enclosed, a list of the 50 negroes left to me in the will, with their increase.

Pray let me hear from you as soon as convenient. Direct your letter to Waynesville.

My kind regards to Mrs Couper

Very respectfully

Your obt Servt, Anna Matilda King

EDS. E.O. HELLERSTEIN *ET AL*, *VICTORIAN WOMEN* (1981)

Money Problems over Social Work

Florence Nightingale received an allowance of £500 a year from her father, which she used to support her social work. Although her mother had a generous allowance and two houses, she never ceased to resent her daughter's expenses. In this letter Florence complains to her father.

12 Jan 1857

In a difficult life (and mine has been more difficult than most) it is always better clearly to decide for oneself

what grievances one will bear being unavoidable
what grievances one will escape from
what grievances one will try to remove

you have mentioned and do mention to me the perpetual grievance it is to you to have such expenses in the female part of your family. . . . London

. . . they say they do it on my account. I will just once, say it is *not* so. You say they spent four months in London last year. Did they stay in London on my account while I was in Russia? If they did so it must have been to buy me one bonnet. . . . Everything else was ordered through the post. . . .

I am sure my dear mother has a dim and vague perception of this viz – that her motherly feeling owes me something more (in the way of facilities to carry out those objects which they approve, now, and which the world approves) than £500 and leave to visit at Embley and Lea Hurst. . . . She tries to smuggle my accounts into hers. She tries in various ways to do me a little contraband good – then when you complain of the confusion and extravagance, also too truly, of her accounts, she forgets this and says 'Oh, it's all Flo's boys' [Miss Nightingale was educating four orphan boys who lived at Embley] or 'It's all Florence's bills.' And she sits down and writes items against me, almost at random, often over charged. . . .

FAWCETT LIBRARY

A Writer's Winter Work

The difficulties of writing for money while nursing children are described by Louisa May Alcott, author of Little Women.

November 1872

Work is my salvation. H.W. Beecher sent one of the editors of the 'Christian Union' to ask for a serial story. They have asked before, and offered $2,000, which I refused; now the offered $3,000, and I accepted.

Got out the old manuscript of 'Success,' and called it 'Work.' Fired up the engine, and plunged into a vortex, with many doubts about getting out. Can't work slowly; the thing possesses me, and I must obey till it's done. One thousand dollars was sent as a seal on the bargain, so I was bound, and sat at the oar like a galley-slave.

F. wanted eight little tales, and offered $35 apiece; used to pay $10. Such is fame! At odd minutes I wrote the short ones, and so paid my own expenses. 'Shawl Straps,' Scrap-Bag, No. 2, came out, and went well.

Great Boston fire; up all night. Very splendid and terrible sight.

December – Busy with 'Work.' Write three pages at once on impression paper, as Beecher, Roberts, and Low of London all want copy at once.

(This was the cause of the paralysis of my thumb, which disabled me.)

Roberts Brothers paid me $2,022 for books. S.E.S. invested most of it, with the $1,000 F. sent. Gave C.M. $100 – a thank-offering for my success. I like to help the class of 'silent poor' to which we belonged for so many years – needy, but respectable, and forgotten because too proud to beg. Work difficult to find for such people, and life made very hard for want of a little money to ease the necessary needs.

– Anna very ill with pneumonia; home to nurse her. Father telegraphed to come home, as we thought her dying. She gave me her boys; but the dear saint got well, and kept the lads for herself. Thank God!

Back to my work with what wits nursing left me.

Had Johnny for a week, to keep all quiet at home. Enjoyed the sweet little soul very much, and sent him back much better.

Finished 'Work,' – twenty chapters. Not what it should be – too many interruptions. Should like to do one book in peace, and see if it wouldn't be good.

The job being done I went home to take Mary's place. Gave her $1,000, and sent her to London for a year of study. She sailed on the 26th, brave and happy and hopeful. I felt that she needed it, and was glad to be able to help her.

I spent seven months in Boston; wrote a book and ten tales; earned $3,250 by my pen, and am satisfied with my winter's work.

ED. E.D. CHENEY, *LOUISA MAY ALCOTT: HER LIFE, LETTERS AND JOURNALS* (1889)

Work as a Writer

We have many letters about the work of writing, because women writers were skilled at penning their problems, and had occasional free moments, denied to servants and labourers. Hildegard in the twelfth century expressed humility at the task of describing her visions. She dictated many of her letters, as did Margaret Paston during the War of the Roses. These first letters in English are direct, about the affairs of the family and the estate. She mentioned no worries about self-expression nor did the skilful Elizabeth I, whose letters were obviously the product of much thought – she needed skill with words to save her own life, and others. I include the first letter we have about a governess. It is Elizabeth's plea for her beloved governess to be released from the Tower of London. Though only fifteen she had been so well taught that K. Ashley was released.

By the seventeenth century women were beginning to be published. Lady Margaret Cavendish had sufficient means not to worry about sales, and could address her audience with assurance. Aphra Behn, dependent on her pen to make a living, had to use it to persuade, in an amazing range of ways. I include three: to her Spymaster, who failed to pay her; to a 'sugar-candied reader'; and to a patron. A patron was an essential social and financial support during tough times.

Women were accepted a trifle less ruefully as professional writers by the nineteenth century. George Eliot analyses her work as an editor, and its many drawbacks. Louisa May Alcott gives us invaluable details of the daily life and the financial rewards for a worker-mother. They include being able to send 'Mary to London for a year of study' and 'money to ease the necessary needs' of the 'needy and respectable, forgotten because too proud to beg' (see pp. 170–1).

Edith Wharton, friend of Henry James, and with many of his qualities as novelist, gained fame in her own time, which involved answering letters from other writers, which she did sympathetically. In the letter included here she comforts Bernard Berenson on his writer's block. I end with Dorothy Richardson (novelist and lesbian) on the difficulties of a woman writer, spiritual as well as social.

Elizabeth I Defends her Governess

Elizabeth I was one of the first daughters to have had her own governess in Britain. In 1536, when Henry VIII's second daughter was three years old, Katheryn Ashley was appointed to govern Princess Elizabeth's household. Later she became Elizabeth's tutor. After Henry VIII's death in 1547, the Court was full of intrigue and suspicion. The power-seeking Protector Somerset wished to prevent a marriage between Seymour and Catherine Parr – or Elizabeth. He considered, erroneously, that Katheryn Ashley supported his rival for the highest office, and had her imprisoned with her husband. Elizabeth promptly wrote to Somerset in Ashley's defence. She was fifteen.

I am the bolder to speak for another thing; the other was because peradventure your Lordship and the Council will think that I favour her evil doing whom I shall speak for, which is for Katheryn Ashley, that it will please your Grace and the Council to do good unto her. Which thing I do not favour her in any evil (for that I would be sorry to do) but for these considerations which follow . . . First because she hath been a long time with me, and many years, and hath taken great labour, and pain in bringing me up in learning and honesty – therefore I ought of my duty to speak for her, for Saint Gregory sayeth that we are more bound to them that bring us up well, than to our parents, for our parents do that which is natural to them, that is, bringeth us into the world, but our bringers up are a cause to make us live well in it . . .

R. WEIGALL, *AN ELIZABETHAN GENTLEWOMAN* (1911)

They were both released.

Poorly Paid Work as a Spy

Aphra Behn was the first professional woman writer in England. When her husband died, she was asked to go to Antwerp, to obtain information for Whitehall. Not even her expenses were paid. She was forced to borrow, and sent these pleas to Whitehall.

16 Aug 1666

I protest to you, sir, I am and was as frugal as possibly I could be, and have many times refused to eat as I would, only to save charges.

WILLIAMSON'S STATE PAPERS, P.R.O., S.P. 29/167 No. 160, 16 AUGUST 1666.NS

I do therefore intreat you, Sir, to let me have some more money . . . Pray, sir, be pleased to consider me very speedily for the longer I stay without it the more time I waste in vain for want of it, and if I did not really believe I should accomplish my business, I would not stay here, it being no delight at all for me so to do, but much the contrary, pray sir, let me not want the main and only thing that is to further my design.

29/169, No. 38, 27 AUGUST

I confess I carried no more upon bill but fifty pounds, and I have not only spent all that upon mere eating and drinking, but in borrowing of money to accomplish my desires of seeing and speaking with this man. I am as much more in debt, having pawned my very rings rather than want supplies for getting him hither.

29/170, No. 75, 15 SEPTEMBER

No money was forthcoming, and by 11 March 1667, when she returned to England, she was forced to borrow £150 from Edward Butler, to help pay her debts. Compare this letter with her completely different discourse in the next, where she defends her comedies from unkind male critics, and with her epistolary poem, where she is attempting to please a potential patron.

Problems for a Restoration Playwright

Aphra Behn became an extremely popular playwright during the reign of Charles II. A widow, she lived on her earnings, which even helped her support her lover when necessary. She wrote witty comedies about sexual encounters which often ran foul of critics nurtured under the puritanical Commonwealth. Her third play The Dutch Lover, *produced in 1673 was so disparaged by academics that she defended comedies in this prefatory epistle to woo potential readers.*

6 February 1673

Good Sweet, Honey, Sugar-Candied Reader,
Which I think is more than anyone has called you yet, I must have a word or two with you before you do advance into the treatise; but 'tis not to beg your pardon for diverting you from your affairs by such as idle pamphlet as this is . . . for I have dealt pretty fairly in the matter, told you in the title-page what you are to expect within. Indeed, had I hung a sign of the immortality of the soul, or the mystery of godliness, or of ecclesiastical policie, and then had treated you with indiscerpibility and essential spissitude (words, though I am no competent judge, for want of languages, yet I fancy strongly ought to mean just nothing) . . . or had presented you with two of three of the worst principles transcribed out of the peremptory and ill-natured, though pretty ingenious Doctor Hobbes, I were then sufficiently in fault; but having inscribed comedy on the beginning of my book, you may guess pretty near what penny-worths you are like to have, and ware your money and your time accordingly.

I would not yet be understood to lessen the dignity of plays, for surely they deserve among the middle if not the better sort of books; for I have heard the most of that which bears the name of learning, and which has abused such quantities of ink and paper, and continually employs so many ignorant, unhappy souls for ten, twenty, years in the University (who yet poor wretches think they are doing something all the while) as logick etc, & several other things that shall be nameless lest I misspell them, are much more absolutely nothing than the errantest play that was ever writ.

A. BEHN, PREFATORY LETTER TO *THE DUTCH LOVER*

Praise for a Patron

Letters sometimes took the form of poems. Here Aphra Behn successfully uses the verse stanza of the ode in order to praise a patron, Dr Burnet. Patrons were needed by many artists in the way subsidies, and good reviews, are today.

(1)

WHEN Old *Rome's* Candidates aspir'd to Fame,
And did the Peoples Suffrages obtain
For some great Consul, or a *Caesar's* Name;
The Victor was not half so Pleas'd and Vain,
As I, when given the Honour of your Choice,
And Preference had in that one single Voice;
That Voice, from whence Immortal Wit still flows;
Wit that at once is Solemn all and Sweet,
Where Noblest Eloquence and Judgment shows
The Inspiring Mind Illustrious, Rich, and Great;
A Mind that can inform your wound'rous Pen
In all that's Perfect and Sublime:
And with an Art beyond the Wit of Men,
On what e're Theam, on what e're great Design,
It carries a Commanding Force, like that of Writ Divine.

(2)

With Pow'rful Reasoning drest in finest Sence,
A thousand ways my Soul you can Invade,
And spight of my Opinions weak Defence,
Against my Will, you Conquer and Perswade.

Your Language soft as Love, betrays the Heart,
And at each Period fixes a Resistless Dart,
While the fond Listner, like a Maid undone,
Inspir'd with Tenderness she fears to own;
In vain essays her Freedom to Regain:
The fine Ideas in her Soul remain,
And Please, and Charm, even while they Grieve and Pain.

(3)

But yet how well this Praise can Recompense
For all the welcome Wounds (before) you'd given!
Scarce any thing but You and Heaven
Such Grateful Bounties can dispense,
As that Eternity of Life can give;
So fam'd by you my Verse Eternally shall live:
Till now, my careless Muse no higher strove
T'inlarge her Glory, and extend her Wings;
Than underneath *Parnassus* Grove,
To Sing of Shepherds, and their humble, Love;
But never durst, like *Cowly*, tune her Strings,
To sing of Heroes and of Kings.

EDS. D. SPENDER AND J. TODD, *ANTHOLOGY OF BRITISH WOMEN WRITERS*
(1989)

George Eliot as Editor

*For two years George Eliot worked virtually unpaid, as assistant editor of
the* Westminster Review, *helping her friend J. Chapman. This letter to
him shows how conscientiously she tried to keep the standards of J.S.
Mill.*

24 July 1852

Dear Friend,

Don't suggest 'Fashion' as a subject to any one else – I should like to keep it.

I have noticed the advertisement of the British Q[uarterly] this morning.
Its list of subjects is excellent. I wish you could contrive to let me see the
number when it comes out. They have one subject of which I am jealous –

'Pre-Raphaelism in Painting and Literature.' We have no good writer on such subjects on our staff. Ought we not, too, to try and enlist David Masson, who is one of the Br[itish] Q[uarterly] set? He wrote that article in the Leader on the Patagonian Missionaries, which I thought very beautiful. Seeing 'Margaret Fuller' among their subjects makes me rather regret having missed the first moment for writing an article on her life myself, but I think she still may come in as one of a triad or quaternion.

I feel that I am a wretched helpmate to you, almost out of the world and incog. so far as I am in it. When you can afford to pay an Editor, if that time will ever come, you must get one. If you believe in Free Will, in the Theism that looks on manhood as a type of the godhead and on Jesus as the ideal Man, get one belonging to the Martineau 'School of thought,' and he will drill you a regiment of writers who will produce a Prospective on a large scale, and so the Westminster may come to have 'dignity' in the eyes of Liverpool.

If not – if you believe, as I do, that the thought which is to mould the future has for its root a belief in necessity, that a nobler presentation of humanity has yet to be given in resignation to individual nothingness, than could ever be shewn of a being who believes in the phantasmogoria of hope unsustained by reason – why then get a man of another calibre and let him write a fresh Prospectus, and if Liverpool theology and ethics are to be admitted, let them be put in the 'dangerous ward,' *alias*, the Independent Section.

The only third course is the present one, that of Editorial compromise.

J.S. Mill and so on can write more openly in the Westminster than anywhere else – It is good for the world that they should have every facility for speaking out. Each can't have a periodical to himself. The grand mistake is to make the Editors responsible for everything. . . .

I congratulate you on your ability to keep cheerful.

Yours etc

Marian Evans

ED. G. HAIGHT, *THE GEORGE ELIOT LETTERS* (1954)

Work of a Writer

Edith Wharton (1862–1937), the American novelist, enjoyed living in France, like her friend Henry James. Here she writes to comfort art historian Bernard Berenson when he complained of writer's block. ('la source a tari' means 'the spring has dried up'.)

Sainte-Claire
January 12, 1937

Dearest B.B.,

This is just a flying line, first to thank you for your good letter, & secondly to tell you that Gillet proposes to come here for a brief holiday (three or four days) on Feb. 17 or 18, & that it wd be delightful if you & Nick could coincide with him – that is to say, if his visit cd fall somewhere, it doesn't matter where, within the circle of yours –

I'm very sorry que la source a tari (the Book-source) for the moment, but I'm so used to this break of continuity in my work that I can't take it very tragically in your case. It is probably just the tank filling up. A propos of which, in looking this morning through an old diary-journal I have a dozen time began & abandoned, I found this: (Dec. 10. 1934.)

'What is writing a novel like?

The beginning: A ride through a spring wood.

The middle: The Gobi desert.

The end: Going down the Cresta run.'

The diary adds: 'I am now' (p. 166 of 'The Buccaneers') in the middle of the Gobi desert.' –

Since then I've been slowly struggling toward the Cresta run, & don't yet despair of sliding down. – Meanwhile, Robert is reading us (in the intervals of political news on the wireless) Granville-Barker's 'Hamlet.' But last night we made him break away & read us the 3 great – greatest – scenes in Esmond. And great they are.

EDS. R.W.B. AND NANCY LEWIS, THE LETTERS OF EDITH WHARTON
(1988)

Difficulties of Working in Male Areas and Systems

These three letters are from Dorothy Richardson, the novelist. Despite poverty, the hostility of the literary establishment, low sales figures and relative obscurity, Dorothy remained undaunted, pursuing her massive, self-appointed task of presenting female realism throughout the latter half of her long life. Nor was she ambivalent about the central social cause of her embattlement.

Art demands what, to women, current civilization won't give. There is for a Dostoyevsky writing against time on the corner of a crowded kitchen table a greater possibility of detachment than for a woman artist no matter how placed. Neither motherhood nor the more continuously exacting and indefinitely expansive responsibilities of even the simplest housekeeping can so effectively hamper her as the human demand, besieging her wherever she is, for an inclusive awareness, from which men, for good or ill, are exempt.

EDS. G. HANSCOMBE, AND V.L. SMYERS, *WRITING FOR THEIR LIVES* (1987)

More than twenty years later, she held to the same view, explaining to her sister-in-law Rose Odle:

27 Nov 1949

most Englishmen dislike women . . . The English pub is alone in being, primarily, a row of boys of all ages at a bar, showing off. That of course is a bit harsh & insufficient. Volumes would be required to investigate & reveal the underlying factors. Vast numbers of Englishmen are so to say spiritually homosexual. Our history, our time of being innocently piratical, then enormously, at the cost of the natives in our vast possessions, wealthy & 'prosperous' so that our culture died, giving place to civilization (!), is partly responsible. For it made millions of women unemployed, vacuous, buyers of commercialised commodities, philistine utterly . . . [men's] picture of 'the Absolute' is male entirely, as is that of the Churches, who all moan & groan & obsequiously supplicate an incense-loving divinity. Mary Baker Eddy's picture is essentially feminine. Is that not why the Christian Science churches grow & spread & are hated, unexamined, by all clerics?

EDS. G. HANSCOMBE AND V.L. SMYERS (1987)

Nor, in her old age, did she change her mind, writing to the poet Henry Savage:

11 Mar 1950

I am not 'literary' Henry. Never was. Never shall be. The books that for you, perhaps for most men, come first, are for me secondary. Partly perhaps because they are the work of men, have the limitations, as well as the qualities of the masculine outlook. Men are practitioners, dealing with things (including 'ideas') rather than with people . . . knowing almost nothing of women save in relation to themselves.

EDS. G. HANSCOMBE AND V.L. SMYERS (1987)

eight

War and Alleviating Suffering

Women have taken a greater part in war than historians have acknowledged until recently. Some dressed as soldiers to be near their husbands, some followed in the baggage train like Brecht's *Mother Courage*, some actually took part in fighting, as this letter from Petrarch to Cardinal Giovanni Colonna proves.

23 November 1343

Of all the wonders of God, 'who alone doeth great wonders,' he has made nothing on earth more marvelous than man. Of all we saw that day, of all this letter will report, the most remarkable was a mighty woman of Pozzuoli, sturdy in body and soul. Her name is Maria, and to suit her name she has the merit of virginity. Though she is constantly among men, usually soldiers, the general opinion holds that she has never suffered any attaint to her chastity, whether in jest or earnest. Men are put off, they say, more by fear than respect. Her body is military rather than maidenly, her strength is such as any hardened soldier might wish for, her skill and deftness unusual, her age at its prime, her appearance and endeavour that of a strong man. She cares not for charms but for arms; not for arts and crafts but for darts and shafts; her face bears no trace of kisses and lascivious caresses, but is ennobled by wounds and scars. Her first love is for weapons, her soul defies death and the sword. She helps wage an inherited local war, in which many have perished on both sides. Sometimes alone, often with a few companions, she has raided the enemy, always, up to the present, victoriously. First into battle, slow to withdraw, she attacks aggressively, practises skilful feints. She bears with incredible patience hunger, thirst, cold, heat, lack of sleep, weariness; she passes nights in the open, under arms; she sleeps on the ground, counting herself lucky to have a turf or a shield for pillow.

She has changed much in a short time, thanks to her constant hardships. I saw her a few years ago, when my youthful longing for glory brought me to Rome and Naples and the king of Sicily. She was then weaponless; but I was amazed when she came to greet me today heavily armed, in a group of soldiers. I returned her greeting as to a man I didn't know. Then she laughed, and at the nudging of my companions I looked at her more closely; and I barely recognized the wild, primitive face of the maiden under her helmet.

They tell many fabulous stories about her; I shall relate what I saw. A number of stout fellows with military training happen to have come here from various quarters. (They were diverted from another expedition.) When they heard about this woman they were anxious to test her powers. So a great crowd of us went up to the castle of Pozzuoli. She was alone, walking up and down in front of the church, apparently just thinking. She was not at all disturbed by our arrival. We begged her to give us some example of her strength. After making many excuses on account of an injury to her arm, she finally sent for a heavy stone and an iron bar. She then threw them before us, and challenged anyone to pick them up and try a cast. To cut the story short, there was a long, well-fought competition, while she stood aside and silently judged the contestants. Finally, making an easy cast, she so far outdistanced the others that everyone was amazed, and I was really ashamed. So we left, hardly believing our eyes, thinking we must have been victims of an illusion.

ED. C. MORIARTY, *THE VOICE OF THE MIDDLE AGES* (1989)

Women in power sometimes had to control fighting forces. Elizabeth I was sensibly economical, but had sufficient men at Tilbury to face Spain's 'Invincible Armada'. In the letter to Essex she displays her ability to take command and be decisive when necessary (see p. 258).

Madame de Sévigné gives witness to the interest women felt in relatives involved in warfare. At almost the same time Aphra Behn attempted to earn a living as a spy while England fought Holland.

Mary Wollstonecraft, like Wordsworth, felt enthusiasm for the French Revolution in 1789. She went to live there for five years, and here recounts her reaction to the Terror.

Florence Nightingale is so well known for her work in the Crimea that I have used only a few extracts. There follows a letter protesting against the suffering of Afrikaners during the Boer War. It can be argued that if male politicians had listened to her criticism of the first concentration camps, South African history might have been less confrontational.

The twentieth century shows writers such as Edith Wharton attempting to get close to the experience of the trenches. Gertrude Bell, the Arabist, found herself imprisoned for two months because her adventurous spirit took her to 'Ha'il', a desert town in Saudi Arabia, where 'murder is like the spilling of milk'. Marina Tsvetayeva, in the Second World War, demonstrates that most women were fully involved in the suffering caused by all wars and revolutions, as individuals and as mothers. Her daughter was imprisoned merely on suspicion; as in so many dictatorships, this was an area in which women were granted equality of suffering.

The Paston Estate is Ransacked

The Pastons gained large estates in Norfolk by dint of hard work and skill. Needless to say, their rapidly increasing property was the envy of local barons, some of whom attacked during the Wars of the Roses. Margaret Paston here tells her husband in London of the capture of their Hellesdon estate.

27 October 1465

. . . Please you to know that I was at Hellesdon on Thursday last and saw the place there, and, in good faith, nobody would believe how foul and horrible it appears unless they saw it. There come many people daily to wonder at it, both from Norwich and many other places, and they speak of it with shame. The Duke would have been £1000 better off if it had not happened, and you have the more good will of the people because it was so foully done. They made your tenants of Hellesdon and Drayton, with others, break down the walls of both the place and the lodge – God knows full much against their wills, but they dare not refuse for fear. I have spoken with your tenants of Hellesdon and Drayton and comforted them as well as I can. The Duke's men ransacked the church and bore away all the goods that were left there, both of ours and of the tenants, and even stood upon the high altar and ransacked the images and took away those that they could find, and put the parson out of the church till they had done, and ransacked every man's house in the town five or six times . . . As for lead, brass, pewter, iron, doors, gates and other stuff of the house, men from Costessey and Cawston have it, and what they might not carry away they have hewn asunder in the most spiteful manner . . .

At the reverence of God, if any worshipful and profitable settlement may be made in your matters, do not forsake it, to avoid our trouble and great costs and charges that we may have and that may grow hereafter . . .

ED. ALICE D. GREENWOOD, *SELECTIONS FROM THE PASTON LETTERS*
(1920)

The Pastons tried to get Hellesdon back, fighting for years through the lawcourts, as John Paston was a lawyer, but they were unsuccessful.

Margaret Paston was frequently left to guard the estate against powerful local barons who threatened to attack. Her husband and sons were in London.

11 July 1467

. . . Also this day was brought me word from Caister that Rising of Fritton had heard in divers places in Suffolk that Fastolf of Cowhawe gathers all the strength he may and intends to assault Caister and to enter there if he may, insomuch that it is said that he has five score men ready and daily sends spies to know what men guard the place. By whose power or favour or support he will do this I know not, but you know well that I have been afraid there before this time, when I had other comfort than I had now: I cannot guide nor rule soldiers well and they set not by [do not respect] a woman as they should by a man. Therefore I would that you should send home your brothers or else Daubeney to take control and to bring in such men as are necessary for the safeguard of the place . . . And I have been about my livelode to set a rule therein, as I have written to you, which is not yet all performed after my desire, and I would not go to Caister till I had done. I do not want to spend more days near thereabouts, if I can avoid it; so make sure that you send someone home to keep the place and when I have finished what I have begun I shall arrange to go there if it will do any good – otherwise I had rather not be there . . .

. . . I marvel greatly that you send me no word how you do, for your enemies begin to grow right bold and that puts your friends in fear and doubt. Therefore arrange that they may have some comfort, so that they be not discouraged, for if we lose our friends, it will be hard in this troublous world to get them again . . .

ED. ALICE D. GREENWOOD (1920)

Preparations for War in the Court of Louis XIV

Madame de Sévigné comments, in this letter to her cousin, Bussey-Rabutin, on an aristocratic woman visiting a warring army during the long and unnecessary war against Germany.

12 October 1678

M. de Luxembourg's army is not yet disengaged; the orderlies even talk of the siege of Trèves or Juliers. I shall be in despair if I have to start thinking about war all over again. I very much wish that my son and my property were no longer exposed to their *glorious sufferings*. It is wretched to be moving on into the land of misery, which is inevitable in your trade.

You do know, I believe, that Mme de Mecklenburg, on her way to Germany, passed through her brother's army [that of M. de Luxembourg]. She spent three days there, like Armida, amid all these military honours which don't give in without a lot of noise. I can't understand how she could think of me in those conditions. She did more, she wrote me a very nice letter, which surprised me very much indeed, for I have no contact with her and she could do ten campaigns and ten journeys in Germany without my having any cause for complaint. I wrote to her that I had often read about princesses in armies being adored and admired by all the princes, who were so many lovers, but that I had never come across one who in the midst of such a triumph thought of writing to an old friend who was not in the princess's confidence. People are trying to read things into her journey. It is not, so they say, to see her husband, whom she doesn't love at all, and it is not that she hates Paris. It is, then, to find a wife for Monsieur le Dauphin. There are some people who are so mysterious that you can never believe that their actions are not equally so.

Monsieur de Brandenburg and the Danes have so thoroughly cleared the Swedes out of Germany that that Elector has nothing left to do but join our enemies. It is feared that that will delay peace for the Germans.

TRANS. L. TANCOCK, *MADAME DE SÉVIGNÉ: SELECTED LETTERS* (1982)

A Husband's Absence at War

Wives suffered great hardships when their husbands 'enlisted' for fighting. Often governments failed to pay them any money, even when the men's wages were promised them. Lack of universal education until recently also meant the added misery of not knowing what had happened. However, there are a few letters, including some from Sarah Hodkins, a 26-year-old mother of two. She had just given birth to the second child when her husband enlisted in the militia in Boston in 1775.

I cannot reconcile myself to your absence. I look for you almost every day, but I don't allow myself to depend on any thing, for I find there is nothing . . . but trouble and disappointments.

My respectful regards to your commanding officer. Tell him I have wanted his bed fellow pretty much these cold nights. I must reproach you for leaving your wife and children. I have got a Swete Babe, almost six months old, but have got no father for it. Above all dear husband I must urge you not to enlist for another three years. . . .

ED. B. HILL, *EIGHTEENTH CENTURY WOMEN* (1984)

The husband for whom her 'heart aked' finally came home – unharmed.

The French Revolution

Mary Wollstonecraft lived in France for a time, as she found French intellectual life less repressive. She felt enthusiasm for the French Revolution at first. This is part of a long letter to a friend, Everina.

Le Havre 1794

My Dear Girl,

It is extremely uncomfortable to write to you thus without expecting, or even daring to ask for an answer, lest I should involve others in my difficulties, or make them suffer for protecting me. The French are, at present, so full of suspicion that had a letter of James's imprudently sent to me, been opened, I would not have answered for the consequences. I have just sent off a great part of my M.S. which Miss Williams would fain have had be burn [sic], following her example, and to tell you the truth, my life would not have been worth much, had it been found. It is impossible for you to have any idea of the impression the sad scenes I have been a witness to have left on my mind. The climate of France is uncommonly fine, the country pleasant, and there is a degree of ease, and even simplicity in the manners of the common people, which attaches me to them – Still death and misery in every shape of terror haunts this devoted [meaning 'doomed' or 'cursed'] country – I certainly am glad I came to France because I never would have had else a just opinion of the most extraordinary event that has ever been recorded – AND I have met with some uncommon instances of friendship which my heart will ever gratefully store up, and call to mind when the remembrance is keen of the anguish it has endured for its fellow-creatures at large – for the unfortunate beings cut off around me and the still more unfortunate survivors.

It is, perhaps, in a state of comparative idleness – pursuing employments not absolutely necessary to support life, that the finest polish is given to the mind, and those personal graces, which are instantly felt, but cannot be described: and it is natural to hope, that the labour of acquiring the substantial virtues, necessary to maintain freedom, will not render the French less pleasing, when they become more respectable.

CLAIRE TOMALIN, *THE LIFE AND DEATH OF MARY WOLLSTONECRAFT*
(1974)

War Work

Here Florence Nightingale writes to her Aunt Mai from the Crimea.

September 1855

The pressure of work is enormous: getting up at 6 a.m. and copying until 11 p.m, and next day getting up at 5 a.m. and copying again until 11 p.m.

November 1855

A women obtains that from military courtesy (if she does not shock either their habits of business or their caste prejudice), which a man who pitted the civilian against the military element and the female against the doctors, partly from temper, partly from policy, effectually hindered.

The hopes she placed in her female wiles in that letter were disappointed. A year later, in September 1856, she wrote again:

I have been appointed a twelvemonth today, and what a twelvemonth of dirt it has been, of experience which would sadden not a life but eternity. Who has ever had a sadder experience. Christ was betrayed by one, but my cause has been betrayed by everyone – ruined, destroyed, betrayed by everyone, excepting Mrs Roberts, Rev. Mother and Mrs Stewart. All the rest, Weare, Clough, Salisbury, Stanley *et id genus omne* where are they? And Mrs Stewart is more than half mad. A cause which is supported by a mad woman and twenty fools must be a falling house . . . Dr Hall [the doctor in official charge of hospitals] is dead against me, justly provoked but not by me. He descends to every meanness to make my position more difficult.

As if I had not enough to endure I was taken ill again and forced to enter the Castle Hospital with severe sciatica. Minus the pain, which was great, the attack did not seem to have damaged me much. I have now had all that this climate can give, Crimean fever, Dysentery, Rheumatism and believe myself thoroughly acclimatised and ready to stand out the war with any man. . . .

From April until November, every egg, every bit of butter, jelly, ale and Eau de Cologne which the sick officers have had has been provided out of my or Mrs. Shaw Stewart's private pockets. Dr Hall would like to broil me slowly on the fires of his own diet kitchen. There is not an official who would not burn me like Joan Of Arc if he could, but they know the War Office cannot turn me out because the country is with me.

FAWCETT LIBRARY

Criticism of The Boer War

Women have been more involved in war than is generally acknowledged. Here Emily Hobhouse criticizes the Boer War in an open letter to the Secretary of State for War, sent to the Press.

1903

Will nothing be done? Will no prompt measures be taken to deal with this terrible evil? Three months ago I tried to place the matter strongly before you, and begged permission to organise immediately alleviatory measures. . . . My request was refused. . . . The repulse to myself would have mattered nothing, had only a large band of kindly workers been instantly despatched with full powers to deal with each individual camp as its needs required. The necessity was instant if innocent human lives were to be saved. Instead we had to wait a month while six ladies were chosen. During that month 576 children died. The preparation and journey of these ladies occupied another month, and in that interval 1,124 more children succumbed. In place of at once proceeding to the great centres of high mortality, the bulk of yet a third month seems to have been spent in their long journey to Mafeking, and in passing a few days at some of the healthier camps. Meanwhile, 1,545 more children died. This is not immediate action; it was very deliberate enquiry, and that too at a time when death, which is unanswerable, was at work; nay, when the demands of death, instead of diminishing, were increasing. Will you not now, with the thought before you of those 3,245 children who have closed their eyes for ever since I last saw you on their behalf, will you not now take instant action, and endeavour thus to avert the evil results of facts patent to all, and suspend further enquiry into the truth of what the whole world knows?

It is monstrous that two of the Ladies chosen for your Commission are known to be in favour of the policy of the concentration camps.

My opinions were discounted and barely tolerated, because I was known to feel sorry for the sickly children, and to have shown PERSONAL sympathy to broken, destitute Boer women in their PERSONAL troubles. Sympathy shown to any of Dutch blood is the one unpardonable sin in South Africa.

RAY. STRACHEY, *MILLICENT FAWCETT* (1931)

Conflict in the Middle East

Gertrude Bell (1868–1926) was the beloved daughter of Sir Hugh Bell, son of a wealthy colliery owner. After an excellent education she went in 1892, when she was twenty-four, to visit her many relations in the Middle East. She fell in love with it, and learned Arabic, becoming a powerful Arabist. In 1914 she set out for Ha'il, a desert city, 800 kilometres south of Damascus, now in Saudi Arabia. Bell underestimated the possibility of local political conflict, because she had long dreamed of this journey.

January 1914

Dearest beloved father, my plans are developing and luck seems to be on my side. An almost incredible tranquillity reigns in the desert – the oldest enemies are at peace and there have been excellent autumn rains, so I shall find both grass and surface water. Bassan found me some riding camels going cheap in Damascus, a stroke of luck as I thought I should have to transport myself into the wilds and haggle for camels there. I now have 20 camels of my own, and feel like an Arab sheikh.

G. BELL, *THE LETTERS OF GERTRUDE BELL* (1930)

However, instead of being greeted by the Amir when she finally arrived, his uncle (who feared he might be murdered) put her under house arrest.

So I sat in honourable captivity and the days were weary and long. Tales round the fire were all of murder, and the air whispered of murder. In Ha'il murder is like the spilling of milk and not one of the sheikhs but feels his head sitting unsteadily on his shoulders. It gets on your nerves when you sit day after day between high mud walls and I thank heaven that my nerves are not very responsive. They kept me awake only one night out of the ten but I will not conceal from you that there were hours of considerable anxiety.

G. BELL (1930)

She let it be known that she had distinguished powerful Arab friends.

Next day came word from the Amir's mother inviting me to visit her. I went, riding solemnly through the moonlit streets of this strange place, and passed two hours, taken straight from *Arabian Nights*, with the women of the palace. There are few places left where you can see the unadulterated East as it has lived for centuries, but Ha'il is one. Those women were wrapped in Indian brocades, hung with jewels, served by slaves, not one thing about them which betrayed the existence of Europe – except me. I was the blot.

G. BELL (1930)

After this visit she was suddenly freed in March 1914.

The First World War Front

American novelist Edith Wharton drove to the Front in 1915. She wrote twice to Henry James to describe what she saw at Verdun.

February 28

From a garden we looked across the valley to a height about 5 miles way, where white puffs & scarlet flashes kept springing up all over the dark hillside. It was the hill above Vauquois, where there has been desperate fighting for two days. The Germans were firing from the top at the French trenches below (hidden from us by an intervening rise of the ground); & the French were assaulting, & *their* puffs & flashes were half way up the hill. And so we saw the reason why there are to be so many wounded at Clermont tonight!

EDS. R.W.B. AND NANCY LEWIS, *THE LETTERS OF EDITH WHARTON*
(1989)

After a second little tour eleven days later, Edith sketched a scene on the Meuse River, west of Verdun.

Picture this all under a white winter sky, driving great flurries of snow across the mud-and-cinder-coloured landscape, with the steel-cold Meuse winding between beaten poplars – Cook standing with Her [the Mercedes] in a knot of mud-coated military motors & artillery horses, soldiers coming & going, cavalrymen riding up with messages, poor bandaged creatures in rag-bag clothes leaning in doorways, & always, over & above us, the boom, boom, boom of the guns on the grey heights to the east.

EDS. R.W.B. AND NANCY LEWIS (1989)

Henry James responded with enthusiasm.

Your whole record is sublime, and the interest and the beauty and the terror of it all have again and again called me back to it. . . .

EDS. R.W.B. AND NANCY LEWIS (1989)

A Prisoner of War

During the Second World War Marina Tsvetayeva wrote to her daughter who had been imprisoned by Stalin.

Moscow, 12 April 1941
Saturday

Dear Alya,

At last, your first letter – in a blue envelope, dated the 4th. I stared at it from 9 a.m. to 3 p.m. when Moor [her brother] came home from school. It lay on his dinner-plate, and he saw it as soon as he opened the door: and with a contented and even self-satisfied 'A-ah!' – pounced on it. He would not let me read it. Both his own letter and mine he read aloud. But even before the reading, I sent you a postcard. I couldn't wait. That was yesterday, the 11th. And on the 10th I took in a parcel and they accepted it.

I have been industriously at work finding provisions for you. Alya, I already have sugar and cocoa; I am about to have a shot at lard and cheese – the most solid I can find. I shall send you a bag of dried carrots; I dried them in the autumn on all the radiators. You can boil them. At least they are still vegetables. It is a pity, though not unnatural, that you do not eat garlic. I have a whole kilo stored up just in case. But bear in mind that raw potato is a reliable and less unpleasant method. It is effective as lemon – that I know for certain [against diseases of vitamin deficiency].

I have already told you that your belongings are free. I myself was given the job of unlocking them – so we shall rescue everything. Incidentally, the moths have eaten nothing. All your things are intact – books, toys and a lot of photographs. I write nothing of my own. No time. A lot of housework. The cleaning lady comes once a week.

I also re-read Leskov – last winter in Golitzino. And I read Benvenuto in Goethe's translation when I was seventeen. I particularly remember the salamander and the slap.

I visited Nina a few times over the winter. She is constantly unwell, but she works, whenever she is able, and is happy in it. I gave her a short artificial fur jacket – she really had frozen to death – and, for her birthday, one of my metal cups, from which nobody drinks, except her and me.

I want to send this off now, so I shall finish. Keep strong and alert. I hope that Mulia's trip is only a matter of time. I have recently been admitted to the Grupkom of Goslitizdat – unanimous. So you see, I am trying.

Keep well. Kisses . . .

Moor is writing to you himself.

Mama

ELAINE FEINSTEIN, *MARINA TSVETAYEVA* (1989)

Prison Visiting and Helping Prostitutes

Women have always worked to alleviate suffering, as individuals and in communities such as nunneries. Witness to female philanthropy comes from the earliest medieval letters. By the nineteenth century there is more public proof, though the scale of female philanthropic enterprise is impossible to quantify; official reports obviously ignore unofficial individual activities. We know that women such as Elizabeth Fry (1780–1845) dedicated their lives to the helping of other women in prison – or imprisoned by poverty.

In France also there is a tradition of social work, spearheaded by feminists like Flora Tristan (1803–44). In a brief unhappy life, deprived of her children by a murderous husband, she campaigned for emancipation of working-class men as well as women. When she visited London, she succeeded in gaining entry to the notorious Newgate Prison, and gave evidence of conditions. A few of the well-to-do English such as Emily Eden, sister of India's Governor-General, refused to blind themselves to the suffering caused by famine in poorer districts, and gave help to children.

Josephine Butler devoted herself to women less fortunate than herself and campaigned bravely for working-class women shut in prison hospitals under the Contagious Disease Acts of 1864, 1866 and 1869. These Acts, intended to check the spread of venereal disease among the armed forces, left men free, but harassed many working-class women suspected of prostitution. Some were dragged by non-uniformed 'police' before medical inspectors and found still to be virgins! Butler toured British cities, explaining the cruelty of governmental persecution of suspected women. She enlisted the signature of Florence Nightingale, and I include here a hitherto unpublished letter in answer to Butler's petition against these Acts.

Millicent Fawcett also used her name, her pen and her energy to reform the laws which humiliated prostitutes – while allowing their clients to remain 'uninspected' for disease.

Butler was much criticized for employing as a maid a girl who had been seduced, dishonoured and then dismissed by the Master of an Oxford College. A few men supported these campaigns, as shown by the letters from Fawcett, working for the release of humanitarian Mr Stead.

Care for the Suffering

Emily Eden went to India in 1835 when her brother was made Governor-General. She kept house for him, surrounded by luxury. She felt little sympathy with the behaviour of most Englishmen she met and kept a sense of balance by sketching and writing letters home. Her care for Indians is shown by her reaction to the famine in Cawnpore in this letter of 1838 to the rest of her family in England.

It is here that we came into the starving districts. They have had no rain for a year and a half, the cattle have all died and the people are all dying or gone away. The distress is perfectly dreadful, you cannot conceive the horrible sights we see, particularly children; perfect skeletons in many cases, their bones through the skin, without a rag of clothing and utterly unlike human beings. The sight is too shocking; the women look as if they had been buried, their skulls look so dreadful. I am sure there is no sort of violent atrocity I should not commit for food, with a starving baby. I should not stop to think about the rights or wrongs of the case.

E. EDEN, *UP THE COUNTRY: LETTERS FROM INDIA* (1872)

When I went round to the stables yesterday before breakfast I found such a miserable little baby, something like an old monkey, but with glazed stupid eyes. I am sure you would have sobbed to see the way in which the little atom flew at a cup of milk. We have discovered the mother since, but she is a skeleton too and says that she has had no food to give it for a month. Dr Drummond says it cannot live it is so diseased with starvation but I mean to try what can be done with it.

E. EDEN (1872)

A Women's Prison in London

Flora Tristan describes her visit to Newgate in this letter.

1841

I confess I felt very ill at ease in this lodge. There is no fresh air or daylight; the prisoner can still hear the noise of the street outside, and beneath the door he can still see the sunlight shining in the square. What a dreadful contrast, and how he regrets the loss of his liberty! But once past the lodge he hears nothing more; the atmosphere is as cold, damp and heavy as in a cellar; most of the passages are narrow, and so are the stairs leading to the upper wards.

First I was taken to see the women's wing. Over the past few years several changes have been made at Newgate and now it houses only prisoners awaiting trial, not convicted prisoners; in this respect it corresponds to the Conciergerie in Paris. It is here too that most executions take place.

The governor was kind enough to accompany me over the prison; he told me that thanks to the writings of philanthropists and the constant complaints of humanitarians, Newgate had undergone all the improvements of which it was capable. Mr Cox was particularly happy that prisoners were now divided into different classes, whereas formerly they had all been confined together.

The internal arrangement of the prison is not very satisfactory and there is not enough space for individual cells. In each ward the beds, wooden constructions six feet long and two feet wide, are arranged in two or three tiers like berths on board a ship. There is a large table in the middle with wooden benches all round it; this is where the prisoners eat, work, read and write. On close examination I found the wards very clean and well-kept, but as they are dark and poorly ventilated and the floors are very uneven, their general appearance is unpleasing.

Nearly all the women I saw there were of the lowest class; prostitutes, servants or country girls accused of theft. Four were on charges carrying the death penalty for crimes classified as felonies under English law. Most of them seemed to be of low intelligence, but I noticed several whose tight thin lips, pointed nose, sharp chin, deep-set eyes and sly look I took as signs of exceptional depravity. I saw only one woman there who aroused my interest. She was confined with six others in a dark, damp low-ceilinged cell; when we entered they all rose and made us the customary servile curtsey which had embarrassed and irritated me from the moment I set foot in the prison. One alone refrained and it was this sign of independence which attracted my attention. Picture a young woman of twenty-four, small, well-made and tastefully dressed, standing with head held high to reveal a perfect profile, graceful neck. My eyes filled with tears and only the presence of the governor prevented me from going up to her and taking her hand so that she might understand my interest in her fate and so that my sympathy might calm for a few moments the sufferings of her heart.

Beauty can only be supreme when it reflects the noblest qualities of the soul. Without that inner radiance even the most beautiful woman in that sad place would have left me unmoved; but there was such dignity in this beauty which bore the depths of misfortune with pride and courage.

TRANS. J. HAWKES, *THE LONDON JOURNAL OF FLORA TRISTAN* (1982)

Exploitation of the Hungry

Josephine Butler spent years in public speaking to help working-class women. When she heard of a servant girl being made pregnant by the Master of an Oxford College, dismissed and then imprisoned for the death of the child, she took this girl into her own service. 'Mrs Butler takes an interest in a class of sinners whom she had better have left to themselves' remarked a male leader-writer. In 1864 her life was devastated by the death of her five-year-old daughter Eva, who fell from an upper landing.

Soon afterwards she moved to Liverpool when her husband George became a headmaster. She visited Brownlow Hill Workhouse, where 5,000 women worked in the oakum sheds. Impoverished women picked the tough, tarred hemp in return for their food, in damp, unhygienic sheds. She decided to help such women usually termed 'sinners' by society, partly to forget the pain of losing her daughter 'in pain greater than my own'. Butler was horrified at what she learned and wrote letters to newspapers to draw public attention to the exploitation of the hungry.

I have seen girls bought and sold just as young girls were at the time of the slave trade. Are you aware that there are gentlemen among the higher classes who pay so much per girl? When a gentleman sends to a professional brothel for a girl he pays for her. Is that not buying? By such a system the path of evil is made more easy for our sons and for the whole of the youth of this country. In as much as the moral restraint is withdrawn, the moment the government recognises and provides convenience for the practice of a vice which it declares necessary and venial.

Florence Nightingale supported Josephine Butler during her untiring work to repeal the Contagious Diseases Act.

private   London Dec 20 1869

Dear Madam,

I return you my signature to your Circular and Petition, in the objects of which I most heartily and deeply concur.

The only correction I offer, as you have decided it, is to omit the word 'permanent' in the petition – altho' I think, had I had the wording of the petition I should have indicated that no statistics exist, which justify the Acts protested against, (or upon which to have the Acts protested against).

I am afraid that I cannot refer you to the statistics which you desire. They exist in all the Returns & scattered thro' all the Reports on Health which reach the War Office from home, the Colonies, and India. Comparative statistics of Health from foreign armies and foreign civil[ian] life being often included in them.

All these have come to me in the way of business for many years – a

196

very melancholy business it is, I assure you. But it would take me several hours even to collect these Blue Books, to look out the passages in them referring to the subjects and to make a list of them.

The Government however is perfectly aware of their existence – since they are all Government Blue Books. Indeed the opinion of the Medical Officer of the Privy Council was asked by the government on this very subject – and was given in conformity with the facts I have mentioned to you. You will find the last official statement in a pamphlet which you probably have – but if not, I enclose a copy. It is the best reply to your request which I am able to give. The chief points are marked in the margin; but the whole pamphlet is a refutation of the 'Society' mentioned by you in your protest. There are however, things in the pamphlet not based on experience, which are unfortunate.

I am sorry that I am really unable, from the press of business, to enter more fully into the subject in correspondence.

Pray believe me, dear Madam, ever your faithful servant,

Florence Nightingale
FAWCETT LIBRARY

Millicent Fawcett Commends a Helper of Women

It was not only women who went to prison in the late nineteenth century to help women. An editor, Mr Stead, attempted to save a girl who had been forced into prostitution. He was arrested and brought to trial on charge of abducting the girl. Stead was found guilty and sent to prison. Millicent Fawcett immediately wrote to him.

1855

I cannot find words to say how I honour and reverence you for what you have done for the weakest and most helpless among women. I always felt that by some legal quibble you might be tripped up, as it were; but this is as nothing; your work will stand. . . . I really envy you as much as I admire and honour you; very few people, even among heroes and martyrs, have had the happiness of seeing their faithful work so immediately crowned with good results. Everything I have written sounds so cold compared to what I feel; but if gratitude and honour from myself and many hundreds and thousands of your countrymen can help you at this stress, I want you to have that help.

RAY STRACHEY, *MILLICENT FAWCETT* (1931)

Stead needed comfort, as he was treated as a common prisoner. Fortunately Fawcett knew how to make the system work. She wrote promptly to Sir Henry Ponsonby, Secretary of State.

12 November

Your kindness to me and my late husband on more than one occasion emboldens me to ask your advice and assistance as to the propriety and possibility of bringing under Her Majesty's notice the fact that Mr Stead is not being treated as a first-class misdemeanant. I yesterday saw the Rev. F.B. Waugh, after he had had an interview with Mr Stead in prison. Mr Stead was in the ordinary cotton prison dress, and appeared to be extremely cold; his cell is very dark; it contains a Bible, but the cell is so dark that it is impossible to read it. Mr Stead therefore has to remain all day long doing absolutely nothing; he was very cheerful when Mr Waugh saw him, and complains of nothing, and desires his friends not to complain for him; the warder treats him with respect and kindness. . . . Mr Stead's friends, however, cannot help dreading the effect upon his health if he remains during the term of his imprisonment in cold and darkness on a lowering diet, without materials for writing and reading, and they venture to think that the fact that the Judge, both the Juries and the Attorney-General having drawn special attention to the purity of Mr Stead's motives, gives him a claim to be treated during his imprisonment as a first-class misdemeanant. I have written as briefly as possible in order not to intrude too much on your time, begging your indulgence if there is any impropriety in my writing at all. Believe me, etc.

RAY STRACHEY (1931)

Helping Prostitutes

In 1887, Millicent Fawcett wrote to the leader of the Liberal Party about 'the utter rottenness of the whole of pubic opinion on morals.' Little by little, she began to attend less to the details of the rescue work, and more and more to the great political remedies. In the same year she wrote to a friend about one of the local societies for the Protection of Public Morals.

I don't think you show anything like sufficient activity in proceeding against the people who TRADE in vice in the town. If you analyse the accounts you will see that during the year the great sum of £1 9s. 2d. represents the expenses of the Society in its proper work. According to Mr H.'s first letter to me, the town is swarming with houses (the report speaks of one only having been closed). Who keeps them up? Who runs them? Who are the customers? Get at these facts and make them public, and you will have done something to attack the evil at its source. Prosecuting victims, children who are the products of the evil rather than its causes, does absolutely nothing but obscure the real issues.

RAY STRACHEY, MILLICENT FAWCETT (1931)

nine

Travellers and Travelling

The desire to see the world existed, no doubt, long before any accounts, but the desire to write about travel began relatively early. In the fourteenth century a woman who made the voyage to Jerusalem became the first travel writer of whom we have a record. The first travel writer in English is Celia Fiennes (1662–1741). She kept a lively Journal for her family, describing her extensive tours, which has provided the first comprehensive survey of change in the British countryside.

Women have travelled for multifarious reasons. The motives were often to discover themselves, other ways of living their lives, as well as other cultures. Some were precipitated into foreign travel by chance, such as Lady Fanshawe, who accompanied her Royalist husband into exile after the English Civil War, and Lady Mary Wortley Montagu, who travelled with her husband to Turkey when he was made ambassador there. Both these women wrote unusually appreciative accounts of different cultures. Lady Fanshawe noted the generosity and liveliness of the Spaniards, their choice wines, bacon, sausages, bread, 'sallad, roots and fruits'. These women were unaffected by English xenophobia, and might have made our culture more open if they had had a wider audience than friends.

Aphra Behn (1640–89) went to Guyana at the age of nineteen, probably with her Dutch husband, and used her experiences to create the first novel in English, about a handsome black slave, *Oroonoko*; she praised the qualities of the 'noble savage' well before Rousseau developed his influential theory. Left an impoverished widow some years later, Behn used her knowledge of Dutch to try to (though she was, in fact, never paid) earn some money – she worked as a spy while England was at war with Holland.

Some women set out with ideas of service, to become missionaries; Mildred Cable and Francesca French cross the Gobi desert. Others went to study, such as the botanist Marianne North, whose paintings of tropical flora hang at the Royal Botanic Gardens in Kew. Some went to improve their health; the indomitable Isabella Bird suffered migraines in England, but recovered during long hours in the saddle. Even in old age she showed remarkable resistance to appalling weather – as long as she stayed abroad. She travelled to seek, not merely to escape.

Some wished to escape. The public imagination was caught by the wealthy Lady Jane Digby who left her drawing room for a far more exotic and flamboyant existence. She travelled to Corfu, then Syria and eventually scandalized her family by letters home explaining that she had married a Bedouin sheik and lived in his desert tent.

Some used travel to 'work', that is to say, to study foreign cultures. Harriet Martineau and Barbara Bodichon, both dedicated reformers, were so horrified by the conditions of slaves in the southern states of America that they spent time writing public and private letters, describing the ill-treatment. Occasionally women went abroad to work, including the wives of settlers in New England and Canada, whose lives are now being studied through letters home. The writer Frances Trollope (1780–1863) travelled to America in order to support her family, destitute because of her husband's incapacity to manage their financial affairs, either as barrister or farmer. Her *Domestic Manners of the Americans* (1832) made her a bestselling author at the age of fifty-two.

Many travellers had private means. However, there were others who exercised ingenuity to increase their small incomes in order to travel: Freya Stark, born in 1893, successfully gambled the little money she had on the stock-market. Mary Kingsley (1862–1900) had only a tiny inheritance, and traded toothbrushes and fish bait to support her years in the Congo. She lived fearlessly among the Congolese whom she admired for their strength, their hospitality, and their culture. After publishing *Travels in West Africa*, an original and informative account of her journeys and African religions, she was asked to advise the British government, proving extraordinarily enlightened compared with most male politicians.

Some women travelled with retinues of servants; others travelled alone, lived with the natives, or very simply, such as Gertrude Bell, the Arabist. From the time of Byron, the East offered attractive images of a sensuous life with fountains and perfumes, but above all of the capacity to live in the present. Women visitors mentioned losing a sense of time in Arabia and praised a culture which valued being, over having or doing. Such writers anticipate anthropology in observing other cultures with few preconceived ideas, and with an openness to alien values.

Travel could occasionally transform existence, bringing openings and possibilities almost unprecedented in the previous history of women's restricted lives. It took the factory girl Mary Slessor a decade or more of saving and studying to realize her ambition of going out to Africa as a missionary. But when she arrived, she tackled tribal abuses like human sacrifice and twin-murder with such vigour and success that the government made her a ruling magistrate. Though single, she also became the adopted mother of no less than twelve pairs of the twins she saved from ritual sacrifice. Back in Scotland, she would have been still at her loom in the mill.

Adventuring women could escape too, from the rigours of Victorian sexual repression. The redoubtable Isabella Bird, having investigated the menfolk of Australia, the Pacific, China, Iraq and Tibet, and having now become the first woman Fellow of the Royal Geographical Society, lost her heart in the American West to a 'dear desperado', 'Rocky Mountain Jim'. The famous lepidopterist Margaret Fountaine briskly collected more than butterflies in her travels and, when she startled a handsome young dragoman in Syria, made this particularly fine specimen her common-law husband. Louisa Jebb, who with only another woman for company rode through Turkey and Iraq narrowly escaping death at the hands of Islamic fanatics, described coming upon a 'screaming circle of dancing stamping men'. Although vividly remembering 'I once did crochet-work in drawing rooms!', Louisa did not hesitate: 'A feeling of wild rebellion took hold of me: I sprang into the circle. "Make me mad!" I cried out. "I want to be mad too!"'

Some women travelled against their will, to accompany their menfolk. Emily Eden went to India to keep house for her brother and became engrossed in the multifaceted life. Her letters home were published, like Bird's, and both became bestsellers. Vita Sackville-West accompanied her husband to Teheran. Her witty letters offer differing reactions to those of Freya Stark, who was more interested in Arab culture.

The chapter ends with some recent letters, sent by a Buddhist nun to her friends as she travelled around India in 1990.

An Early Tour of England

Celia Fiennes (1662–1741) is one of our liveliest travel-writers. For eighteen years she toured England extensively, initially for her health. She wrote a Journal for her family, an incomplete version of which was published in 1888. Her style is breathless, but direct, the spelling erratic, the enthusiasm genuine, as in this prefatory letter.

As this was never designed, soe not likely to fall into the hands of any but my near relations, there needs not much to be said to excuse or recommend it. Something may be diverting and proffitable tho' not to Gentlemen that they have travelled more about England, staid longer in places, might have more acquaintance and more opportunity to be inform'd.

My Journeys, as they were begun to regain my health by variety and change of aire and exercise, soe whatever promoted that was pursued; and those informations of things as could be obtain'd from inns *en passant* or from some acquaintance, inhabitants of such places, could furnish me with for my diversion, I thought necessary to remark.

Now thus much without vanity may be asserted of the subject, that if all persons, both Ladies, much more Gentlemen, would spend some of their tyme in Journeys to visit their native Land, and be curious to inform themselves and make observations of the pleasant prospects, good buildings, different produces and manufactures of each place, with the variety of sports and recreations they are adapt to, would be a souveraign remedy to cure or preserve from these epidemick diseases of vapours, should I add Laziness?

It would also form such an Idea of England, add much to its Glory and Esteem in our minds and cure the evil itch of over-valueing foreign parts; at least furnish them with an equivalent to entertain strangers when amongst us, or inform them when abroad of their native Country. . . .

It must be owned that many Gentlemen, in general service of their country are most ignorant of anything but the name of the place for which they serve in parliament; how then can they speake for or promote their Good or redress their Grievances? I shall conclude with the hearty wish and recommendation to all, but especially my own Sex, the studdy of those things which tends to improve the mind and makes our Lives pleasant and comfortable, as well as profitable in all the Stages and Stations of our Lives, and render Suffering and Age supportable and Death less formidable and a future State more happy.

C. FIENNES, *THROUGH ENGLAND ON A SIDE SADDLE IN THE TIME OF WILLIAM AND MARY* (1888)

First Visit to a Turkish Bath

After her first visit to a Turkish bath, Lady Mary Wortley Montagu wrote enthusiastically to her sister. Unlike most male travellers, she did not take her culture's ideas to an 'exotic' east, but studied what she saw.

Adrianople 1 April 1717

I must not omit what I saw remarkable at Sophia, one of the most beautiful towns in the Turkish Empire and famous for its hot baths that are resorted to both for diversion and health. I stopped here one day on purpose to see them. Designing to go incognito, I hired a Turkish coach. These *voitures* are not at all like ours, but much more convenient for the country, the heat being so great that glasses would be very troublesome. They are made a good deal in the manner of the Dutch coaches, having wooden lattices painted and gilded, the inside being painted with baskets and nosegays of flowers, intermixed commonly with little poetical mottoes. They are covered all over with cloth, lined with silk and very often richly embroidered and fringed. This covering entirely hides the persons in them, but may be thrown back at pleasure and the ladies peep through the lattices. They hold four people very conveniently, seated on cushions, but not raised.

In one of these covered wagons I went to the bagnio about ten o'clock. It was already full of women. It is built of stone in the shape of a dome with no windows but in the roof, which gives light enough. There was five of these domes joined together, the outmost being less than the rest and serving only as a hall where the porteress stood at the door. Ladies of quality generally give this woman the value of a crown or ten shillings, and I did not forget that ceremony. The next room is a very large one, paved with marble, and all round it raised two sofas of marble, one above another. There were four fountains of cold water in this room, falling first into marble basins and then running on the floor in little channels made for that purpose, which carried the streams into the next room, something less than this, with the same sort of marble sofas, but so hot with steams of sulphur proceeding from the baths joining to it, 'twas impossible to stay there with one's clothes on. The two other domes were the hot baths, one of which had cocks of cold water turning into it to temper it to what degree of warmth the bathers have a mind to.

I was in my travelling habit, which is a riding dress, and certainly appeared very extraordinary to them, yet there was not one of 'em that showed the least surprise or impertinent curiosity, but received me with all the obliging civility possible. I know no European court where the ladies would have behaved themselves in so polite a manner to a stranger. I believe in the whole there were two hundred women and yet none of those disdainful smiles or satiric whispers that never fail in our assemblies when anybody appears that is not dressed exactly in fashion. They repeated over and over to me, '*Uzelle, pek uzelle*', which is nothing but, 'Charming, very charming'. The first sofas were covered with cushions and rich carpets, on which sat the ladies, and on the second their slaves behind 'em, but without any distinction of rank by their dress, all being in the state of nature, that is, in plain English, stark naked, without any beauty or defect concealed, yet there was not the least wanton smile or immodest gesture amongst 'em. They walked and moved with the same majestic grace which Milton describes of our General Mother. There were many amongst them as exactly proportioned as ever any goddess was drawn by the pencil of Guido or Titian, and most of their skins shiningly white, only adorned by their beautiful hair divided into many tresses hanging on their shoulders, braided either with pearl or riband, perfectly representing the figures of the Graces.

I was here convinced of the truth of a reflection that I had often made, that if 'twas the fashion to go naked the face would be hardly observed. I perceived that the ladies with the finest skins and most delicate shapes had the greatest share of my admiration, though their faces were sometimes less beautiful than those of their companions. . . .

In short, 'tis the women's coffee-house, where all the news of the town is told, scandal invented, etc. They generally take this diversion once a week, and stay there at least four or five hours without getting cold by immediate coming out of the hot bath into the cool room, which was very surprising to me. The lady that seemed the most considerable amongst them entreated me to sit by her and would fain have undressed me for the bath. I excused myself with some difficulty, they being all so earnest in persuading me. I was at last forced to open my skirt and show them my stays, which satisfied 'em very well, for I saw they believed I was so locked up in that machine that it was not in my own power to open it, which contrivance they attributed to my husband. I was charmed with their civility and beauty and should have been very glad to pass more time with them.

ED. R. HALSBAND, *THE COMPLETE LETTERS OF LADY MARY WORTLEY MONTAGU* (1965)

Lady Mary Wortley Montagu made the most of her two years in Turkey. This letter to her sister describes both the feelings and tremendous riches of the Sultan's favourite wife.

10 March 1718

I went to see the Sultana Hafise, favourite of the last Emperor Mustafa, who, you know (or perhaps you don't know), was deposed by his brother, the reigning Sultan, and died a few weeks after, being poisoned, as it was generally believed. This lady was immediately after his death saluted with an absolute order to leave the Seraglio and choose herself a husband from the great men at the Porte. I suppose you imagine her overjoyed at this proposal. Quite contrary; these women, who are called and esteem themselves queens, look upon this liberty as the greatest disgrace and affront that can happen to them. She threw herself at the Sultan's feet and begged him to poniard her rather than use his brother's widow with that contempt. She represented to him in agonies of sorrow that she was privileged from this misfortune by having brought five princes into the Ottoman family, but all the boys being dead and only one girl surviving, this excuse was not received and she compelled to make her choice. She chose Ebubekir Efendi, then secretary of state, and above fourscore year old, to convince the world that she firmly intended to keep the vow she had made of never suffering a second husband to approach her bed, and since she must honour some subject so far as to be called his wife she would choose him as a mark of her gratitude, since it was he that had presented her at the age of ten year old to her lost lord. But she has never permitted him to pay her one visit, though it is now fifteen year she has been in his house, where she passes her time in uninterrupted mourning with a constancy very little known in Christendom, especially in a widow of twenty-one, for she is now but thirty-six. She has no black eunuchs for her guard, her husband being obliged to respect her as a queen and not enquire at all into what is done in her apartment, where I was led into a large room, with a sofa the whole length of it, adorned with white marble pillars like a *ruelle*, covered with pale *bleu* figured velvet on a silver ground, with cushions of the same, where I was desired to repose till the Sultana appeared, who had contrived this manner of reception to avoid rising up at my entrance, though she made me an inclination of her head when I ris up to her. I was very glad to observe a lady that had been distinguished by the favour of an Emperor to whom beauties were every day presented from all parts of the world. But she did not seem to me to have ever been half so beautiful as the fair Fatima I saw at Adrianople, though she had the remains of a fine face more decayed by sorrow than time.

But her dress was something so surprisingly rich I cannot forbear describing it to you. She wore a vest called *dolaman*, and which differs from a caftan by longer sleeves, and folding over at the bottom. It was of purple cloth strait to her shape and thick set, on each side down to her feet and round the sleeves, with pearls of the best water, of the same size as their buttons commonly are. You must not suppose I mean as large as those of my Lord – but about the bigness of a pea; and to these buttons, large loops of diamonds in the form of those gold loops so common upon birthday coats. This habit was tied at the waist with two large tassels of smaller pearl, and round the arms embroidered with large diamonds; her shift fastened at the bosom with a great diamond shaped like a lozenge; her girdle as broad as the broadest English riband entirely covered with diamonds. Round her neck she wore three chains which reached to her knees, one of large pearl at the bottom of which hung a fine coloured emerald as big as a turkey egg, another consisting of two-hundred emeralds close joined together, of the most lively green, perfectly matched, every one as large as a half-crown piece and as thick as three crown pieces, and another of small emeralds perfectly round. But her earrings eclipsed all the rest; they were two diamonds shaped exactly like pears, as large as a big hazel nut. Round her *talpack* she had four strings of pearl, the whitest and most perfect in the world, at least enough to make four necklaces every one as large as the Duchess of Marlborough's, and of the same size, fastened with two roses consisting of a large ruby for the middle stone, and round them twenty drops of clean diamonds to each. Besides this, her headdress was covered with bodkins of emeralds and diamonds. She wore large diamond bracelets and had five rings on her fingers, all single diamonds, (except Mr Pitt's) the largest I ever saw in my life. 'Tis for jewellers to compute the value of these things, but according to the common estimation of jewels in our part of the world, her whole dress must be worth above £100,000 sterling. This I am very sure of, that no European queen has half the quantity.

ED. R. HALSBAND (1965)

Camping with the Army in India

Emily Eden's experiences of camping with the Army in India made entertaining reading, but it was clearly less enjoyable for the participants. 'G' is George, her brother, the Governor-General.

Camp near Allahabad, Nov. 30, 1837

I sent off one journal to you two days ago from a place that, it since appears, was called Bheekee. Yesterday we started at half-past five, as it was a twelve miles' march, and the troops complain if they do not get in before the sun grows hot, so we had half an hour's drive in the dark. I came on in the carriage, as I did not feel well, and one is sick and chilly naturally before breakfast. Not but that I like these morning marches; the weather is so English, and feels so wholesome when one is well. The worst part of a march is the necessity of everybody, sick or well, dead or dying, pushing on with the others. Luckily there is every possible arrangement made for it. There are beds on poles for sick servants and palanquins for us, which are nothing but beds in boxes. G. and I went on an elephant through rather a pretty little village in the evening, and he was less bored than usual, but I never saw him hate anything so much as he does this camp life. I have long named my tent 'Misery Hall.'

'Mine,' G. said 'I call Foully Palace, it is so very squalid-looking.' He was sitting in my tent in the evening, and when the purdahs are all down, all the outlets to the tents are so alike that he could not find which *crevice* led to his abode; and he said at last, 'Well! it is a hard case; they talk of the luxury in which the Governor-General travels, but I cannot even find a covered passage from Misery Hall to Foully Palace.'

This morning we are on the opposite bank of the river to Allahabad, almost a mile from it. It will take three days to pass the whole camp.

Most of the horses and the body-guard are gone to-day.

E. EDEN, *UP THE COUNTRY: LETTERS FROM INDIA* (1872)

Emily Eden only went to India to keep house for her brother. Her letters give a varied picture of their life there.

October 1838

This day fortnight we are to be in our wretched tents – I could have a fit of hysterics when I think of it. The work of packing progresses and there are no bounds to the ardour with which everybody labours to make us uncomfortable. Already there are horrible signs of preparation with camel trunks and stores going off. A great many people have to go down to the plains this week. Poor things, it is about as rational as if a slice of bread were to get off the plate and put itself on the toasting fork.

E. EDEN (1872)

On 9 November 1838, after seven months in Simla, they returned to the tramping way of life. Emily's desperation was compounded by the weather.

We have been six days in camp and it is pouring as it only pours in India. It is impossible to describe the squalid misery; little ditches run round or through each tent with a slosh of mud that one invariably steps into; the servants look soaked and wretched, the camels slip down and die in every direction; I have to go under an umbrella to George's tent and we are carried in palanquins to the dining tent. How people who might by economy and taking in washing and plain work have a comfortable back attic in the neighbourhood of Manchester Square, with a fireplace and a boarded floor, can come and march about India, I cannot guess.

E. EDEN (1872)

The meeting between the Governor-General and the Lion of the Punjab had been arranged for Ferozepore on the border between British India and the Punjab. On 26 November Lord Auckland and his party arrived to discuss averting war – unsuccessfully.

Today was the great day. George and all the gentlemen went on their elephants to meet Ranjit who arrived on an equal number of elephants – indeed there were so many that the clash at meeting was very destructive to howdahs and hangings. George handed the Maharajah into the large tent where he sat down for a few minutes on the sofa between George and me.

E. EDEN (1872)

Slavery in the Southern States

Harriet Martineau devoted most of her life to helping women achieve greater rights. When she visited the southern states of America in the 1850s she was appalled at what she saw.

A lady from New-England, staying in Baltimore, was one day talking over slavery with me, her detestation of it being great, when I told her I dreaded seeing a slave. 'You have seen one,' said she. 'You were waited on by a slave yesterday evening.' She told me of a gentleman who let out and lent out his slaves to wait at gentlemen's houses, and that the tall handsome mulatto who handed the tea at a party the evening before was one of these. I was glad it was over for once; but I never lost the painful feeling caused to a stranger by intercourse with slaves. No familiarity with them, no mirth and contentment on their part, ever soothed the miserable restlessness caused by the presence of a deeply-injured fellow-being. No wonder or ridicule on the spot avails anything to the stranger. He suffers, and must suffer from this, deeply and long, as surely as he is human and hates oppression. . . .

There is something inexpressibly disgusting in the sight of a slave woman in the field. I do not share in the horror of the Americans at the idea of women being employed in outdoor labour. It did not particularly gratify me to see the cows always milked by men (where there were no slaves); and the hay and harvest fields would have looked brighter in my eyes if women had been there to share the wholesome and cheerful toil. But a negro woman behind the plough presents a very different object from the English mother with her children in the turnip-field, or the Scotch lassie among the reapers. In her pre-eminently ugly costume, the long, scanty, dirty·woollen garment, with the shabby large bonnet at the back of her head, the perspiration streaming down her dull face, the heavy tread of the splay foot, the slovenly air with which she guides her plough, a more hideous object cannot well be conceived, unless it be the same woman at home, in the negro quarter, as the cluster of slave dwellings is called.

ED. MARIA W. CHAPMAN, *HARRIET MARTINEAU'S AUTOBIOGRAPHY AND MEMORIALS OF HARRIET MARTINEAU* (1877)

The Lives of Slaves

Barbara Bodichon also dedicated much of her time to reform, even when travelling. She visited the southern states of America soon after Harriet Martineau, and felt impelled to record her varied reactions:

Letter to Albany Fonblanque   4 March 1853

The happiness of these niggers is quite a curiosity to witness. I don't mean that Slavery is right but that if you want to move your bowels with compassion for human unhappiness, that sort of aperient is to be found in such plenty at home that it's a wonder people won't seek it there. Every person I have talked to here about it deplores it and owns that is the most costly domestic machinery ever devised. In a house where four servants would do with us (servants whom we can send about their business too, when they get ill and past work, like true philanthropists as we are) there must be a dozen blacks here. The hire of a house slave from his master is 120 dollars – £25 – besides of course his keep, clothing etc. To be sure that leaves the great question untouched that Slavery is wrong. Of course they feel the cruelty of flogging and enslaving a negro – Of course they feel here the cruelty of starving an English labourer, or of driving an English child into a mine. Brother, Brother, we are kin.

ENGLISH WOMAN'S JOURNAL 8, DECEMBER 1861

Letter from Savannah   Sunday 7th March 1858

I have been to the Methodist Church. It is a pleasant-looking, white, Noah's ark kind of building, very large, very white, very cheerful, with windows all round. As I approached I heard singing. The minister, a slave and a very black negro, gave a good sermon on the Communion. In the evening I went to my Baptist Church close by, and heard another slave preach. I asked a few questions of a very old man who seemed to be an authority. He said the minister could read and write and had studied. I asked how he could study if he worked all day and I was told: 'He studied at night. Of course he can't do as well as white men who have all their time, but he worries so gets a little learning.'

I found the congregation as polite as usual. I have talked to a good many and cannot say they look unhappy even when their circumstances would naturally have made them so. For instance a woman told me today that she is the property of a gentleman in the country who hires her out – to a white washerwoman. Here she always stays unless she is going to have a child, and then she goes to the plantation till her child can toddle; then out to work again. She has had five children, but never sees them except under these circumstances. 'Well, I said, How do you get along?' 'Splendidly; of course I must get along. You see there ain't no other way.' Sometimes, it is true I meet faces which are tragedies to look on; but these are generally mulattoes.

– 12th – In the beautiful fir wood where I have been several times to paint, I heard a pleasant voice singing hymns. Yesterday the singer appeared, a young negro girl very slight and small, but she says she is eight years of age. She and her little sister of four or five sang to me negro songs and hymns. A boy came and joined them; and after much conversation I found he was given to running away and was often whipped for it. The girl said she would never do anything so wicked. I was amused with these children and they were amused with me. 'Never was anybody like you.' They were not sure whether I was Indian or not. They peeled off the inner bark of the fir, and chewed it like tobacco; but the girl said 'If master seed us do that He'd whip us, because it spoils the teeth.'
March 13
Polly my servant is black, a real black woman. I said to her, 'Polly, how many times have you been sold?' 'Twice.' 'Have you any children?' 'I had three; God only knows where two of them are – my master sold them. We lived in Kentucky; one, my darling, he sold South. She is in one of those fields perhaps, picking with one of those poor creatures you saw. Oh, dear! Mum, we poor creatures have need to believe in God; for if God Almighty will not be good to us some day, why were we born? When I hear of His delivering His people from bondage, I know it means the poor African.' Her voice was so husky I could hardly understand her; but it seems her master promised to keep *one* child, and then sold it without telling her. When she asked in agony 'Where is my child?' the master said it was 'hired out'. But it never came back. I found she was a member of the church I had visited in Louisville. She said to me on parting 'Never forget me; never forget what we suffer. Do all you can to alter it.'

ENGLISH WOMAN'S JOURNAL 8, DECEMBER 1861

Egypt in the Mid-nineteenth Century

Lucy Duff Gordon went to Upper Egypt for seven years, a longer stay than any other European. Her sympathy for the Arabs contrasts with many English attitudes of the time; she proved the only contemporary

*witness to the disastrous governments of Ismail praised as Viceroy by
English male politicians. Her* Letters from Egypt *(1865), reprinted three
times in their first year, remain a valuable historical document and a lively
account of one remarkable individual's view of another culture. Here she
tells her husband of Egyptian food and drink.*

Thebes 11 Feb 1863

Dearest Alick

We got quite intimate over our leather cup of sherbet (brown sugar and
water), and the handsome jet-black men, with features as beautiful as
those of the young Bacchus, described the distant lands in a way which
would have charmed Herodotus. They proposed to me to join them, 'they
had food enough,' and Omar and I were equally inclined to go. It is of no
use to talk of the ruins; everybody has said, I suppose, all that can be said,
but Philae surpassed my expectations. No wonder the Arab legends of
Ans el Wogood are so romantic, and Abou Simbel and many more. The
scribbling of names is quite infamous, beautiful paintings are defaced by
Tomkins and Hobson, but worst of all Prince Pückler Muskau has
engraved his and his *Ordenskreuz* in huge letters on the naked breast of
the august and pathetic giant who sits at Abou Simbel. I wish someone
would kick him for his profanity.

I have eaten many odd things with odd people in queer places, dined in
a respectable Nubian family (the castor-oil was trying), been to a Nubian
wedding – such a dance I saw. Made friends with a man much looked up
to in his place (Kalabshee – notorious for cutting throats), inasmuch as he
had killed several intrusive tax-gatherers and recruiting officers. He was
very gentlemanly and kind and carried me up a place so steep I could not
have reached it. Just below the cataract – by-the-by going up is nothing
but noise and shouting, but coming down is fine fun – *Fantasia khateer* as
my excellent little Nubian pilot said. My sailors all prayed away manfully
and were horribly frightened. I confess my pulse quickened, but I don't
think it was fear. Well, below the cataract I stopped for a religious fête,
and went to a holy tomb with the darweesh, so extraordinarily handsome
and graceful – the true *feingemacht* noble Bedaween type. He took care of
me through the crowd, who never had seen a Frank woman before and
crowded fearfully, and pushed the true believers unmercifully to make
way for me. He was particularly pleased at my not being afraid of Arabs;
I laughed, and asked if he was afraid of us. 'Oh no! he would like to come
to England; when there he would work to eat and drink, and then sit and

sleep in the church.' I was positively ashamed to tell my religious friend that with us the 'house of God' is not the house of the poor stranger. I asked him to eat with me but he was holding a preliminary Ramadan (it begins next week), and could not; but he brought his handsome sister, who was richly dressed, and begged me to visit him and eat of his bread, cheese and milk. Such is the treatment one finds if one leaves the highroad and the backsheesh-hunting parasites. There are plenty of 'gentlemen' barefooted and clad in a shirt and cloak ready to pay attentions which you may return with a civil look and greeting, and if you offer a cup of coffee and a seat on the floor you give great pleasure, still more if you eat the dourah and dates, or bread and sour milk with an appetite.

At Koom Ombo we met a Rifaee darweesh with his basket of tame snakes. After a little talk he proposed to initiate me, and so we sat down and held hands like people marrying. Omar sat behind me and repeated the words as my 'Wakeel,' then the Rifaee twisted a cobra round our joined hands and requested me to spit on it, he did the same and I was pronounced safe and enveloped in snakes. My sailors groaned and Omar shuddered as the snakes put out their tongues – the darweesh and I smiled at each other like Roman augurs. I need not say the creatures were toothless.

L. Duff Gordon, Letters from Egypt (1865)

A Home in Brazil

Isabel Burton accompanied her adventurer husband to Brazil in 1865. These extracts come from letters to her mother.

1865

It was fortunate that I had the foresight to take iron bedsteads along, as already at Lisbon three-inch cockroaches seethed about the floor of our room. I jumped onto a chair and Burton growled 'I suppose you think you look very pretty standing on that chair and howling at those innocent creatures'. My reaction was to stop screaming and reflect that he was right; if I had to live in a country full of such creatures, and worse, I had better pull myself together. I got down among them, and started lashing out with a slipper. In two hours I had a bag full of ninety-seven, and had conquered my queasiness.

Santos:
Here in Brazil there are spiders as big as crabs. In the matter of tropical diseases it ranks with darkest Africa; there are slaves, too, often maintained in conditions of utmost savagery. . . . I am becoming painfully acclimatised. There is cholera, and the less dramatic but agonising local boils so close you could not put a pin between them. I battle through these boils on frequent draughts of stout! However I have now unpacked my fifty-nine trunks, set my house in order, and given my first dinner-party – successfully. I believe that the Emperor considers Burton a great addition to the country, because his wonderful conversation holds his audience spell-bound. . . .

Some of these chic Brazilians look askance at me, wading barefoot in the streams, bottling snakes, painting, furbishing up a ruined chapel, or accompanying my husband on expeditions to the virgin interior. The ladies are namby-pamby: They have taken exception, as improper, to four puny English railway clerks rowing at the Regatta, in jerseys. I often think a *parvenue*, or half-bred woman would burst if she had to do as I do, keeping up appearances, lancing boils, coping with insects, with Richard, with everything. I do hate Santos. The climate is beastly, the people fluffy. The stinks, the vermin, the food, the niggers are all of a piece. There are no walks, if you go one way you sink knee-deep in mangrove swamps; another, you are covered with sandflies. Fortunately Richard has even taught me to fence. And with him I do gymnastics, have cold baths, go to Mass and market. Above all I help Richard with Literature. I copy out all the pages of his reports to the Foreign Office. Thirty-two pages on Cotton Report, one hundred and twenty-five on Geographic Report – & cheerfully!

L. BLANCH, *THE WILDER SHORES OF LOVE* (1954)

A Traveller's Life

Isabella Bird, born in 1831, rejected conventional life in order to travel to some of the remotest regions of the world. Yet she had been a frail child and suffered from severe back-pain all her life. On foot, horseback, yak, even elephant, she visited Japan, Korea, Kurdestan, Persia, and the Rocky Mountains. She wrote nine books about her dangerous journeys, which became bestsellers in her time. She gave most of the profits to charities, declaring her travels 'vindicated the right of a woman to do anything which she can do well'. She rode through the Rocky Mountains in 1873.

Ranch, Plum Creek   October 24.

You must understand that in Colorado travel, unless on the main road and in the larger settlements, there are neither hotels nor taverns, and that it is the custom for the settlers to receive travellers, charging them at the usual hotel rate for accommodation. It is a very satisfactory arrangement. However, at Ranch, my first halting-place, the host was unwilling to receive people in this way, I afterwards found, or I certainly should not have presented my credentials at the door of a large frame house, with large barns and a generally prosperous look. The host, who opened the door, looked repellant, but his wife, a very agreeable, lady-like-looking woman, said they could give me a bed on a sofa. The house was the most pretentious I have yet seen, being papered and carpeted, and there were two 'hired girls.' There was a lady there from Laramie, who kindly offered to receive me into her room, a very tall, elegant person, remarkable as being the first woman who had settled in the Rocky Mountains. She had been trying the 'camp cure' for three months, and was then on her way home. She had a waggon with beds, tent, tent-floor, cooking-stove, and every camp luxury, a light buggy, a man to manage everything, and a most superior 'hired girl.' She was consumptive and frail in strength, but a very attractive person, and her stories of the perils and limitations of her early life at Fort Laramie were very interesting. Still I 'wearied,' as I had arrived early in the afternoon, and could not out of politeness retire and write to you. At meals the three 'hired men' and two 'hired girls' eat with the family. I soon found that there was a screw loose in the house, and was glad to leave early the next morning, although it was obvious that a storm was coming on. I saw the toy car of the Rio Grande Railroad whirl past, all cushioned and warmed, and rather wished I were in it, and not out among the snow on the bleak hill-side. I only got on four miles when the storm came on so badly that I got into a kitchen where eleven wretched travellers were taking shelter, with the snow melting on them and dripping on the floor. I had learned the art of 'being agreeable' so well at the Chalmers's, and practised it so successfully during the two hours I was there, by paring potatoes and making scones, that when I left, though the hosts kept 'an accommodation house for travellers,' they would take nothing for my entertainment.

I. BIRD, *A LADY'S LIFE IN THE ROCKY MOUNTAINS* (1982)

Her last journey was to the Atlas Mountains, from where she wrote this letter in 1901, aged seventy, to relatives at home.

I left Tangier and had a severe two days' voyage to Mazagan, where the landing was so terrible and the sea so wild that the captain insisted on my being lowered into the boat by the ship's crane, in a coal basket. The officers and passengers cheered my pluck as the boat mounted a huge breaking surge – no cargo could be landed. Before leaving the steamer I had a return of fever; and when the camping-ground turned out to be a soaked field with water standing in the furrows, and the tent was pitched in a storm of wind and rain, and many of the tent-pegs would not hold, and when the head of my bed went down into the slush, I thought I should die there – but had no more illness or fever. After an awful night when the heavy wet end of my tent, having broken loose, flapped constantly against my head, things mended. The rain ceased, and we left with camel, mule, donkey and horse and travelled here, 126 miles in six days.

Marakesh is awful; an African city of 80,000 people, the most crowded, noisiest, filthiest, busiest city I have seen in the world. It terrifies me. It is the great Mohammedan feast, lasting a week, and several thousand tribesmen, sheiks and retainers, are here, all armed, mounted on their superb barbs, splendidly caparisoned, men as wild as the mountains and deserts from which they come to do homage to the Sultan.

I have seen several grand sights: the Sultan in the midst of his brilliant army, receiving the homage of the sheiks and on another day, similarly surrounded, killing a sheep, in memory of Abraham's sacrifice of Isaac, and as an atonement for the sins of the year. I was at the last in Moorish disguise, pure white and veiled.

I have a Moorish house to myself with a courtyard choked with orange-trees in blossom and fruit. I also have what is a terror to me, a magnificent barb, the property of the Sultan; a most powerful black charger, a huge fellow far too much for me, equipped with crimson trappings and a peaked crimson saddle, 18 inches above his back. I have to carry a light ladder for getting on and off!

With mules, horses and soldiers I left the din and devilry of Marrakesh, as the Sultan's guest. We have been travelling six hours daily since, camping four nights and sleeping two in the castles of these wild tribes till tonight, when we are camped in the fastnesses of the great Atlas range at the height of 1000 feet, in as wild a region as can be imagined. This journey differs considerably from any other as it is as rough as the roughest. I never expected to do such travelling again. You would fail to recognise your infirm friend astride a superb horse in full blue trousers and a short full skirt with brass spurs belonging to a generalissimo of the Moorish army, and riding down places awful even to think of, where a rolling stone or slip would mean destruction. In these wild mountains we are among tribes which Rome failed to conquer. It is evidently air and riding which do me good. I never realised this so vividly as now.

This is an awful country, the worst I have been in. The oppression and cruelty are hellish – no one is safe. The country is rotten to the core, eaten up by abominable vices, no one is to be trusted. Every day deepens my horror of its deplorable and unspeakable vileness.

The journey of twenty-one days is over. The last day I rode thirty miles and walked two. Is it not wonderful that even at my advanced age this life should affect me thus? We were entertained everywhere as guests of the Sultan. The bridle tracks on the Atlas are awful, mere rock ladders, or smooth faces of shelving rock. We lamed two horses, and one mule went over a precipice, rolling over four times before he touched the bottom. We had guides, soldiers and slaves with us. The weather was dry and bracing. Today I had an interview with the Sultan, the first European woman to see the Emperor of Morocco! It was very interesting, but had to be secretly managed, because of the fanatical hatred to Christians.

ED. C. PALSER HAVELY, *THE TRAVELS OF ISABELLA BIRD* (1971)

'My Cannibal Friends Never Eat Human Heads'

Mary Kingsley was born in 1862, to a middle-class family, and lived a respectable Victorian life until her parents died in 1892. For the next eight years she travelled in West Africa, alone, making copious notes of her adventures. Considering herself an anthropologist, she studied African religion and law. As the family money had been spent educating her brother, she paid her way by trading fish-hooks and matches. She preferred traders to missionaries, since they did not try to change African customs. She enjoyed staying with traders, as this gave her freedom to criticize, which she eschewed in her published works, but not in private letters, such as this undated one to the trader John Holt.

I could not be a parson's guest and then abuse them, so seeing staying with missions tied my hands I settled with traders to their great alarm at times. I don't mean to say I could ever half pay them, but I spent my money at their stores to the tune of £500 while in West Africa. The three missions I stayed at are the Mission Evangelique. I hold my tongue for the sake of those men and women I respect, but I have never forgiven one of the best of the white women from saying to me when I said I was going down that night to nurse a sick man, white, who was ill with fever, with no other Christian close by, 'Miss Kingsley, you can not, it's not respectable'.

She enjoyed teasing, as here to Professor E.B. Taylor in 1898:

'My cannibal friends never eat human heads unless for religious purposes. By the way, did I tell you of my friend James Irvine, the Elder of the Presbyterian Church, late of Calabar, now Liverpool, who came across a black friend boiling human heads in an oil cauldron – he expressed his opinion and the African let him run on and laughed and finally demonstrated he was not soup-making but only preparing the skulls to keep in a way that would not attract flies.'

VALERIE GROSVENOR MYER, *A VICTORIAN LADY IN AFRICA* (1989)

A Himalayan Journey

Alexandra David-Néel (1868–1969) toured the Middle East and North Africa as an opera singer. In 1904 she married a distant cousin, Philippe Néel, but she felt trapped by marriage, and they separated within a matter of days. Nevertheless, they continued to correspond, and he supported her financially, enabling her to study and travel abroad. In 1911, when the Dalai Lama was in exile in Darjeeling, she became the first Western woman to interview him. Her meeting with him inspired her to concentrate on Tibetan Buddhism in her studies. These letters were sent to her husband.

7 December 1913 Sikkim

Dear Philippe,

I love you very much for what you have done to support me. I know you make sacrifices to provide me with a life that displeases you. This journey to Sikkim [in the Himalayas] has restored my spirits. I visited villages and monasteries with the Prince, travelling much in the manner of a medieval court, like a dream of a very old world. The Prince encouraged me to exhort the monks to practice a purer Buddhism. I took to the task with zeal, lecturing at the monasteries on the pure doctrine. I have been given a lama's red robe to wear and the designation of 'lamina' [woman lama].

I have found a tutor to instruct me in Tibetan. At my age [forty-four] I must not delay learning the language. I am in a singular position as a woman, and a militant practising Buddhist. Orientalists in the West would be severely critical of my writing. What I want above all is to be completely accurate and document my findings so thoroughly that I'll be able to return home a person of some importance in the world of Orientalists. All I need is a bit more time and experience. Don't you think, given our situation and our characters, we can make the sacrifice to be separated a little longer? My hope is to spend time in Tibet if the authorities will let me. Then I'll leave India, and travel home via Japan, with my cycle of studies on Buddhism in northern Asia completed.

March 1914

Now the Prince's father has died he has become ruler so I travelled alone, except for my interpreter and a few porters to carry my camping gear through the azalea and rhododendron forests. We went up and down nearly vertical hills on my way to the north, where Sikkim borders Tibet. It was one of my most memorable journeys. The track enters a fantastic region near the frontier passes. In the intense silence of these wild solitudes only brooks chat gently. Up and up we went, skirting glaciers, catching occasional glimpses of valleys filled by huge clouds. And then, without any transition, as we issued from the mists, the Tibetan tableland appeared before us, immense, void and resplendent under the luminous sky of Central Asia. . . . Nothing can dim that first sight of Tibet in my mind.

A. DAVID-NÉEL, *MY JOURNEY TO LHASA* (1938)

Illegally entering Tibet in 1914, she spent time in a monastery, lived as a hermit in a cave, and became a lama herself. In 1923, disguised as a Tibetan beggar on pilgrimage with her adopted son, Yongden, she became the first Western woman to enter the 'Forbidden City' of Lhasa, where she remained for two months before her identity was discovered. This letter, written in 1923, is again to her husband.

Next morning, leaving my old friend, the Mekong, we turned westward through the rocky gorge at the entrance of which we had slept. Soon it opened out into a narrow, densely wooded valley. The weather was sunny and walking easier. We passed two mounted Tibetan traders, who gave us scarcely a glance. Perhaps they thought we were Chinamen, for Yongden and I both wore Chinese dresses. Nevertheless this first meeting, precursor of the many which were to follow, gave us a little shock. Although we were yet in that part of Tibet, still under Chinese rule, wherein foreigners can travel freely, though at their own risk, it was most important that rumours of my wanderings in the neighbourhood of the border should not spread. For the Tibetan officials, once warned and on the alert, would have the road carefully watched, which would greatly increase the difficulties of our entering the forbidden area.

A little before noon we came in sight of Londre. Had we been alone, Yongden and I, we could have easily avoided passing through the village by hiding ourselves in the wood until evening. It would have saved us much trouble and fatigue, for between the steep slopes of the Kha Karpo range which we were about to climb, there was but the width of this torrential river which we had followed upwards and crossed several times in the narrow gorge. But such a thing was out of the question, for I had expressly told the coolies that I intended to go into the country of the Loutze tribes to collect plants, and the road to Lutze-Kiang went through Londre and there turned in a direction exactly opposite to the Kha Karpo.

Very disturbed, and reflecting that each step added a difficulty to my approaching flight, I followed the two Tibetans who meant to take me to a wooded tableland about ten miles higher, where they knew of a good camping-ground. As far as they could see, Yongden and I scarcely cast a glance at the country in the direction of the Dokar Pass; but in reality we did our best to impress on our memory the shape and peculiarities of the landscape which would help us when we had to cross it on the next night.

Our passage in Londre was as inconspicuous as we could have wished. Not one of the villagers whom we met appeared to take any particular notice of us. This most happy circumstance was perhaps due to the fact that an American naturalist worked in the vicinity and employed a large number of people. No doubt the villagers thought that we were on our way to join him as assistants.

After having proceeded for a few miles on the Lutze-Kiang path, turning my back to my real goal, I thought it imprudent to proceed farther. Safety required that plenty of time be allowed for the long tramp on the opposite side of Londre, so that dawn should find us far away from the village, having, if possible, reached the pilgrimage road. Once there, we could easily pretend to have come from any northern Tibetan part we cared to name, in order to get round the Sacred Mountain.

I had hesitated a long time in choosing the road I would take in order to enter independent Tibet. The one I preferred, or perhaps I should say the one which circumstances seemed to be thrusting upon me, is followed every autumn by many travellers. By taking it I foresaw that I should run the danger of frequent meetings. Not that this inconvenience was without its favourable aspect, since our tracks could be more easily lost amongst those of pilgrims from various Tibetan regions, each of whom spoke in different dialect, and whose womenfolk had a variety of different dress and coiffures. The little peculiarities of my accent, my features, or my clothes would more easily be overlooked on such a road, and if enquiries were to be made, they would have to embrace so many people that confusion might very likely follow to my advantage. But of course I sincerely hoped that no enquiry would be made!

A. DAVID-NÉEL (1938)

Diplomatic Life, Teheran

Vita Sackville-West admired, liked and loved Virginia Woolf. She missed her when she accompanied her husband Harold Nicholson to Teheran when he was appointed Ambassador to Persia. This letter to Woolf was written in 1926.

Teheran

15 March

Today being the birthday of the Shah, (though common report has it that he knows neither his birthday nor his age, being of low extraction,) last night a dinner was given in his honour at the Foreign Office. So at 8.15, an immense yellow motor draws up at the door: Harold in uniform and gold lace, little sword getting between his legs; Vita derisive, but decked in emeralds; escort in scarlet and white (the Minister is all for swank, – thinks it impresses the Persians;) the yellow motor proceeds down the street. Pulls up at the Foreign Office. Sentries present arms. The scarlet *escort escorts.* The sentries' boots are muddy; everything is very shoddy here. Seventy people to dinner; the china doesn't match, – not enough to go round, – the Persian ministers wear their robes of honour: grubby old cashmere dressing-gowns, with no collars to their evening shirts; dinner cold; I escape the awful fate of sitting between two Persians who talk nothing but their own language, and get Sir Percy, who is nice, and the Belgian minister, who tells me about the Emperor of Korea. (I never knew there was such a person; he sounds incredibly romantic; Hakluyt's voyages, and all that.) Suddenly, an awful pause, and we stand up to drink the health of the eleven states represented. But first their national anthems must be played; and, glass in hand, we endure God Save the King, the Brabançonne, (I feel the Belgian minister at my side stiffen to attention,) the International Soviet Hymn, the Marseillaise, the Wacht am Rhein, and six unidentifiable minor powers. An unfortunate incident ushers in the ceremony: all the dirty plates have been stacked under Sir Percy's chair, all the dirty knives and forks under mine, so as we rise to our feet shoving back our chairs there is a clatter. . . . Having drunk to our respective sovereigns and presidents, we drink to the Shah. We adjourn. There are fireworks. Now the Persians are really good at fireworks. The garden, from the balconies, coruscates with wrestling babies of Herculean promise, taxi-cabs with revolving wheels, aeroplanes with revolving propellers, catherine wheels, and VIVE SA MAJESTÉ IMPÉRIALE PAHLEVI in letters of gold reflecting in the central tank, – all very lovely, really, and fantastic, seen through clouds of smoke from above; while Tamur Tasch, officially Minister of Works, but really the Power behind the Throne, enquires in my ear as to the merits of Thos. Goode and Son, South Audley Street, and the Army & Navy Stores.

This is diplomatic life.

This morning, the yellow motor again; and Sir Percy and Harold, both in uniform again, with fluttering plumes in their hats, (Sir Percy loving it, and Harold wretched,) going off to the Shah's reception, the scarlet-and-white servants and the Indian lancers trotting before and behind the car.

Do not imagine, however, that life is all like that. There are days of going into the mountains, and eating sandwiches beside a stream, and picking wild almonds, and of coming home by incredible sunsets across the plain. And every morning at seven we ride, and the freshness and beauty of the morning are inconceivable.

Then once a fortnight the muddy car comes in, and there are letters: the only rift opening on the outside world. Otherwise it is all very self-contained, – what with the old white horse who goes his rounds every morning, bringing two barrels of water to every house in the compound, and the Sanitary Cart, which drawn by a donkey performs a sordid emptying function.

EDS. L. DESAHO AND M. LEASKA, *THE LETTERS OF VITA SACKVILLE-WEST TO VIRGINIA WOOLF* (1984)

Freya Stark Explores

Freya Stark (1893–   ) decided she must travel in the Middle East. She gambled her small income, successfully, on the stock-market to pay for her travels. She went to Lebanon in 1927, fell in love with it and began learning Arabic. By 1930 she was adventurously exploring Persia, seeing far more than Sackville-West. Here she writes to her mother, whom she called 'B'.

Nr. Khurramabad
23 May 1930

Dearest B,

It is a most extraordinary sight to come out on to the Caspian after all the forest – all yesterday afternoon and six hours today riding through it, lovely in the lower parts like some lonely bit of Pyrenees with its rushing streams and enormously tall trees. One leaves the big river, the two Hizars they are, which have joined their waters and rush down foaming together: one crosses a small col which the Emir Sipahsalar paved with boulders before he was asked by the government to commit suicide: then one crosses the Valmirud – a broad slow stream in a big bed: up another steep, short col – and there is the Caspian, and between you and it a landscape that has walked out of a lacquered tray: a flat landscape shining like a dull mirror with endless little sub-divisions of rice plots divided by tiny mud barriers: islands of green trees, oranges and pomegranates in flower, rise all among these water plots, and every island has a few houses under enormous beehive roofs of rice thatching. Little observatories on four pillars, under a dome of thatching, stand about in the water, and beyond it all is a pale streak of sea without shadows that also might come out of a Japanese print. Blue dragonflies, with the outer half of their wings velvety black, dart about doing their little best with the mosquitoes: but, of course, this is a perfect trap for malaria and even the poorest house has a veranda which you climb to by a ladder and are supposed to be out of their way. I am sitting on one now, after lunch, and the centre of an interested row of onlookers who look very much more Russian than Persian, with darker eyes, and pretty oval faces, and a generally softer expression. Their language is quite incomprehensible – and especially today because my cold is so bad that I could scarcely understand English if there were any to be heard within fifty miles.

My coming has evidently been heralded by the muleteers who went ahead, for I was greeted with looks of expectant surprise by all we met. It is quite a shock when you are jogging along amiably absent-minded to see people meeting you suddenly petrified with surprise.

I had quite a good night having rediscovered the Keatings; and a nice airy balcony: and in the early light could see the caravans getting under way, the mules being groomed down and the packs fixed on, all in the cold wet light with mist overhead and everything drenched in dew. The men wore woollen stockings and a bit of leather or fur gathered round their feet by way of shoes. I believe these people used to be very wild and a man who is now political officer in Fars was kept a year or so as a prisoner tied to a tree: at least that is what Captain Holt told me, and said I should get to know him as he is as mad as me. Anyway they seem friendly enough now.

24 May 1930

I am waiting to know whether or no a motor is going to take me to Resht or not this evening. I had been hearing so long of Tunakabun as the centre of all things here, and was thinking of it as a kind of metropolis where civilisation, films and chairs were flourishing. What it is, is a peaceful little village with a market twice a week where people from Resht spread awnings and all sorts of bright cottons, buttons, beads, elastic, and such European oddments for the rice growers round to buy. It would be a charming spot with its green gardens and the row of wooded slopes rising to snow behind, if it were not a perfect death-trap for malaria; I dose myself with quinine which may explain why I feel so peculiar – but I shall be glad to get away to a drier country.

I felt rather depressed: having come to the end of my objective, and also having left the hills. The hill people are all gentlefolk in their way; one likes to be with them; on the plains, if you go into the same sort of house, you find just peasants, and it isn't good enough.

Resht
26 May 1930

I had just got so far when a motor car finally turned up. Two in fact; one which had been ordered from Shahzavar came along, but with the intention of taking me only half-way and then stopping: so we took the other one, which had a charming chauffeur like a Mujik with an enormous beard. The first car wanted to be paid for coming so far, but even the easy benevolence of the Doctor came to the conclusion that a car which comes to take you to a place where you haven't asked to go, needn't be paid. To make all sure we appealed to a village Elder with a red hennaed beard: and the verdict being in favour, started off without more ado. Most affectionate farewells. I felt I was leaving quite a familiar place: having sat under the orange trees, drinking tea in the Emir's garden: and spent the morning with a little procession of Bahai notables behind me, visiting the bazaar (and buying a silk bedcover which I regret, for the sum would have just prevented me from being impecunious now): and having visited the school, which is a lonely old dilapidation in a garden with a tank and big trees where the little boys read out short moral stories in high sing-song voices. It was good to make for the coast and see the Caspian, grey in the grey evening, stretching away shallow and flat. The mountains were hidden, and it was drizzling now and then, but it is a magnificent coast. We got to a place called Ab-i-Garm, where some pools of steaming water spring up by the roadside and you can see the skinny Persians bathing while a little circle of *chaikhanas* and cars and crowd make it into a sort of fair: there was even a conjurer with his wares spread on the floor making the same jokes in Persian which his colleagues make in their European languages. I lost my people, who disappeared to drink tea, and when at last they reappeared it was with a fat blond chauffeur and a really nice car.

It was now about seven o'clock, and I had discovered that it would be another four hours at least to Resht, and was not too pleased when it turned out that the fat chauffeur was taking me alone through the Caspian jungle. It did seem very lonely: the forest here reaches almost to the water's edge; the sea lay very quiet and dull with a last light in it; and this road drifted along through sand or gravel, with not a soul on it. Luckily the chauffeur was a really good man and not fond of talking: his only remark was as we came to a particularly shadowy bit under the trees, that there used to be a lot of robbers here. We met a woodcutter or two trudging home: a horseman now and then: and about one car an hour coming the opposite way. Here and there were clearings for rice fields. We punctured conveniently in one of these clearings – and the chauffeur turned out really capable and put it right quickly. After that I saw no more of the country; we went through like a dream, and it was extraordinarily like England – the green hedges, and trees, and thatched roofs. Only the little towns with their bazaars still busy looked foreign enough – shoemakers and tailors stitching away at ten o'clock at night round a big lantern, and the tea-shops handing round their little glasses. About 10.30 we waded up to the footboards through the first branch of the Safid Rud which I had crossed a week before near Chala; when we got across, a man in a little hut sounded a gong, and by the time we reached the second branch the ferry was waiting and a posse of men ready to get us across. It was so like a dream. I could not help wondering all the time how I came to be there on the edge of the Caspian in the middle of the night. A little after eleven I got here and asked for the Grand Hotel, an awful little place, with nothing clean but its noticeboard. I was too exhausted to care much, but refreshed next day.

Dear love to you   Freya

EDS. C. AND L. MOOREHEAD, *THE LETTERS OF FREYA STARK* (1974–82)

A Buddhist Nun Returns to India

A Buddhist nun, travelling around India in 1990, here describes her reactions to the country in this letter to friends.

To you all,   19.11.90 6.30 a.m.
Arrive in New Delhi Airport and after some bewilderment, finally fix up a taxi – direction Karmarpa Institute. The driver has a little picture of the Hindu god Hanuman by the wheel. I figure we'll be alright, as he's one of my favourite Hindu deities. Driving through the streets – Amazement. I'd forgotten how mind-blowing India is. We pass a large dead cow on its back, legs extended, it's mouth wide open as if the spirit had been knocked from its throat. It was in the middle of the main dual carriage-way into Delhi. No one seemed bothered about it.

Dusty sidewalks, rubbish strewn everywhere, people milling about amongst cows, dogs, even pigs. Erratic driving with horns hooting, motor rickshaws, taxis colourful but tatty buses and lorries crammed with people. Brown eyes staring at us with curiosity, need and sometimes bewilderment – sometimes friendliness and interest. Chai shops and wallas squatting selling anything that's saleable, dusty grey-looking beings, thin and wrapped in rags, sometimes carrying bundles on their heads. Motor scooter with whole families perched precariously on top. Colourful saried women, men in groups, talking, laughing, sometimes holding hands. Little stalls with charcoal burners cooking dosas, samosas, iddlies and of course large aluminium kettles filled with hot tea, milk and loads of sugar – Ahh, that famous Chai, one taste and memories come flooding back. Smell of urine, wood smoke, sewerage beedies and the sweet air of a hot climate.

I feel a happiness well up inside and a smile transform my face. I'm just happy to be back in India, I really don't know why I love it, it's a total affront to my western conditioning – our slightly uptight, neurotic, prepackaged, tidy and neat and usually subliminally negative approach to life. It's hard for me to fathom why I feel so much at home here, but I recognise the feeling after a few hours. I realize how, on some impercept-able level, I find it a strain to live within the Western psyche, where some-how we've forgotten to be what we are, possibly through so much expha-sis on individuality which always gives the result of isolation. We finally make it to the Karmarpa Institute.

Sister Thanissara

AUTHOR'S COLLECTION

Later, in November that year, she describes a meeting with the Dalai Lama in India.

Dear Friends,

At 12 o'clock a message comes that we're to go to H.H. residence. We have to fill out a form, have our passports checked, then be searched. Finally we're allowed to go up to his reception room, with a group of Westerners. There's also a group of Western monks and nuns. H.H. Dalai Lama comes in and smiles at us all with that real friendliness he has. He sits and talks with us for 1^{1}/2 hours about, answering questions on Dhamma [Buddha's teaching]. He talks on karma, overcoming depression and fear, meditation on the mind, and especially about realizing the 'natural mind' when thought, memory and future expectation cease. That its own nature remains pure in spite of the reflections of all types of phenomena.

This is the way to realize Shunyata, where the mind is like a multi-dimensional infinite mirror which is empty of any particular quality. He said this state needs to be realized more fully. The Tibetans call this natural mind, when realized, the Clear Light, and that its nature is peace-ful, blissful and the source of Bodhi Citta, the heart of compassion. I find this similar to our understanding. They have practices of realizing this 'natural mind' when entering and leaving sleep consciousness and also during the death process. I think in our practice we can develop this, moment by moment when we abandon self view or when we practise non-attachment to the ephemeral world of samsara [suffering].

He was also asked whether all religions lead to enlightenment. He replied that only those where the total eradication of ignorance was the result. He said people don't want to face emptiness so there's subtle grasping and therefore ignorance. It was a wonderful opportunity to hear H.H. reflecting on Dhamma. He likes to back his reflections with logic, sometimes his thought processes would get quite technical and involved. I wondered how much the group really understood what he was talking about. Nevertheless everyone enjoyed his presence. Afterwards, we had the opportunity to make our offerings. I gave him a photo of the community and explained we were disciples of Ajahn Chah, he seemed very interested. Also I gave him a personal gift of the lovely butterfly cup. He blessed the holy relics we're carrying and all the holy bits and bobs that people have given me.

My respect and love and gratitude to you all, Sister Thanissara.

AUTHOR'S COLLECTION

ten

Illness and Ageing

Women's medical knowledge was more frequently appealed to in the past than men's. Wives such as Margery Paston were asked for remedies by their family. Nuns such as Hildegard of Bingen were famous for preparing herbal remedies for their community. Women acted as midwives until men proclaimed themselves as experts even in this field in the nineteenth century.

Women studied medicine and acted as surgeons in medieval Italy, but were increasingly marginalized by university faculties of medicine. In the nineteenth century, just as men were taking over every area of medical treatment, by demanding paper qualifications, a few thoughtful women were reacting against male textbooks. Male books included the invaluable knowledge that women must be mad if they wanted sexual pleasure (because they could not feel it) and that they were aged by the time of the menopause. An American reformer, Eliza Farnham (1815–64) proclaimed the far more optimistic and verifiable view that the menopause offered relief from the burdens of maternal labour.

These letters are remarkable for their constructive common sense, based both on observation of women and respect for the ways in which natural forces can be used to help tackle disease. Hildegard's *Book of Herbal Remedies* is eight hundred years old, but still efficacious today. Her female preparedness to study the best usage is seen also in Lady Mary Wortley Montagu's approach to smallpox vaccination. She implemented this on her son, three centuries before its widespread use. Her open mind realized that study of other cultures can teach us a great deal. Many lives would have been saved if only doctors had listened to her. She and Hildegard advocated a gentle balanced use of body and nature which is continued in the letter of the Buddhist nun, written in 1990 during illness in India.

Sickness was more widespread among the poorer classes than the rich, though we know that many aristocrats were killed by viral diseases, smallpox, 'flu, appendicitis and illnesses which have only been conquered recently. Sewerage systems in England were only constructed in the nineteenth century, after the second cholera epidemic, which affected so many middle-class families in Manchester and London. As well as disease, the poor were stricken by malnutrition and lack of decent housing.

For all ranks, the death rate was high; mothers died as young as twenty-nine, on average, until the end of the nineteenth century. Expectation of old age was a luxury for most of the poor. Poor relief had begun under Elizabeth I, and was later replaced by the workhouse. However, working-class women often preferred to die on their own than to face the humiliation and deprivation of a workhouse.

Literate women were relieved of that fear, but acknowledge in their writings the suffering caused by the process of ageing. Society offered little comfort to older women: either to be religious or a grandmother. Yet instead of limiting themselves to cultural role models, these letters show women using the space for spirituality in radical ways. Queen Victoria, like other grandmothers, enjoyed ordering her many grandchildren's lives through her letters (to which most paid scant attention). George Sand rejected societal roles, both in her sex life and vigorous old age.

Though deaths in the family were frequent in the past, and women often in charge of the laying-out of the corpse, by the nineteenth century they were increasingly excluded from the actual funeral, told they were too sensitive to bear public display of grief. Death was not the great leveller of gender. However, their letters show an ability to face up to death, and to help others to face the equally disturbing processes of ageing.

The final part of this chapter deals with ways of facing death. Lady Mary Wortley Montagu makes typically acute, brave observations as she prepares to leave 'this dirty world'. Over a hundred years later the feminist Harriet Martineau is equally tough in refusing facile consolation.

The Dauphin Dies

Madame was the wife of Monsieur, the brother of Louis XIV. In these letters to the Duchess of Hanover, she describes male doctors' treatment of illness and contrasts it with that of untrained governesses.

10th March, 1712, Versailles

You, too, will certainly be aghast when you hear how sorrow continues to smite us here. The doctors have made the same mistake again as they did in the case of the Dauphiness, because while the little Dauphin was all flushed with measels and in a sweat they bled him and then gave him an emetic, with the result that the poor child died during the operation, which shows clearly that it was the doctors who killed him. His little brother had exactly the same illness, but while the nine doctors were busy with the elder brother the younger one's nurse shut herself up with her little prince and gave him some wine and a biscuit. Yesterday the child was very feverish, and the doctors wanted to bleed him also, but Madame de Ventadour and the prince's under-governess, Madame de Villefort, protested vigorously against it. They absolutely refused to allow it to be done, and contented themselves with keeping the child nice and warm. He is now, by the grace of God, and to the doctor's shame, recovering, but he would have been dead as surely as his brother if they had been allowed to have their way.

13th March, 1712, Versailles

I am sure there are at least a hundred duly canonised saints who were less worthy of canonisation than our late Dauphin, the second one, I mean, because, horrible to relate, we have lost three Dauphins in eleven months. One was forty-nine, one twenty-six, and the other five years old. I don't think there can be another such instance in history. The Dauphin most certainly died of grief. He was extraordinarily fond of his wife, and it was sorrowing for her death that gave him his fever. For several days the fever ran an irregular course, but afterwards it returned every fourth day. They bled him. After his wife's death his forehead came out in spots, which, however, did not prevent him from going out. It was not until Monday evening that he took to his bed. His skin became discoloured with many purple stains and spots, which were larger and quite different from the ordinary measles rash. They gave him stimulants and tried to make him sweat, but the perspiration would not flow freely. On Wednesday night, after everyone had gone to bed, he caused an altar to be brought to his bedroom and partook of holy communion with great devotion.

TRANS AND ED. G.S. STEPHENSON, *LETTERS OF MADAME* (1937)

The Use of a Smallpox Vaccination

Lady Mary Wortley Montagu here admires Turkish skill in inventing a vaccination for smallpox, when it was still a killer in Europe. This letter is to a friend.

Adrianople, 1 April 1717

In my opinion, dear Sarah, I ought rather to quarrel with you for not answering my Nijmegen letter of August till December, than to excuse my not writing again till now. I am sure there is on my side a very good excuse for silence, having gone such tiresome land journeys, though I don't find the conclusion of 'em so bad as you seem to imagine. I am very easy here and not in the solitude you fancy me; the great quantity of Greek, French, English and Italians that are under our protection make their court to me from morning till night, and I'll assure you are many of 'em very fine ladies, for there is no possibility –for a Christian to live easily under this government but by the protection of an ambassador, and the richer they are the greater their danger.

Those dreadful stories you have heard of the plague have very little foundation in truth. I own I have much ado to reconcile myself to the sound of a word which has always given me such terrible ideas, though I am convinced there is little more in it than a fever, as a proof of which we passed through two or three towns most violently infected. In the very next house where we lay, in one of 'em, two persons died of it. Luckily for me I was so well deceived that I knew nothing of the matter, and I was made believe that our second cook who fell ill there had only a great cold. However, we left our doctor to take care of him, and yesterday they both arrived here in good health and I am now let into the secret that he has had the plague. There are many that 'scape of it, neither is the air ever infected. I am persuaded it would be as easy to root it out here as out of Italy and France, but it does so little mischief, they are not very solicitous about it and are content to suffer this distemper instead of our variety, which they are utterly unacquainted with.

Apropos of distempers, I am going to tell you a thing that I am sure will make you wish yourself here. The smallpox, so fatal and so general amongst us, is here entirely harmless by the invention of engrafting (which is the term they give it). There is a set of old women who make it their business to perform the operation. Every autumn, in the month of September, when the great heat is abated, people send to one another to know if any of their family has a mind to have the smallpox. They make parties for this purpose, and when they are met (commonly fifteen or sixteen together) the old woman comes with a nutshell full of the matter of the best sort of smallpox and asks what veins you please to have opened. She immediately rips open that you offer to her with a large needle (which gives you no more pain than a common scratch) and puts into the vein as much venom as can lie upon the head of her needle, and after binds up the little wound with a hollow bit of shell and in this manner opens four or five veins. The Grecians have commonly the superstition of opening one in the middle of the forehead, in each arm, and on the breast to mark the sign of the cross, but this has a very ill effect, all these wounds leaving little scars, and is not done by those that are not superstitious, who choose to have them in the legs, or that part of the arm which is concealed. The children or young patients play together all the rest of the day and are in perfect health till the eighth. Then the fever begins to seize 'em and they keep to their beds two days, very seldom three. They have very rarely above twenty or thirty in their faces, which never mark, and in eight days' time they are as well as before the illness. Where they are wounded there remains running sores during the distemper, which I don't doubt is a great relief to it. Every year thousands undergo this operation, and the French ambassador says pleasantly that they take the smallpox here by way of diversion as they take the waters in other countries. There is no example of anyone who has died from it, and you may believe I am well satisfied of the safety of this experiment, since I intend to try it on my dear little son.

I am patriot enough to take pains to bring this useful invention into fashion in England, and I should not fail to write to some of our doctors very particularly about it, if I knew any one of them that I thought had virtue enough to destroy such a considerable branch of their revenue for the good of mankind. But that distemper is too beneficial to them, not to expose to all their resentment the hardy weight that should undertake to put an end to it. Perhaps, if I live to return, I may, however, have courage to war with them. Upon this occasion admire the heroism in the heart of your friend, etc, etc.

ED. R. HALSBAND, *THE COMPLETE LETTERS OF LADY MARY WORTLEY MONTAGU* (1965)

She carried out her decision and had her son vaccinated a year later.

Preparing for the Last Journey

The year before she died, Lady Mary Wortley Montagu wrote to Sir James Stewart, vividly depicting the trials of infirmity. Lord Bute is her son-in-law.

Venice, 12 April 1761

Sir,

Though I am preparing for my last and longest journey, and stand on the threshold of this dirty world, my several infirmities like post horses ready to hurry me away, I cannot be insensible to the happiness of my native country, and am glad to see the prospect of a prosperity and harmony that I never was witness to. I hope my friends will be included in the public joy; and I shall always think Lady Fanny and Sir James Stewart in the first rank of those I wish to serve. Your conversation is a pleasure I would prefer to any other; but I confess even that cannot make me desire to be in London, especially at this time when the shadow of credit that I should be supposed to possess would attract daily solicitations, and gain me a number of enemies who would never forgive me the not performing impossibilities. If all people thought of power as I do, it would be avoided with as much eagerness as it is now sought. I never knew any person that had it who did not lament the load, though I confess (so infirm is human nature) they have all endeavoured to retain it at the same time they complained of it.

You observe justly there is no happiness without an alloy, nor indeed any misfortune without some mixture of consolation, if our passions permitted us to perceive it. But alas! we are too imperfect to see on all sides; our wisest reflections (if the word wise may be given to humanity) are tainted by our hopes and fears: we all indulge views almost as extravagant as those of Phaeton, and are angry when we do not succeed in projects that are above the reach of mortality. The happiness of domestic life seems the most laudable as it is certainly the most delightful of our prospects, yet even that is denied, or at least so mixed 'we think it not sincere or fear it cannot last'. A long series of disappointments have perhaps worn out my natural spirits and given a melancholy cast to my way of thinking. I would not communicate this weakness to any but yourself, who can have compassion even where your superior understanding condemns.

I confess that though I am (it may be) beyond the strict bounds of reason pleased with my Lord Bute's and my daughter's prosperity I am doubtful whether I will attempt to be a spectator of it. I have so many years indulged my natural inclinations to solitude and reading, I am unwilling to return to crowds and bustle, which would be unavoidable in London. The few friends I esteemed are now no more; the new set of people who fill the stage at present are too indifferent to me even to raise my curiosity.

I now begin (very late, you'll say) the worst effects of age, blindness excepted: I am grown timorous and suspicious; I fear the inconstancy of that goddess so publicly adored in ancient Rome and so heartily inwardly worshipped in the modern. I retain, however, such a degree of that uncommon thing called commonsense not to trouble the felicity of my children with my foreboding dreams, which I hope will prove as idle as the croaking of ravens or the noise of that harmless animal distinguished by the odious name of screech-owl. You will say, why then do I trouble you with my old wives' prophecies? Need I tell you that it is one of the privileges of friendship to talk of our own follies and infirmities? You must then, nay you ought to, pardon my tiresome tattle in consideration of the real attachment with which I am unalterably, sir, your obliged and faithful humble servant,

M.W. Montagu

ED. R. HALSBAND, THE COMPLETE LETTERS OF LADY MARY WORTLEY
MONTAGU (1965)

Grief in Leaving This World

This (undated) letter was found, in the eighteenth century, among the papers of Lady Betty, aunt of the younger Lady of Llangollen, Sarah Ponsonby. Lady Betty was an affectionate, naïve woman who did not realize that her husband was hoping for her early death, so that he could remarry, and produce an heir.

My dear Sir Wm, the greatest Grife I have in leaving this World is parting with you and the thoughts of your sorrow for me. Don't grive my dear Sir Wm, I am, I trust in God going to be happy. You have my sincear Prayers and thanks for your tenderness to me and good behaviour to my dear Child. May God grant you happiness in her. If you Marry again I wish you much happiness. If I ever offended you forgive me. I have never meant any offence, I have always ment to be a good Wife and Mother and hope you think Me so. As to my Funeral I hope youl allow me to be Buried as I like, which is this: When the Women about me are sure I am dead, I would be Carried to the Church and kept out of Ground two days and nights, four Women to sitt up with me. To each Woman give five pound. I would have twenty Pound laid out in Close for the poor People, in all forty. No body to be at My Funeral but my own poor, who I think will be sorry for me. If Nelly be wt me at the time of my death give her fifty Pound, she deserves it much. Take care of yourself (live and do all the good you can) and may God almighty give you as peacefull and happy an End as I think I shall have . . .

COLLECTION OF MS K. KENYON

She was not, however, to go first; Sir William died seven years before she did.

Facing Bereavement

Jane Austen loved her sister Cassandra and lived with her for some years. Here Cassandra describes what the death of Jane means to her, writing to their niece.

Chawton: Tuesday [July 29, 1817]

My dearest Fanny,
I have just read your letter for the third time, and thank you most sincerely for every kind expression to myself, and still more warmly for your praises of her who I believe was better known to you than to any human being besides myself. Nothing of the sort could have been more gratifying to me than the manner in which you write of her, and if the dear angel is conscious of what passes here, and is not above all earthly feelings, she may perhaps receive pleasure in being so mourned. Had *she* been the survivor I can fancy her speaking of *you* in almost the same terms. There are certainly many points of strong resemblance in your characters; in your intimate acquaintance with each other, and your mutual strong affection, you were counterparts.

Thursday was not so dreadful a day to me as you imagined. There was so much necessary to be done that there was no time for additional misery. Everything was conducted with the greatest tranquillity, and but that I was determined I would see the last, and therefore was upon the listen, I should not have known when they left the house. I watched the little mournful procession the length of the street; and when it turned from my sight, and I had lost her for ever, even then I was not overpowered, nor so much agitated as I am now in writing of it. Never was human being more sincerely mourned by those who attended her remains than was this dear creature. May the sorrow with which she is parted with on earth be a prognostic of the joy with which she is hailed in heaven!

I continue very tolerably well – much better than any one could have supposed possible, because I certainly have had considerable fatigue of body as well as anguish of mind for months back; but I really am well, and I hope I am properly grateful to the Almighty for having been so supported. Your grandmamma, too, is much better than when I came home.

I did not think your dear papa appeared unwell, and I understand that he seemed much more comfortable after his return from Winchester than he had done before. I need not tell you that he was a great comfort to me; indeed, I can never say enough of the kindness I have received from him and from every other friend.

ED. R.W. CHAPMAN, JANE AUSTEN: LETTERS (1932)

Illness and Death in India

Illness in India killed many people when they were young. Fortunately Emily Eden was tough, even able to joke about the different fevers affecting each place they visited. She writes home from Gugga in 1839.

Wednesday, Jan. 30.

It is four days since I have been able to write. I was 'took so shocking bad' with fever on Sunday, caught, it is supposed, at that river-side – that eternal Gugga. Captain L.E. was seized just in the same way, and several of the servants, so we all say we caught it there; but it is all nonsense – every inch of the plains in India has its fever in it, only there is not time to catch them all. I think the Gugga fever is remarkably unpleasant, and I did not know that one head and one set of bones could hold so much pain as mine did for forty-eight hours. But one ought to be allowed a change of bones in India: it ought to be part of the outfit. I hope it is over to-night; but as things are, I and L.E., with Captain C. and the doctor, are going straight to Hansi to-morrow – only a short march of ten miles, thereby saving ourselves two long marches of sixteen miles, which G. makes to Hissar, and giving ourselves a halt of three days to repair our shattered constitutions.

It is so absurd to hear people talk of their fevers. Mr M. was to have joined us a month ago, but unfortunately caught 'the Delhi fever' coming up: he is to be at Hansi. Z. caught 'the Agra fever' coming up; hopes to be able to join us at Hansi, but is doubtful. Then N., our Hansi magistrate, looks with horror at Hansi: he has suffered and still suffers so much from 'that dreadful Hansi fever.' I myself think 'the Gugga fever' a more awful visitation, but that is all a matter of opinion. Anyhow, if N. wished us to know real hardship, fever in camp is about the most compendious definition of intense misery I know. We march early each morning; so after a racking night – and I really can't impress upon you the pain in my *Indian* bones – it was necessary at half-past five – just when one might by good luck have fallen asleep – to get up by candle-light and put on a bonnet and cloak and – one's *things* in short, to drive over *no* road. I went one morning in the palanquin, but that was so slow, the carriage was the least evil of the two. Then on arriving, shivering all over, we were obliged to wait two hours till the beds appeared; and from that time till ten at night, I observed by my watch that there was not one minute in which they were not knocking tent-pins, they said into the ground, but by mistake they all went into my head – I am sure of it, and am convinced that I wear a large and full wig of tent-pins. Dr D. put leeches on me last night, and I am much better to-day. L.E. is of course ditto: the Gugga fevers are all alike.

E. EDEN, *UP THE COUNTRY: LETTERS FROM INDIA* (1872)

Fanny Burney Faces Loss

Fanny Burney, the novelist, here writes to her niece, Mrs Barrett, about loss and facing illness.

March 5, 1839

Ah! My dearest! how changed, changed I am, since the irreparable loss of your beloved mother! that last original tie to native original affections!

Wednesday. I broke off and an incapable unwillingness seized my pen; but I hear you are not well, and I *hasten* – if that be a word I can ever use again – to make personal inquiry how you are.

I have been very ill, very little *apparently*, but with nights of consuming restlessness and tears. I have now called in Dr Holland, who understands me marvellously, and am now much as usual; no, not that – still tormented with nights without repose – but better.

My spirits have been dreadfully saddened of late by whole days – nay weeks – of helplessness for any employment. They have but just revived. How merciful a reprieve. How merciful is *all* we know! *The ways of Heaven* are not *dark* and intricate, but unknown and unimagined till the great teacher, Death, develops them.

ED. A. DOBSON, *THE DIARY AND LETTERS OF MME D'ARBLAY* (1904)

Charlotte Brontë on her Brother's Death

Charlotte Brontë here writes to W.S. Williams, reader at Smith & Elder and first admirer of Jane Eyre. *Branwell Brontë had died on 24 September.*

October 2nd, 1848

My Dear Sir,

'We have buried our dead out of sight.' A lull begins to succeed the gloomy tumult of last week. It is not permitted us to grieve for him who is gone as others grieve for those they lose. The removal of our only brother must necessarily be regarded by us as rather in the light of a mercy than a chastisement. Branwell was his father's and his sister's pride and hope in boyhood, but since manhood the case has been otherwise. It has been our lot to see him take a wrong bent; to hope, expect, wait his return to the right path; to know the sickness of hope deferred, the dismay of prayer baffled; to experience despair at last – and now to behold the sudden early obscure close of what might have been a noble career.

I do not weep from a sense of bereavement – there is no prop withdrawn, no consolation torn away, no dear companion lost – but for the wreck of talent, the ruin of promise, the untimely dreary extinction of what might have been a burning and a shining light. My brother was a year my junior. I had aspirations and ambitions for him once, long ago – they have perished mournfully. Nothing remains of him but a memory of errors and sufferings. There is such a bitterness of pity for his life and death, such a yearning for the emptiness of his whole existence as I cannot describe. I trust time will allay these feelings.

My poor father naturally thought more of his *only* son than of his daughters, and, much and long as he had suffered on his account, he cried out of his loss like David for that of Absalom – my son! my son! – and refused at first to be comforted. And then when I ought to have been able to collect my strength and be at hand to support him, I fell ill with an illness whose approaches I had felt for some time previously, and of which the crisis was hastened by the awe and trouble of the death-scene – the first I had ever witnessed. The past has seemed to me a strange week. Thank God, for my father's sake, I am better now, though still feeble. I wish indeed I had more general physical strength – the want of it is sadly in my way. I cannot do what I would do for want of sustained animal spirits and efficient bodily vigour.

My unhappy brother never knew what his sisters had done in literature – he was not aware that they had ever published a line. We could not tell him of our efforts for fear of causing him too deep a pang of remorse for his own time misspent, and talents misapplied. Now he will *never* know. I cannot dwell longer on the subject at present – it is too painful.

I thank you for your kind sympathy, and pray earnestly that your sons may all do well, and that you may be spared the sufferings my father has gone through. – Yours sincerely,

C. Brontë

EDS. T.J. WISE AND J.A. SYMINGTON, THE BRONTES: THEIR LIVES,
FRIENDSHIPS AND CORRESPONDENCE IN FOUR VOLUMES (1932)

George Eliot's Despair

When George Eliot was editing Westminster Review *it caused her many headaches. In 1854 when she became attracted to George Lewes, she was completing her translation of Feuerbach's* Das Wesen des Christenthums? *'Poor Lewes' fell ill and she probably completed all his articles, as well as her own. That summer she wrote to her sympathetic friend Cara Bray about her own ailments.*

1854

My various aches determined themselves into an attack of rheumatism which sent me to bed yesterday; but I am better this morning and, as you see, able to sit up and write. My troubles are purely psychical – self-dissatisfaction and despair of achieving anything worth the doing. I can truly say, they vanish into nothing before any fear for the happiness of those I love. . . . When I spoke of myself as an island, I did not mean that I was so exceptionally. We are all islands –

'Each in his hidden sphere of joy or woe,
Our hermit spirits dwell and roam apart' –

and this seclusion is sometimes the most intensely felt at the very moment your friend is caressing you or consoling you. But this gradually becomes a source of satisfaction instead of repining. When we are young we think our troubles a mighty business – that the world is spread out expressly as a stage for the particular drama of our lives and that we have a right to rant and foam at the mouth if we are crossed. I have done enough of that in my time. But we begin at last to understand that these things are important only to one's own consciousness, which is but as a globule of dew on a rose-leaf that at midday there will be no trace of. This is no high-flown sentimentality, but a simple reflection which I find useful to me every day.

ED. G. HAIGHT, *SELECTED LETTERS OF GEORGE ELIOT* (1968)

Queen Victoria Faces Prince Albert's Illness with Courage

Queen Victoria found greater strength to face Prince Albert's final illness than his death a few weeks later. Here she writes to the King of the Belgians.

Windsor Castle, 11th December 1861
Dearest Uncle, I can report another good night, and *no* loss of strength, and continued satisfactory symptoms. But more we dare *not* expect for some days; *not* losing ground is a *gain, now*, of *every* day.

It is very sad and trying for me, but I am well, and I think really *very* courageous; for it is the first time that *I* ever witnessed anything of this kind though *I* suffered from the same at Ramsgate, and was much worse. The trial in every way is so very trying, for I have lost my guide, my support, my all, *for a time* – as we can't ask or tell him anything. Many thanks for your kind letter received yesterday. We have been and are reading Von Ense's book to Albert; but it is *not* worth much. He likes very much being read to as it soothes him. W. Scott is also read to him. You shall hear again to-morrow, dearest Uncle, and, please God! each day will be more cheering.

Ever your devoted Niece,

Victoria R.

Windsor Castle, 12th December 1861

My Beloved Uncle, – I can again report favourably of our *most* precious invalid. He maintains his ground well – had another very good night, takes plenty of nourishment, and shows surprising stength. I am constantly in and out of his room, but since the *first four dreadful* nights, *last* week, *before* they had declared it to be *gastric fever* – I do not sit up with him at nights as I could be of no use; and there is nothing to cause alarm. I go out twice a day for about an hour. It is a very trying time, for a fever with its despondency, weakness, and occasional and *invariable* wandering, is most painful to witness – but we have *never* had *one unfavourable* symptom; to-morrow, reckoning from the 22nd, when dear Albert first fell ill – after going on a wet day to look at some buildings – having likewise been unusually depressed with worries of different kinds – is the *end* of the *third week*; we *may* hope for improvement *after* that, but the Doctors say they should *not* be *at all disappointed if* this did *not* take place till the *end* of the *fourth week*. I cannot sufficiently praise the skill, attention, and devotion of Dr Jenner, who is the *first fever* Doctor in Europe, one may say – and good old Clark is here every day; good Brown is also *most* useful. . . . We have got Dr Watson (who succeeded Dr Chambers) and Sir H. Holland has also been here. But I have kept clear of these two. Albert sleeps a good deal in the day. He is moved every day into the next room on a sofa which is made up as a bed. He has only *kept* his bed entirely since Monday. Many, many thanks for your dear, kind letter of the 11th. I knew how *you* would *feel* for and think of me. I am very wonderfully supported, and excepting on three occasions, have borne up very well. I am sure Clark will tell you so. Ever your most devoted Niece,

Victoria R.

ED. A.C. BENSON, *LETTERS OF QUEEN VICTORIA* (1907)

She could scarcely bear Prince Albert's death, however.

Osborne, 24th December 1861

My Beloved Uncle, – Though, please God! I am to see you so soon, I must write these few lines to prepare you for the trying, sad existence you will find it with your poor forlorn, desolate child – who drags on a weary, pleasureless existence! I am also anxious to repeat *one* thing, and *that one* is *my firm* resolve, my *irrevocable decision*, viz. that *his* wishes – *his* plans about everything, *his* views about *every* thing are to be *my law*! And *no human power* will make me swerve from *what he* decided and wished – and I look to *you* to *support* and *help* me in this. I apply this particularly as regards our children – Bertie, etc. – for whose future he had traced everything *so* carefully. I am *also determined* that *no one* person, may *he* be ever so good, ever so devoted among my servants – is to lead or guide or dictate *to me.* I know *how he* would disapprove it. And I live *on* with him, for him; in fact *I* am only *outwardly* separated from him, and *only* for a *time.*

No one can tell you more of my feelings, and can put you more in possession of many touching facts than our excellent Dr Jenner, who has been and is my great comfort, and whom I would *entreat* you to *see and hear* before you see *any one else.* Pray do this, for *I fear much* others trying to see you first and say things and wish for things which I *should not* consent to.

Though miserably weak and utterly shattered, my spirit rises when I think *any* wish or plan of his is to be touched or changed, or I am to be *made to do* anything. I know you will help me in my utter darkness. It is but for a short time, and *then* I go – *never, never* to part! Oh! that blessed, blessed thought! He seems so *near* to *me,* so *quite my own* now, my precious darling! God bless and preserve you.

Ever your wretched but devoted Child,

Victoria R.

What a Xmas! I won't think of it.

ED. A.C. BENSON (1907)

Advice on Depression to Flaubert

George Sand (1804–76), the French novelist, born Aurore Dupin, maintained lifelong friendships with many well-known men. She often cheered the ageing Flaubert, seventeen years her junior, with her advice on how to deal with depression and pain.

5 July 1872   Nohant

My old troubadour,

I must write to you today. Sixty-eight years old. Perfect health in spite of the cough which lets me sleep now that I plunge daily in a furious little torrent, cold as ice. The doctor says it's madness. I let him talk, too; I am curing myself while his patients look after themselves and croak. I am like the grass of the fields: water and sun, that is all I need . . .

15 March 1873   Nohant

Well, my old troubadour, we can hope for you very soon, I was worried about you. I am always worried about you. To tell the truth, I am not happy over your ill tempers, and your *prejudices*. They last too long, and in effect they are like an illness, you recognize it yourself. Now, forget; don't you know how to forget? You live too much in yourself and you get to consider everything in relation to yourself. If you were an egoist, and a conceited person, I would say that it was a normal condition; but with you who are so good and so generous it is an anomaly, an evil that must be combatted. Rest assured that life is badly arranged, painful, irritating for everyone; but do not neglect the immense compensations which it is ungrateful to forget.

That you get angry with this or that person, is of little importance if it is a comfort to you; but that you remain furious, indignant for weeks, months, almost years, is unjust and cruel to those who love you, and who would like to spare you all anxiety and all deception.

You see that I am scolding you; but while embracing you, I shall think only of the joy and the hope of seeing you flourishing again. We are waiting for you with impatience, and we are counting on Turgeneff [to visit] whom we adore also.

I have been suffering a good deal lately with a series of very painful hemorrhages; but they have not prevented me from amusing myself writing tales and from playing with my *little children*. They are so dear, and my big children are so good to me, that I shall die, I believe, smiling at them. What difference does it make whether one has a hundred thousand enemies if one is loved by two or three good souls? Don't you love me too, and wouldn't you reproach me for thinking that of no account? When I lost Rollinat, didn't you write to me to love the more those who were left? Come, so that I may *overwhelm* you with reproaches; for you are not doing what you told me to do.

We are expecting you, we are preparing a mid-Lent fantasy; try to take part. Laughter is a splendid medicine. We shall give you a costume; they tell me that you were very good as a pastry cook at Pauline's! If you are better, be certain it is because you have gotten out of your rut and have distracted yourself a little. Paris is good for you, you are too much alone yonder in your lovely house. Come and work, at our house; how perfectly easy to send on a box of books!

ED. E. DREW, *LETTERS OF GEORGE SAND* (1930)

Harriet Martineau Faces her End

Harriet Martineau (1802–76) wrote on women's issues and supported herself from the proceeds of her numerous books and articles. She suffered from ill-health throughout her life and in 1854 developed heart disease, which her doctors predicted would soon prove fatal. Despite this incurable illness, she continued her prodigious activities for the rest of her life. She was brought up a Christian, but rejected the idea of salvation, believing in eternal and irreversible laws in the universe. In this letter, written to a close friend a month before her death, Martineau calmly faces her end.

To Maria Weston Chapman   May 17, 1876

My dearest Friend, I am very ill. I leave it to J—— to show you how nearly certain it is that the end of my long illness is at hand. The difficulty and distress to me are the state of my head. I will only add that the condition daily grows worse, so that I am scarcely able to converse or to read, and the cramp in the hands makes the writing difficult or impossible; so I must try to be content with a few lines I can send, till the few days become none. We believe that time to be near; and we shall not attempt to deceive you about it. My brain feels under the constant sense of being not myself, and the introduction of this new fear into my daily life makes each day sufficiently trying to justify the longing for death which grows upon me more and more. I feel sure of your sympathy about this. You enter into my longing for rest, I am certain, and when you hear, some day soon, that I have sunk into my long sleep, you will feel it as the removal of a care, and as a relief on my account.

. . . I have no wish for further experience, nor have I any fear of it. Under the weariness of illness I long to be asleep; but I have not set my mind on any state. Above all I wish to escape from the narrowness of taking a merely human view of things, from the absurdity of making God after man's own image.

On my side I have suffered much anxiety on your account; and if you can tell me that you are no longer suffering physically under the peculiar feebleness that attends bronchial mischief, you will make me happier than anything else could make me. Farewell for today, dearest friend! While I live, I am your grateful and loving H.M.

ED. Maria W. Chapman, *Harriet Martineau's Autobiography and Memorials of Harriet Martineau* (1877)

A Muslim Husband's Death

After the death of a husband a Muslim wife in Senegal has to face not only the family of the second wife (Binetou) but public revelations of her husband's behaviour. This letter is from the novel So Long a Letter *(1982) by Mariama Bâ.*

Dear Aissatou, my friend, perhaps I bore you by relating what you already know: that a dead person be stripped of his most intimate secrets. This is what we crudely learned:

This house and its chic contents were acquired by a bank loan granted on the mortgage of 'Villa Fallene', where I live. Although the title deeds of this house bear his name, it is nonetheless our common property, acquired by our joint savings. Insult upon injury!

Moreover, he continued the monthly payments of seventy-five thousand francs to the SICAP. These payments were to go on for about ten years before the house would become his.

Four million francs borrowed with ease because of his privileged position, which had enabled him to pay for Lady Mother-in-Law and her husband to visit Mecca to acquire the titles of *Alhaja* and *Alhaji*; which equally enabled Binetou to exchange her Alfa Romeos at the slightest dent.

Now I understand the terrible significance of Modou's abandonment of our joint bank account. He wanted to be financially independent so as to have enough elbow room.

And then, having withdrawn Binetou from school, he paid her a monthly allowance of fifty thousand francs, just like a salary due to her. The young girl, who was very gifted, wanted to continue her studies, to sit for her *baccalauréat*. So as to establish his rule, Modou, wickedly, determined to remove her from the critical and unsparing world of the young. He therefore gave in to all the conditions of the grasping Lady Mother-in-Law and even signed a paper committing himself to paying the said amount. Lady Mother-in-law brandished the paper, for she firmly believed that the payments would continue, even after Modou's death, out of the estate.

As for my daughter, Daba, she waved about a bailiff's affidavit, dated the very day of her father's death, that listed all the contents of the SICAP Villa. The list supplied by Lady Mother-in-Law and Binetou made no mention of certain objects and items of furniture, which had mysteriously disappeared or had been fraudulently removed.

You know that I am excessively sentimental. I was not at all pleased by this display on either side.

TRANS. M. BODÉ-THOMAS, MARIAMA BÂ, *So Long a Letter* (1982)

Illness on Pilgrimage in Northern India

A Buddhist nun based at Chithurst Monastery, and involved in setting up a Buddhist school, visits North India on pilgrimage in November 1990. She writes to her friends on how she copes with illness there.

23 November

That night I woke after midnight with a fever, sore throat, stinging eyes and generally feeling rotten. I lay for a while wondering what it could be. A lot of anxiety came up, getting sick in Asia is no fun. My mind went a bit wild, thinking of all sorts of possibilities. Images of all the beggars and filth and poverty. I seemed to be face to face with the total insecurity of life, that feeling is more raw here. I felt assailed by the dark side of India. We have a false sense of security in the west, whereas in reality the shadow of death is always on us. I started to repeat the Bud dho mantra and decided just to let go. As I calmed down, I realised it was important to allow this quite natural response to insecurity. India is overwhelming and one can't pretend to meet it with our usual rational responses which come from a set world view. I realised how cushioned our life is – and fancied some of that cushioning now! Maybe the west isn't so bad with its hygiene and medical resources. . . .

I drank a lot of purified water, took some paracetamol and homoeo-pathy for fever, and lay down for a few hours just observing sensations in the body and calming the mind. I reflected on the inevitability of death and separation from the loved. Quite awesome, this impermanence. No wonder we cushion ourselves so much. In the morning the fever had subsided leaving me with a fluey cold, not too bad.

25 Nov. Today I went to see the local Tibetan doctor as I've been feeling a bit rough. He put it down to general readjustment and has given me some strange looking herbal pills to take three times a day. One shouldn't take any heavy drugs or antibiotics unless it's something serious, but rather just give one's body time to build up its own immunity.

26 Nov. The sickness seems to be subsiding. Feel like I've been through a massive clean out. The Tibetan medicine seems to be working. I went to the temple, only 5 minutes walk, to join in prostrations with the elderly ladies. Almost any time of day or night one can see the Tibetan monks, nuns and laity alike doing prostrations. One aspect that's strongly emphasised is that everything should be undertaken with the view of benefiting all sentient beings. . . .

With respects, gratitude and loving thoughts to you all, Sister Thanissara.

AUTHOR'S COLLECTION

eleven

Political Skills

This final chapter demonstrates female capacity for reasoning and logical argument in many areas: skill in argument demonstrated by women in power, or addressing those in power, in an attempt to persuade; skill in expounding ethical or theological ideas, and in analysing other people. All these writers possess the ability to deploy 'patriarchal' discourses together with female responsiveness to individuals.

The chapter opens with two letters from Hildegard of Bingen. Respected for her visions and sermons, she was often asked for advice. Here she takes the initiative, to persuade the young king 'readily to do good, for your mind is well-disposed, except when the foul habits of others overwhelm you'. She uses bold biblical images to frighten a Pope with her warning. The second letter is proof of the power possessed by a woman when in charge of a large independent nunnery.

There are a fair number of letters available from queens, who were in a position to wield power, and negotiate. I include the first translation in English of a letter by Isabella la Católica, mother of Catherine of Aragon, to her brother, King Enrique, to persuade him to let her marry the man of her choice. This was Ferdinand of Aragon who proved an excellent consort, and who was possibly a model for Machiavelli's *The Prince*. Together they reunited Spain, making it the most powerful country in the known world: Isabel had the foresight, alone among Europeans, to back Columbus.

The two letters of Elizabeth I demonstrate her skill in adapting her discourse to the topics on which she wished to legislate or persuade. Her faith is as strong as her sister's, but vastly distinct in tone and content. Both took power as Head of the Church, and displayed patriarchal ability to use that power forcefully. Distinct in tone, but not in common sense, are the letters of Empress Maria Theresa of Austria, who used her influence to stop the Franco-Austrian war, and Queen Victoria. Both sound naïve, but they carried out their duty better than most monarchs.

The working-class is not omitted, with two brave, skilful letters from groups petitioning men in power to improve their pitiful earning position.

Every century offers evidence of the skill with which women used 'patriarchal' discourse to convince their readers, such as Aphra Behn who deployed many different types of language in order to earn a living (see Chapter Seven). By the eighteenth century groups of intellectual women were corresponding with each other; and far more so as the century drew to its revolutionary close.

Mary Wollstonecraft is the best-known among many who argued for women's equality, as in the letter to Talleyrand earlier. Women novelists, in less argumentative vein, possessed the ability to pronounce balanced judgements on the awesomely distinguished, as Fanny Burney on Dr Johnson.

By the nineteenth century, women wrote on public issues and social reform, from Elizabeth Fry on prisons to Beatrice Webb for the Fabians. Suffragette views are so well known that I have included only one – a farseeing argument for a Women's Movement from Christabel Pankhurst – because of its classlessness. Anaïs Nin argues for honesty in wartime, in a letter to a homosexual friend. Finally, La Pasionaria links her personal grief for the death of her son with public support of the Revolution.

Abbess at Work

Hildegard of Bingen had mystic visions, composed moving plainsong and ran a large convent. Yet she always found time to help powerful men with her letters of advice. The first letter is to Henry II of England. He had been crowned king in 1154. He greatly admired the Emperor, Barbarossa, and a marriage was planned between the babies of the two royal houses, which Henry cancelled when his future son-in-law was passed over in the imperial succession. King Henry supported the antipope, while the English bishops, Thomas à Becket among them, supported Pope Alexander. Henry became Thomas's enemy, but did penance after his murder at Canterbury in 1170. The archbishop was canonized three years later.

To a certain man who holds a certain office, the Lord says: 'Yours are the gifts of giving: it is by ruling and defending, protecting and providing, that you may reach heaven.' But a bird, as black as can be, comes to you from the North and says: 'You have the power to do whatever you want. So do this and do that; make this excuse and that excuse. It does not profit you to have regard for Justice; for if you are always attentive to her, you will not be a master but a slave.'

Yet you should not listen to the thief who gives you this advice; the thief who, in your infancy, when you had become, from ashes, a thing of beauty, after receiving the breath of life, stripped you of great glory. Look, instead, more attentively upon your Father who made you. For your mind is well-disposed, so that you readily do good, except when the foul habits of others overwhelm you and you become entangled in them for a time. Shun this, with all your might, beloved son of God, and call upon your Father, since willingly he stretches out his hand to help you. Now live forever and remain in eternal happiness.

Following Eugenius, Anastasius IV reigned briefly as Pope between 12 July, 1153 and 3 December, 1154. Although an upright figure himself, he won a reputation for tolerating lesser men in positions of influence.

Note Hildegard's bravery in criticizing the Pope, in spite of his position as leader of the Church.

So it is, O man, that you who sit in the chief seat of the Lord, hold him in contempt when you embrace evil, since you do not reject it but kiss it, by silently tolerating it in depraved men. And so the whole earth is disordered by a great succession of heresies; for man loves what God has destroyed. And you, Rome, like a man lying at the point of death, will be so confounded that the strength of your feet, on which up till now you have stood, will ebb away. For you love the King's daughter, Justice, not with a burning love, but as though in the numbness of sleep; so that you drive her from you. But she herself will flee from you if you do not call her back.

But the high mountains will still hold out to you the jaw-bone of assistance. They will lift you up, supporting you with the massive timbers of tall trees, so that you will not be despoiled completely of all your honour – the glory of your betrothal to Christ. You will keep some wings to adorn you, until the snow of manifold mockeries arrives, producing much folly. Beware, therefore, of wanting to associate yourself with the ways of the pagans, lest you fall.

ED. M. FOX, *LETTERS OF HILDEGARD OF BINGEN* (1987)

Advice to a Son

Hardworking Margaret Paston not only ran a large estate whenever her husband was away, she helped her children with their financial problems. In this letter Margaret writes to her son with serious news about her husband's will.

1450

This is to let you know that I am sending you by the bearer of this letter £40 in gold coin, which I have borrowed for you on pledge, because I would not take the money laid aside for you at Norwich; for, so I am told by the chancellor, Master John Smith, and others, we have all been cursed for administering a dead man's goods without licence or authority, and I think matters are going all the worse with us because of it. For the reverence of God, get a licence from my lord of Canterbury, to ease my conscience and yours, to administer goods to the value of three or four hundred marks, and explain to him how your estates have been in such trouble these past two years that you could get nothing at all from them, nor can take anything now without hurting your tenants. They have been so harrassed by unjust means before now, and you have so much important business in hand, that you cannot afford to be forebearing with them or keep your rights without using your father's goods for a time. This I hope, will ease our conscience in respect of what we have administered and spent before; because we have no more money to pay off this £40 and all other charges than the £47 which you and your uncle know about, which is laid aside at Norwich.

By your mother

ED. ALICE D. GREENWOOD, *SELECTIONS FROM THE PASTON LETTERS* (1920)

Isabella of Castile Argues for her Own Choice of Husband

Isabella of Castile (1451–1501) transformed a peninsula of disparate, warring kingdoms into the nation-state of Spain, much as we know it today. Only eighteen when she wrote this letter to her brother, King Enrique, she displays many skills in argument: she underlines her position and rights, as sister and heir to the throne; as sister, she stresses her love for the brother; as princess, she renounces civil war, in order to bring peace to their kingdoms. She gives many reasons why the man she favours as her future husband would prove better than her brother's choices for her, which he had endeavoured to impose by keeping her under house arrest.

October 1470

My worthy Lord and powerful King: your lordship knows full well that after the illustrious King Alonso, my brother and your lordship's, had passed from this life, many nobles, prelates and knights, who had served and followed him, remained in my service in Avila; I might well have retained the titles and land which Alonso, our brother, won before his death. But I have always placed my great, true love at the service of your majesty's person and welfare, and the peace and security of these kingdoms. Conscious of your Majesty's desire to put an end to the wars, riots, dangers, deaths and disturbances, I wished to defer everything which seemed to strengthen my power and authority in order to further the will and disposition of your Excellence. Nevertheless it must be recognised that the lawful succession of these kingdoms always belonged, and still belongs, to me, as legitimate successor and inheritor . . . since you, in the presence of many nobles and the Papal Nuncio, as I have been informed, had sworn on the Holy Bible, and publicly announced, throughout your kingdoms, and much of Christendom, that I am your Heir and legitimate successor.

F. FERNÁNDEZ-ARNESTO, *FERDINAND AND ISABELLA* (1975) TRANS. OLGA
KENYON

Lucrezia Borgia to her Lover

Lucrezia Borgia, sister of the infamous Pope, enjoyed a certain amount of power through him. But he was jealous of her relationships which forced her to be circumspect, as this witty letter to her lover Pietro Bembo, shows. As with many women, she expresses 'powerlessness' to match his wording, so partly absolving herself from the rashness of a longer missive which could have been intercepted. However, she is aware that when a man falls in love, it is the one moment when a woman in patriarchal society has a modicum of power – which she seems to enjoy in her playing on words. Thesauriero is a pun on a title meaning both thesaurus and treasurer.

[1517]

My dearest Misser Pietro,
I know that the very expectation of something awaited is the greater part of satisfaction because the hope of possessing it lights up desire. The rarer it is, the more beautiful it seems, the commoner, the less so. I decided to put off writing to you until this moment, with the result that by awaiting some exquisite reward to your most exquisite letters, you have become the source of your own satisfaction; you are both creditor and payer.

Nevertheless I have in two of my letters, confessed to Monsignor Thesauriero of my debt to you and this may have constituted no small part of that which I can pay. As far as the rest is concerned, I do not believe that I can be held bound. In your letters you express with such ease all that you feel for me, but, I, just because I feel so well disposed towards you, am unable to do so. It is this feeling of powerlessness which absolves me from the debt. However as it would be unsuitable for me to be both prosecutor and judge of my own cause, I submit to the weighty judgement of the aforesaid Monsignor Thesauriero, commending myself to his Lordship and you. Ferrara the seventh day of August.

Your own Duchess of Ferrara
A. FRASER, *LOVE LETTERS* (1976)

The Promotion of Catholicism against Protestantism

Mary Tudor (1516–1558) was imbued with the intense Catholic faith which had supported her mother during the long years of rejection by Henry VIII. After the persecution of Catholics, she was determined to reimpose her faith. Her resolve was strengthened by her marriage to Philip II of Spain. By January 1555 she felt secure with the re-establishment of Catholicism, and an apparent pregnancy. She determined to persecute a few well-known Protestants, but without the processions and public confessions demanded by the Spanish Inquisition at that time. This letter is far more humane in approach than attitudes in Rome, though she might be accused of Jesuitical rationalization. Compare it with her sister's humanistic approach, in the next letter.

To Pole, her legate   January 1555

. . . touching good preaching, I wish that may supply and overcome the evil preaching in time past. And also to make a sure provision that none evil books shall either be printed bought or sold without just punishment therefore. I think it should be well done that the universities and churches of this realm should be visited by such persons as my Lord Cardinal with the rest of you may be well assured to be worthy and sufficient persons . . . Touching punishment of heretics me thinketh it ought to be done without rashness, not leaving in the meanwhile to do Justice to such as by learning would seem to deceive the simple, and the rest so to be used that the people might well perceive them not to be condemned without just occasion, whereby they shall both understand the truth and beware to do the like. And especially within London I would wish none to be burnt without some of the Council's presence and both there and everywhere good sermons at the same. I verily believe that many benefices should not be in one man's hands but after such sort as every priest might look to his own charge and remain resident there, whereby, they should have but one bond to discharge towards God whereas now they have many, which I take to be the cause that in most parts of the realm there is overmuch want of good preachers and such as should with their doctrine overcome the evil diligence of the abused preachers in the time of the schism; not only by their preaching but also by their good example without which in mine opinion their sermons shall not so much profit as I wish. And like as their good example on their behalf shall undoubtedly do much good, I account myself bound on my behalf also to show some example in encouraging and maintaining those persons well doing their duty (not forgetting in the meanwhile to correct and punish them which do contrary) that it may be evident to all this Realm how I discharge my conscience therein and minister true justice in so doing.

BL HARLEIAN MS 444, F. 27; COTTON MS, TITUS C VIII, F. 120

Supreme Governor of the Church

Elizabeth I had seen religious persecution of Catholics under her brother, and burning of Protestants during her sister's reign. She was determined to keep a middle way between destructive extremes. Her people could believe what they wished, she demanded no window on their souls, but she insisted on social behaviour that would not promote fanatical reaction. Here she writes to the bishops, stressing her responsibilities as Supreme Governor of the Church, and pointing out her own unique responsibilities for the post.

1584

One matter touches me so near as I may not overskip. Religion is the ground on which all other matters ought to take root, and being corrupted may mar all the tree; and that there be some fault finders with the order of the clergy, which so may make a slander to myself and the Church whose overruler God hath made me, whose negligence cannot be excused if any schisms or errors heretical were suffered.

Thus much I must say that some faults and negligence may grow, as in all other great charges it happeneth; and what vocation without? All which if you, my Lords of the clergy, do not amend, I mean to depose you. Look ye therefore well to your charges.

I am supposed to have many studies but most philosophical. I must yield this to be true, that I suppose few that be no professors have read more. And I need not tell you that I am so simple that I understand not, nor so forgetful that I remember not. And yet amidst so many volumes I hope God's book hath not been my seldomest lectures; in which we find that which by reason, for my part, we ought to believe, that seeing so great wickedness and griefs in the world in which we live but as wayfaring pilgrims, we must suppose that God would never have made us but for a better place and of more comfort than we find here. I know no creature that breatheth whose life standeth hourly in more peril for it than mine own; who entered not into my state without sight of manifold dangers of life and crown, as one that had the mightiest and the greatest to wrestle with. Then it followeth that I regarded it so much as I left myself behind my care. And so you see that you wrong me too much if any such there be as doubt my coldness in that behalf. For if I were not persuaded that mine were the true way of God's will, God forbid I should live to prescribe it to you. Take you heed lest *Ecclesiastes* say not too true; they that fear the hoary frost the snow shall fall upon them.

ED. G. HARRISON, *LETTERS OF QUEEN ELIZABETH I, 1558–1570* (1935)

Elizabeth I's Defence of the Realm

Elizabeth I also gave forceful orders when war threatened. In this first letter she orders Essex back to London, which he had left without her permission, just after the storm's destruction of the Spanish Armada in 1588.

Essex,
Your sudden and undutiful departure from our presence and your place of attendance, you may easily conceive how offensive it is, and ought to be, unto us. Our great favours, bestowed on you without deserts, hath drawn you thus to neglect and forget your duty; for other constructions we cannot make of those your strange actions. Not meaning therefore to tolerate this your disordered part, we give directions to some of our Privy Council to let you know our express pleasure for your immediate repair hither; which you have not performed, as your duty doth bind you, increasing greatly thereby your former offence and undutiful behaviour, in departing in such sort without our privity, having so special office of attendance and

charge near our person. We do therefore charge and command you forth-
with, upon receipt of these our letters, all excuses and delays set apart, to
make your present and immediate repair unto us to understand our further pleasure. Whereof see you fail not, as you will be loth to incur our
indignation, and will answer for the contrary at your uttermost peril.

MARIA PERRY, *THE WORD OF A PRINCE: A LIFE OF ELIZABETH I* (1990)

*The queen decided that Parliament's desire to declare war on Spain was
unnecessarily aggressive – and too expensive. She preferred Drake's plan
of hit-and-run attacks on what remained of the Spanish fleet. Sir Roger
Williams set sail, with her beloved Essex, to attack and plunder before her
order was received. Her angry letter demands the death of the disobedient
Sir Roger.*

1589

Although we doubt not but of yourselves you have so thoroughly weighed
the heinousness of the offence lately committed by Sir Roger Williams,
that you have both discharged him from the place and charge which was
appointed him in that army and committed the same to some other meet
person, yet you should also know from ourself by these our special letters
our just wrath and indignation against him and lay before you his intolerable contempt against ourself and the authority you have from us in that
he forsook the army and conveyed also one of our principal ships from
the rest of the fleet. His offence is in so high degree that the same
diserveth by all laws to be punished by *death*, which if you have not
already done then we will and command you sequester him from all
charge and service. Therefore consider well of your doings herein.

MARIA PERRY (1990)

A Sense of Responsibility

*Maria Theresa, wife of Emperor Joseph of Austria and the mother of
Marie Antoinette, writes to her sister, in October 1744, about her
attempts to persuade her husband not to go to war, she was twenty-seven;
Franz Joseph was thirty-six. In the end she got her way.*

I was sick with anger and pain, and I made *mon vieux* [her husband] ill
with my wickedness. I fell back on our usual refuge, caresses and tears;

259

but they did not work, although he is the best husband in the world. . . . In the end I got into another temper, to such effect that now we are both ill. I can't move him at all, and at the same time I have to confess to myself that his reasons are plausible enough. All the same, if he really goes off I shall either follow him or shut myself up in a convent.

E. CRANKSHAW, *MARIA THERESA* (1969)

She also drew up a programme for her daily life. Though young, she took her duties and responsibilities seriously.

. . . The Queen must learn to economise her time; method was half the battle. She must allow time for dressing properly, for eating properly and for retreat; only thus could she keep her end up and the world at bay. Very well then, assuming that she got up at eight o'clock she was to give herself an hour for dressing, breakfast and hearing Mass. After Mass, half an hour with her children. Then, from 9.30 to 12.30 it would be solid work; documents to read and initial, ministers to confer with, audiences to take. At 12.30 she was to stop everything, to relax before the midday meal at 12.45. Above all she must be punctual at meals, and she must eat her food before it got cold – and drink up her after-dinner coffee before *that* got cold. After the meal an hour for herself, her children.

E. CRANKSHAW (1969)

A Frenchwoman Works for Fraternity

In this open letter Flora Tristan persuades English workers to fight to improve their rights, towards the end of the Chartist movement.

Be sure of this, that your freedom and progress depend entirely on spreading throughout your ranks a thorough knowledge of every law and institution which either harms or benefits the workers' interests.

History shows us that urban and rural workers have been slaves for thousands of years. Their servitude might have endured for ever had not the advent of printing brought books within their reach. Reading has spread slowly among the working classes, but greater freedom has always followed in its wake. When people could read the Bible and the Gospels, they rejected the domination of Rome and the priests; when they had newspapers to instruct them in the *rights of man*, they demanded that their rulers should be accountable for their actions, that public office should be open to all, and that all (or at least all males) should have equal civil and political rights. I will acquaint you with the callous egotism, revolting hypocrisy and monstrous excesses of the powerful Engligh oligarchy and its unpardonable crimes against the people. I will prepare you for the inevitable and terrible struggle between the proletariat and the aristocracy, and help you to judge whether the English people are destined to throw off the yoke and rise again, or whether this great nation must remain forever divided between a cruel and corrupt aristocracy on the one hand and a wretched and degraded people on the other.

Through the English example you will see how precarious is the existence of a people whose civil liberties are not guaranteed by political rights and social institutions, established *in the equal interests of all*. You will see how important it is for you to obtain these two guarantees and fit yourselves through education to make proper use of them.

Workers, if you would persevere in the study and investigation of these evils and reflect on them calmly, you will need to steel your hearts and summon up all your courage, for you will uncover wounds too deep to heal.

I clasp your hands in mine, all you men and women who up to this day have *counted for nothing* in the world. I join with you in the common task, I live in you through love,

I am your sister *in humanity*,

Flora Tristan, 1842
TRANS. J. HAWKES, *THE LONDON JOURNAL OF FLORA TRISTAN* (1982)

Fanny Burney meets Dr Johnson

Fanny Burney (1752–1840) met many intellectuals of her time at her father's house, since Dr Burney was a celebrated and hospitable musicologist. Though young when she met the redoubtable Dr Johnson, she penned this unimpressed portrait, addressed to a friend of her father, nicknamed 'Daddy', Samuel Crisp. He advised her 'that trifling, negligence, even incorrectness, now & then in familiar epistolary writing, is the very soul of genius and ease'.

28 March 1777

My Dear Daddy
My dear father seemed well pleased at my returning to my time; and that is no small consolation and pleasure to me. So, to our Thursday morning

party: Mrs and Miss Thrale, Miss Owen came, Mrs Thrale a very pretty woman still; she is extremely lively and chatty, has no supercilious or pedantic airs. Miss Owen, a relation, is good-humoured and sensible, a sort of butt, prodigiously useful in drawing out the wit and pleasantry of others.

My sister Burney was invited to meet and play to them, and in the midst of the performance Dr Johnson was announced. He is *terribly* ill-favoured; is tall and stout; but stoops terribly; he is almost bent double. His body is in continual agitation, see-sawing up and down; his feet are never a moment still; and in short his whole person is in perpetual motion. His dress too, considering the times, and that he had meant to put on his 'best becomes', being engaged to dine in a large company, was as much out of the common road as his figure; he had a large wig, snuff-coloured coat and gold buttons, but no ruffles to his shirt. He is shockingly near-sighted, and did not, till she held out her hand to him, even know Mrs Thrale (whom he loved). He poked his nose over the keys of the harpsichord, then my father introduced him to (sister) Hetty, as an old acquaintance and he kissed her!

His attention, however, was not to be diverted five minutes from the books, as we were in the library; he pored over them, almost touching their backs with his eyelashes, as he read their titles. At last, having fixed on one, he began, without further ceremony, to read, all the time standing at a distance from the company. I question if he even heard the duet.

Chocolate being then brought, we adjourned to the dining-room. And here, Dr Johnson being taken from the books, entered freely and most cleverly into conversation; though it is remarkable that he never speaks at all, but when spoken to; nor does he ever *start*, though he admirably *supports* any topic.

ED. A. DOBSON, *THE DIARY AND LETTERS OF MME D'ARBLAY* (1904)

Queen Victoria and her Government

Queen Victoria treated her uncle Leopold, King of the Belgians, as adviser, confidant and substitute father. In her inimitable childlike discourse she describes a government crisis. As Head of State she took her work of attending to parliamentary matters seriously.

Buckingham Palace, 18th June 1844

My Dearest Uncle, – . . . I can write to you with a light heart, thank goodness, to day, for the Government obtained a majority, which *up* to the *last* moment last night we feared they would not have, and we have been in sad trouble for the last four or five days about it. It is the more marvellous, as, if the Government asked for a *Vote* of Confidence, they would have a *Majority* of 100; but this very strength makes the supporters of the Government act in a *most* unjustifiable manner by continually acting and voting against them, *not* listening to the debates, but coming down and voting against the Government. So that we were generally in the greatest *possible* danger of having a resignation of the Government *without knowing to whom to turn*, and this from the recklessness of a handful of foolish *half* 'Puseyite' half 'Young England' people! I am sure you will agree with me that Peel's resignation would not only be for us (for *we cannot* have a better and a *safer* Minister), but for the whole country, and for the peace of Europe – a *great calamity*. Our present people are all *safe*, and not led away by impulses and reckless passions. We must, however, take care and not get into another crisis; for I assure you we have been quite miserable and *quite* alarmed ever since Saturday.

Since I last wrote to you, I spoke to Aberdeen (whom I should be equally sorry to lose, as he is *so very fair*, and has served *us personally*, so kindly and truly), and he told me that the Emperor has *positively pledged* himself to send a Minister to Brussels the moment those Poles are no longer employed; that he is quite aware of the importance of the measure, and would be disposed to make the arrangement easy, and that he spoke very kindly of *you* personally. Aberdeen says it is not necessary to disgrace them in any way, but only for the present *de les éloigner*. The Emperor has evidently some time ago made some strong declaration on the subject which he feels he cannot get over, and, as I said before, he will not give up what he has once pledged his word to. *Then, no one* on earth *can* move him. *Au fond*, it is a fine *trait*, but he carries it too far. He wrote me a *very* kind and affectionate letter from the Hague.

ED. J. RAYMOND, *QUEEN VICTORIA'S EARLY LETTERS* (1963)

She wrote to politicians in slightly less personal discourse.

To Sir Robert Peel

Pavilion, 18th February 1845

The Queen has received Sir Robert Peel's letter, and is glad that the progress in the House of Commons was so satisfactory.

The Queen was much hurt at Mr Borthwick's most impertinent manner of putting the question with respect to the title of King Consort, and much satisfied with Sir Robert's answer. The title of King is open assuredly to many difficulties, and would perhaps be no *real* advantage to the Prince, but the Queen is positive that something must at once be done to place the Prince's position on a constitutionally recognised footing, and to give him a title adequate to that position. *How* and *when*, are difficult questions. . . .

ED. A.C. BENSON, LETTERS OF QUEEN VICTORIA (1907)

To the King of the Belgians

Windsor Castle, 25th March 1845

. . . I copied what you wrote me about Peel in a letter I wrote him, which I am sure will please him much, and a Minister in these days *does* require a little encouragement, for the abuse and difficulties they have to contend with are dreadful. Peel works so hard and has so much to do, that sometimes he says he does not know *how* he is to get through it all!

You will, I am sure, be pleased to hear that we have succeeded in purchasing *Osborne* in the Isle of Wight, and if we can manage it, we shall probably run down there before we return to Town, for three nights. It sounds so snug and nice to have a place of *one's own*, quiet and retired, and free from all Woods and Forests, and other charming Departments who really are the plague of one's life.

Now, dearest Uncle, adieu. Ever your truly devoted Niece,

Victoria R.

ED. A.C. BENSON (1907)

Women Workers Petition for Better Treatment

These two letters are from groups of women workers seeking improved conditions, the first written during the Revolution of 1848, the second during the American Civil War. Both groups are composed of mothers attempting to support their children; their efforts have been undermined by employers undercutting their already meagre wages. Their language in both cases is forceful, their bravery notable in signing their names and addresses.

Parisian garment workers   August 1848

Gentlemen:

Please consider the request of some poor working women. The convents and the prisons take all our work away from us; they do it for such a low price that we can't compete with them. Almost all of us are mothers of families. We have our keep, our nourishment and our lodgings to pay for and we are not able to make enough to cover these expenses. The employers also wrong us by sending their garment-making orders out of Paris; thus we can find no work and are nearly reduced to begging. Therefore, gentlemen, we urge you to put an end to these injustices. All we want is work.

We hope, Gentlemen, that you will be good enough to consider our request. We salute you with respect.

[Signed by seven women, with their addresses]

EDS. E.O. HELLERSTEIN *ET AL*, *VICTORIAN WOMEN* (1981)

Philadelphia seamstresses   July 1862

We the undersigned formerly doing sewing for the United States Arsenal at Philadelphia most respectfully remonstrate against the action of Col. Crossman in taking the work from us and giving it to contractors who will not pay wages on which we can live – many of us have husbands, fathers, sons & brothers now in the army and from whom we derived our support. Deprived of that as we are our only mode of living was by sewing and we were able by unceasing exertions to barely live at the prices paid by the Arsenal. The Contractors who are speculators offer about fifty per cent of the prices paid heretofore by the arsenal – we respectfully ask your attention to our case. We have all given satisfaction in the work we have done. Then why should the government money be taken from the families of the poor to enrich the wealthy speculator without any gain to the government.

Very Resp^y Yours &c

Anna Long Widow 5 children 121 Mois St.

Louisa Bastian 124 Mirris St.

Mary Hamelton 1673 Front St. Husband at war

[Some 100 signatures followed these – many with the indication that the women were widows with children or had husbands or sons in the army.]

EDS. E.O. HELLERSTEIN *ET AL* (1981)

Work of Men – and Advice on it

George Sand, the novelist, writes to Edmond Planchot, a youngish admirer of her work. He was an enthusiastic botanist.

Nohant, 11 April 1857

I envy your youth and wonderful journeys interwoven, no doubt, with dangers, sufferings and disasters, which are so grandly compensated for, by the vast spectacles of nature and the riches of all Creation. I expect that you take a great many notes and that you keep a journal which will help you to give a full account of your travels.

These vast excursions, however we may look upon them (and the best thing to do is to look at them from all quarters at once) always hold a powerful interest and you will find many resources of your future in them. Take an interest in natural history; even if you are not very well up in it, your collections and observations would have their own usefulness. Please bring me back some butterflies and insects; the humblest and most paltry would mean riches to me; and as I know some collectors, I could introduce you to some interesting people when you come back.

The best way of bringing back butterflies and insects is to put off setting them up. When the butterfly has been killed and has a long pin through its body its wings close up and it dries in that position. One can thus bring back a number, set side by side in a small box, and if they are securely packed and are not touching each other there is no risk of damage. On arrival they can be softened, opened and spread out by very simple processes, which I will undertake. You must stick a little piece of camphor at each end of your box. You can also bring back chrysalises of butterflies and insects in bran. A good number of them die or fail to hatch out on the journey, but there are always a few which can be hatched out here by artificial heat and produce superb specimens.

But I am far more bent on news of you, than butterflies, and if I can be useful to you in any way whatsoever, please remember me.

Adieu monsieur. My best wishes go with you, and I pray God that they may still bring you good luck.

Yours sincerely,

George Sand

G. SAND, *LETTRES D'UN VOYAGEUR* (1987)

'The Maiden Warrior' in full flow

In March 1912 as, under her leadership, the tactics of the WSPU (Women's Social and Political Union) entered a more militant phase (window-smashing, setting fire to or bombing churches, piers, pavilions, letter boxes etc.) Christabel, the eldest of Emmeline Pankhurst's three daughters, fled to Paris to avoid arrest. From there, with the help of couriers who took her orders and inflammatory Suffragette *copy back to London, she continued – some thought with a reckless disregard for political realities and for the prison/forcible feeding ordeals of her dwindling band of hardcore devotees – to direct the Votes for Women campaign. Several would-be male supporters travelled to Paris to urge her to follow her sister Sylvia's example in making a close alliance with the militant Labour movement and its newspaper the* Daily Herald. *She was not to be moved, and in August 1913 one of these envoys, Henry Harben, a wealthy Liberal turned socialist, was warned off in two remarkable letters which show 'the Maiden Warrior' in full radical feminist flow:*

My view of the situation is this. The *Daily Herald* can help us if it will be attacking the Government: firstly on account of the refusal to give votes to women, and secondly on account of the policy of coercion. Between the WSPU and the Daily Herald League and Movement there can be no connection. Ours is a Woman's Movement and the Herald League is primarily a Man's Movement or at any rate a mixed Movement. . . . The great need of the time is for women to learn to stand and act alone. . . . No men, even the best of men, ever view the Suffrage question from quite the same standpoint as women. You speak of the Herald Movement and the WSPU as being akin . . . but there are great psychological differences. . . . The women's rebellion has been in preparation for centuries. It is expressing something deeper and bigger than anything expressed by present-day unrest among men. Women are beginning to realise that they must grow their own backbone before they can be any use to themselves or to humanity as a whole. It is helpful and *it is good for men themselves* when they try to promote women's emancipation; but they have to do it from the outside, and the really important thing is that women are working out their own salvation . . . and are able to do it, even if not a living man takes any part in bringing it about.

Another fundamental difference, is that the Herald League tends to be a Class Movement. Ours is not a Class Movement at all. We take in everybody – the highest and the lowest, the richest and the poorest. The bond is Womanhood! If women, with their greater altruism, had had their due influence from the beginning they might have been able to prevent the existence of abuses which men socialists are now trying to get rid of. [Though she fully agreed that the Parliamentary Labour Party had been a miserable failure, she was not at all sure that workers' control was the answer to the nation's ills.] If it turned out that Britain could only be governed by riot and violence I am game for that sort of thing. But I mean to have a try at the other thing first – when the vote is won! Not that we value it only or chiefly for its political value. We want it far more for its symbolic value – the recognition of our human equality that it will make. This may sound very old-fashioned and nineteenth century, but women have a lot of leeway to make up. When we have done that, then we will help the men to solve the problems of the twentieth century. Plainly they can't settle them without us. But for the time being it comes to this. The men must paddle their canoe and we must paddle ours.

ED. DAVID MITCHELL, *QUEEN CHRISTABEL: A BIOGRAPHY OF CHRISTABEL PANKHURST* (1977) (The originals can be found in the Harben-Tuke papers, British Library Dept. of Manuscripts, Add MSS 58226)

Arabic Ceremony

Freya Stark reveals a gentler vein of female humour, analysing the politics of Arabic manners, in this letter to Venetia Buddicom written on her first visit to the Middle East.

Brumana
4 January 1928

Dearest Venetia,

I have just been taking a rest from perpetual Arabic, looking into Graves' book on Lawrence. Save us from our friends! I begin to feel the man almost unbearable. This attitude of continually saying 'I would like to be modest if only I could' is ridiculous and probably not at all true to the poor man. If only I can get to Baghdad, I have a letter to Mr Woolley who worked with him on the Euphrates and should be full of interesting information. I see with pleasure that it took four years in the country to teach him Arabic: it makes me feel less painfully stupid. I now begin to follow the drift of conversations and to attempt ambitious subjects like Doughty's Arabian travels in my efforts with Miss Audi at lunch. There is plenty of practice: every afternoon we pay a lengthy call (about two hours) and sit on a divan talking gossip interspersed with one of the sixteen formulas of politeness which I have collected so far. After a while a large tray is brought in with all sorts of delicious sweetmeats, wine, tea; we take a little of each – (fearfully bad for my inside) – and say 'May this continue' as we put down the cup; and the hosts say 'May your life also continue', and then we leave. I believe there is no feeling of class in this country at all: you are divided by religions, and as you see nothing practically of any religion but your own, you never have the unpleasant feeling of being surrounded by people who are hostile and yet bound to mix up their lives with yours.

I am very popular here – the one and only person who has ever come to learn Arabic *for pleasure*.

Your loving

Freya

EDS. C. AND L. MOOREHEAD, *THE LETTERS OF FREYA STARK* (1974–82)

Anaïs Nïn advises a Homosexual Friend

In this letter, Anaïs Nin argues for honesty in wartime at the beginning of the Second World War.

To Robert   1939

You refuse to free yourself from serving in the Army by declaring your homosexuality. And by this you will live a double lie, for you are also against war. At the same time you feel burdened with guilt. Our only prison is that of guilt. Guilt is the negative aspect of religion. We lost our religion but we kept the guilt. We all have guilt. Even Henry [Miller, the novelist] has it, who seems the freest of all. Only domestic animals have guilt. We train them so. Animals in the jungle do not have it.

Everything negative should die. Jealousy as the negative form of love, fear the negative form of life.

You speak of suffering, of withdrawal, retreat. Face this suffering, for all the real suffering can save us from unreality. Real pain is human and deepening. Without real pain you will remain the child forever. The legend of Ondine tells of how she acquired a human soul the day she wept over a human love. You were caught in a web of unreality. You choose suffering in order to be awakened from your dreams, as I did. You are no longer the sleeping prince of neurosis. Don't run away from it now. If you run away from it without conquering it (I say accept the homosexuality, live it out proudly, declare it), then you will remain asleep and enchanted in a lifeless neurosis.

ANAÏS NIN, *JOURNALS* (1970)

A Mother and a Communist

La Pasionaria, who fought in the Spanish Civil War, links the personal and the political in this letter written a few weeks after the death of her son, Ruben, to the young workers at Krasnoiarsk, who had named their brigade after him.

Dear Friends and Comrades: September 1942
As both a mother and a communist, I was moved when I was told that a Brigade which has named itself after my son is working on the construction of the great Krasnoiarsk Hydroelectric Power Station. It's difficult to convey what this means to me. My son Ruben is still alive in your dreams, in your hopes and in your heroic work, the construction of the biggest Hydroelectric power station in the Soviet Union!

Even as a child in Spain he was used to hard work and struggle. He always helped us in the difficult life of a worker's family. He distributed banned Party literature and newspapers with us. He took part in demonstrations where workers were attacked more than once! When I was arrested, the leaders of our Party decided to send my two sons to Russia, to let me devote myself to the revolutionary activities of our Party, in the tough living conditions we were facing in Spain, without having the constant worry of leaving them to fend for themselves.

In the Soviet Union, Ruben worked in the Lijachov factory and during the Spanish war he returned to fight alongside his countrymen in the ranks of the People's Army.

When the Spanish Republic was defeated, he was interned by the French government, like thousands of other Republican soldiers, in a French concentration camp – which he was allowed to leave to go back to the Soviet Union, his second homeland. He attended the Military Academy, and joined the Soviet Army to go on to fight from the very first day against the Nazi aggressors. He was gravely wounded while defending

Bielorusia, and was awarded the Order of the Red Flag for bravery. His wounds had not fully healed when he took up arms again, to be killed heroically in the defence of Stalingrad. He was given the title of Hero of the Soviet Union.

Please forgive this short biography of my Ruben, as brief as his life; he was 22 years old. But I wanted to write, so that the friends and comrades who named their Brigade after him should know that Ruben wasn't a rich man's son, but a worker like you and a young communist who fought in Spain and sacrificed his life in defence of the Soviet Union.

Dolores

TRANS. O. KENYON, PRIVATE COLLECTION

The Epistolary Novel

The epistolary novel is composed entirely of letters. It grew out of women's need for creativity, out of their shaping of their experience in correspondence. Letters deal with significant incidents, with problems and possible resolutions, with responses and conflicts between personalities in ways that link them with the pattern-making and character analysis of fiction. Epistolary novels are among the first examples of the novel, the 'new' form.

Histories of literature generally state that Defoe and Richardson were the creators of the English novel, but over a century before them, two women, Aphra Behn and the Duchess of Newcastle, first realized the potential of unifying epistles with a semblance of narrative. In *Sociable Letters* (1664) Margaret Cavendish, Duchess of Newcastle, offered a moral guide, often sought in letters by daughters 'who are but branches which by marriage are broken off from the root'. Behn, the first professional woman playwright, was also a skilful poet. Her *Love Letters Between a Nobleman and his Sister* was probably published as early as 1683. Based on a real scandal, the novel reflects a desire for news reports and contemporary sexual scandal in the traditional discourse of woman as victim of passion.

To Philander.

After I had dismissed my page this morning with my letter, I walked (filled with sad soft thoughts of my brother *Philander*) into the grove, and commanding *Melinda* to retire, who only attended me, I threw myself down on that bank of grass where we last disputed the dear, but fatal business of our souls: where our prints (that invited me) still remain on the pressed greens: there with ten thousand sighs, with remembrance of the tender minutes we passed then, I drew your last letter from my bosom, and often kissed, and often read it over; but oh! who can conceive my torment when I come to that fatal part of it, where you say you gave your hand to my sister? I found my soul agitated with a thousand different passions, but all insupportable, all mad and raving; sometimes I threw myself with fury on the ground, and pressed my panting heart to the earth; then rise in rage, and tear my heart, and hardly spare that face that taught you first to love; then fold my wretched arms to keep down rising sighs that almost rend my breast, I traverse swiftly the conscious grove; with my distracted show'ring eyes directed in vain to pitiless heaven, the lovely silent shade favouring my complaints, I cry aloud, Oh God! *Philander's* married, the lovely charming thing for whom I languish is married! – That fatal word's enough, I need not add to whom. Married is enough to make me curse my birth, my youth, my beauty, and my eyes that first betrayed me to the undoing object: curse on the charms you have flattered, for every fancied grace has helped my ruin on; now, like flowers that wither unseen and unpossessed in shades, they must die and be no more, they were to no end created, since *Philander* is married: married! Oh fate, oh hell, oh torture and confusion! Tell me not it is to my sister, that addition is needless and vain: to make me eternally wretched, there needs no more than that *Philander* is married! Than that the priest gave your hand away from me; to another, and not to me; tired out with life, I need no other pass-port than this repetition, *Philander* is married! 'Tis that alone is sufficient to lay in her cold tomb

The wretched and despairing
Sylvia

Wednesday night,
Bellfont.

To Sylvia
Twice last night, oh unfaithful and unloving *Sylvia*! I sent the page to the old place for letters, but he returned the object of my rage, because without the least remembrance from my fickle maid: in this torment, unable to hide my disorder, I suffered myself to be laid in bed; where the restless torments of the night exceeded those of the day, and are not even by the languisher himself to be expressed; but the returning light brought a short slumber on its wings; which was interrupted by my atoning boy, who brought two letters from my adorable *Sylvia*: he waked me from dreams more agreeable than all my watchful hours could bring; for they are all tortured. —— And even the softest mixed with a thousand despairs, difficulties and disappointments, but these were all love, which gave a loose to joys

undenied by honour! And this way, my charming *Sylvia*, you shall be mine, in spite of all the tyrannies of that cruel hinderer; honour appears not, my *Sylvia*, within the close-drawn curtains; in shades and gloomy light the phantom frights not, but when one beholds its blushes, when it is attended and adorned, and the sun sees its false beauties; in silent groves and grottoes, dark alcoves, and lonely recesses, all its formalities are laid aside; it was then and there methought my *Sylvia* yielded, with a faint struggle and a soft resistance; I heard her broken sighs, her tender whispering voice, that trembling cried, – Oh! Can you be so cruel? – Have you the heart – will you undo a maid because she loves you? Oh!

Letters had the advantage of male acceptance, flexibility, and popularity. They could also incorporate travel reports, enabling the heroine to widen her narrative with tales of adventure in distant countries.

As Dale Spender has shown, in *Mothers of the Novel: 100 Good Women Writers Before Jane Austen*, there were a fair number of women publishing successfully in the eighteenth century. It was Eliza Haywood who established the popularity of the epistolary novel, writing seventeen. She extended the structure while putting the heroine through a moral test. Her works can be seen as a document of the development of the genre, from *Love in Excess* to *The History of Miss Betsy Thoughtless* (1751). This latter novel was much admired by Fanny Burney, who said it inspired her delightful *Evelina* (1776). *Evelina*, a still under-rated work, exploits the supposed veracity of letters, with a girl's fresh reactions to London society, while exploring women's position in that culture.

Letters were acceptable in a protestant culture which advocated introspection and conscience-searching. Elizabeth S. Rowe was one of the authors whose work succeeded in being both religious and easy to read. Her *Letters Moral and Entertaining* (1729) is fiction based on sermons to young ladies; it was often recommended for their moral education. It is a worthy precursor of Samuel Richardson's *Pamela*. In 1773 the *Monthly Review* stated that fiction was almost entirely the domain of women. By then the novel was not only commenting on morals and offering guides to manners, but also offered entertainment to an increasing readership. The

Austen family were 'great novel readers and not ashamed of being so'. Indeed, Jane Austen's first experiments with novel-writing, as a young adolescent, were epistolary: a charming, brief four-page novelette of letters from a young man who sees a pretty girl, asks for her hand in marriage, and gets it.

The nineteenth century gave enforced leisure to middle-class women, who enjoyed longer novels, to read to the family, or on their own. Only a few writers continued with the epistolary form, among them the Irish Lady Morgan (1776–1859), daughter of Owenson, an impoverished actor. To help feed the family she began writing when young. As her *Poems by a Young Lady Between the Ages of 12 & 14* did not sell well she turned to the novel, gaining a reputation as a regional novelist with *The Wild Irish Girl: A National Tale* (1806). Like George Eliot she used the novel to present social issues, though her passionate defence of the Irish cause led to ostracism by some English aristocrats. She may be an inspiration for Thackeray's *Vanity Fair*. She was the first woman to be granted a literary pension – of £300 a year.

In the late twentieth century, after decades of neglect, we find four experimental novelists turning to epistles. Fay Weldon in *Letters to Alice on Reading Jane Austen* (1983) continues the potential to offer advice (see p. 29); Gillian Hanscombe's *Between Friends* (1983) stresses the power of female directness (see p. 30); Alice Walker in *The Color Purple* (1983) demonstrates the vigour of black women's discourse by comparing the letters of two sisters; and Lee Smith, an oral historian, in *Fair and Tender Ladies* (1989) displays the strengths of hitherto despised working-class discourse, its directness, ability to analyse, and dramatize. Women's letter-writing has shaped and re-envisioned female experience – and language.

Extracts from twentieth-century epistolary novels may be found in chapters one, two, four and six.

Select Biographies

Kate Amberley (1842–74) was the mother of Bertrand Russell. She died when he was only two, after a love match with his father, Lord Amberley. Their letter was published by their son.

Emilia Pardo Bazán (1851–1923) was a Spanish novelist of outstanding 'realist' works and feminist sympathies, a friend of Galdós.

Isabella Bird (1831–1904) was a frail child who suffered from back pain all her life. Yet she rejected conventional life to travel to some of the furthest countries. On foot, horseback, yak, even elephant, she visited Japan, Korea, Kurdistan, Persia and the Rocky Mountains. She became the first woman elected to the Royal Geographical Society.

Rosalía de Castro (1837–85) was a fine poet who lived and worked in Galicia, in the north of Spain. She cared so much about this poverty-stricken area that she preferred it to fame in Madrid.

Alexandra David-Néel (1868–1969) was born in Paris. After studying eastern religions, with a particular interest in Buddhism, she worked for a time as a journalist, and then toured the Middle East and North Africa as an opera singer. In 1904 she married a distant cousin, Philippe Neel, but they separated. The Dalai Lama was in exile in Darjeeling in 1911 when Alexandra David-Néel became the first Western woman to interview him. Her meeting with him inspired her to concentrate on Tibetan Buddhism in her studies. Illegally entering Tibet in 1914, she spent time in a monastery, lived as a hermit in a cave, and became a Lama herself. In 1923, disguised as a Tibetan beggar on pilgrimage with her adopted son, Alexandra David-Néel became the first Western woman to enter the 'Forbidden City' of Lhasa, where she remained for two months before her identity was discovered. Her last Asian journey ended in 1944, but she went on to write many books about her travels and about Buddhism.

Lucie Duff Gordon (1821–69) was the only child of a privileged intellectual couple. At eighteen she fell in love with Sir Alexander Duff Gordon, a civil servant. They knew many writers, including Charles Dickens, Caroline Norton, Meredith and Tennyson. The couple had three children. In the 1850s when Lucie began to suffer from tuberculosis, the doctor advised her to go to South Africa, where she wrote *Letters from the Cape* (1864). Then she went to Upper Egypt for seven years, a longer stay than any other European, subsequently publishing *Letters from Egypt* (1865) which was reprinted three times in the first year. She died in Cairo in 1869.

Elizabeth Elstob (1683–1756) is one of the best known governesses, as she wrote the first 'English Saxon Grammar'. Though brought up by a narrow-minded uncle, she was fortunate with her aunt, who taught her languages. She worked in a village school, and for the Duchess of Portland.

Mary Hays (1760–1843) was born to a Dissenting family, which sympathized with the ideals of the Enlightment and the French Revolution. Her fiancé died before their wedding, and she devoted her time to remarkable writing about the wrongs suffered by women.

Hildegard of Bingen (1098–1179) was born in a German province bordering the Rhine, where her family owned estates. She was their tenth child, offered to the local Benedictine monastery as a gift at the age of eight. She lived immured with an anchoress till she was fifteen, learning the liturgy, and to pray in Latin. From childhood she experienced frequent religious visions, and felt called to preach, and she later became well known both for her visions and her spiritual advice. Her writings include three visionary books: *Know the Ways* (1141–51), *The Book of Life's Merits* a moral treatise (1158–63); and her most mature work, *The Book of Divine Works*. She also wrote a book on *Medicine* based on her knowledge of healing herbs, and analysis of the four elements, and was an outstanding composer of plainsong.

La Pasionaria (1895–1980) was born Dolores Ibarruri, in an impoverished district of the Basque country. She and her worker husband joined the communist party when they were young. At the time Spain suffered from oligarchic governments and unjust distribution of wealth. The Basques were particularly discriminated against by the right-wing government of 1934. When Franco led the uprising of soldiers from Africa in 1936, which caused the Civil War, Dolores held meetings all over Spain to persuade workers to support the Republic. Her oratory gained her the name of 'La Pasionaria', passionate.

Lady Honor Lisle (?–1563) was married to Lord Lisle, illegitimate son of Edward IV. He was her second husband, and she hoped to produce a Plantagenet heir. She was disappointed in this, but enlarged her ample estates in Devon, and ensured the worldly success of the children by her first marriage to Basset. Her husband was appointed Lord Deputy of Calais, where she accompanied him. Their correspondence with England, which spans the years 1533 to 1540, gives an unusual insight into the way such a family lived.

Caroline Norton (1808–77), writer, was a granddaughter of the playwright Richard Brinsley Sheridan. In 1827 she married George Norton, a barrister and Member of Parliament. She had an unhappy and violent marriage, was forcibly separated from her children, and devoted years to fight for Parliament to allow divorce.

Margaret Paston (c. 1420–84) inherited property from her father John Mautby of Caister. She had an arranged marriage with John Paston whose father made money by studying law and buying up property near the small Norfolk village of Paston, where he was born. John worked in London, an absence which has provided us with one of the most fascinating collections of letters to survive the Wars of the Roses. They include details about the daily life and requirements of a large estate, and give us unique knowledge of the duties and skills of a lady of the manor, in peacetime, and under siege.

Christine de Pisan (c. 1364–c. 1430), was born in Venice. She was the daughter of an Italian physician in the service of Charles V, and brought up in Paris. She was left a widow at twenty-five with three small children and an elderly mother to support. She became the first professional woman writer. Her prose works include *La Cité des dames* and *Le Livre des Trois Vertus* (a treatise on women's education). In her *Epître au dieu* *d'amour* (1399) and *Dit de la Rose* (1400) she ardently took up the defence of her sex against the strictures of Jean de Meung. Her poetry comprised *ballades* and longer poems on themes of love.

Madame de Sévigné (1626–96) was born in Paris and married at eighteen to the Marquis de Sévigné, who left her a widow at twenty-five. She lived near the brilliant court of Louis XIV at Versailles, hearing of the changes and scandals first hand. These she recounted with unusual vivacity and humour, mainly for her beloved daughter. She was a friend of the writers Madame de la Fayette and La Rochefoucauld, and went to the plays of Corneille, Molière and Racine. Her letters provide an invaluable chronicle of forty years of the French monarchy.

Charlotte Smith (1749–1806) was a prolific novelist, and a poet of considerable skill. She was forced to support her large family when her husband was imprisoned for debt, and she produced fairly popular 'Gothick' novels; the best known is *Emmeline* (1788).

Flora Tristan (1803–44) was a Peruvian Spanish colonel's daughter and her uncle was President of Peru, yet she was brought up in poverty in Paris by her widowed French mother. In 1821 she married her employer, the painter and engraver André Chazel, but left him in 1824, initiating a long battle over custody of their children. From 1825 to 1830 she worked as governess to an English family. In 1830 she went to Peru, in a vain attempt to persuade her uncle to support the family. Eight years later the frank revelations in her autobiography, *Pérégrinations d'une paria*, provoked her husband to attempt murder, for which he was sentenced to twenty-two years' hard labour. On returning to France in 1834 she wrote skilful feminist articles. A great admirer of Mary Wollstonecraft, she was first influenced by the libertarian philosophy of Fourier, and then by the social reformism of Robert Owen, whom she met in 1837. She continued to write, publishing the novel *Mephis* in 1838. During a long visit to England she studied Chartism and made a detailed analysis of social conditions which resulted in her *Promenades dans Londres* (1840). Her travels had crystallized her strong socialist and feminist views and in 1843 she published her *Union ouvrière*, the first proposal for a Socialist International. She died of typhoid in Bordeaux while travelling around France to publicize her ideas.

Nellie Weeton (1776–1844) is one of the few governesses of whom we know detailed experiences, thanks to her letters published in 1936 by E. Day as *Miss Weeton: Journal of a Governess.*

Sources

Place of publication is London unless otherwise stated.

Louisa May Alcott: *Louisa May Alcott: Her Life, Letters and Journals*, ed. E.D. Cheney, Boston, 1889.

Kate Amberley: *The Amberley Papers*, ed. Bertrand Russell, Hogarth Press, 1937.

Jane Austen: *Jane Austen: Letters*, ed. R.W. Chapman, Oxford University Press, Oxford, 1932; New York, 1952.
Jane Austen: Her Life, Honan Park, Weidenfeld, 1987.

Mariama Bâ: *So Long A Letter*, trans. M. Bodé-Thomas, Virago, 1982.

H.E. Back: H. Robinson Papers, A. and E. Schlesinger Library, Radcliffe College, Cambridge, Massachusetts.

Honoré de Balzac: *Lettres de femmes addressées à Honoré de Balzac 1832–6*, Cahiers Balzaciens, pp. 43–4, Paris, 1924.

Jane Bassett: *The Lisle Letters*, ed. M. St Clare Byrne, University of Chicago Press, Chicago, 1983; Penguin, 1985.

Emilia Pardo Bazán: in private collection, trans. O. Kenyon.
For further reading, *Cartas a Benito Pérez Galdós 1889–90*, Madrid, Ediciones Turner, 1975.

Aphra Behn: *Love Letters between a Nobleman and his Sister*, Virago, 1987; first published in three volumes, *c.* 1676–7.
Williamson's State Papers, PRO, SP 29/167.

Gertrude Bell: *The Letters of Gertrude Bell*, selected and edited by Lady Bell, Benn, 1930.

Annie Besant: *An Autobiography*, A. Besant, Philadelphia, 1893.

Isabella Bird: *A Lady's Life in the Rocky Mountains*, I. Bird, Virago, 1982.
The Travels of Isabella Bird, ed. C. Palser Havely, Century Press, 1971.

Barbara Bodichon: 'A Letter from Savannah', in *English Woman's Journal* 8, December 1861, pp. 261–6.

Lucrezia Borgia: in A. Fraser, *Love Letters*, Weidenfeld, 1976.

The Brontë family: *The Brontës: Their Lives, Friendships and Correspondence in Four Volumes*, eds. T.J. Wise and J.A. Symington, Oxford, 1932.
Branwell Brontë, Winifred Gerin, Hutchinson, 1961.
Charlotte Brontë, Winifred Gerin, Oxford University Press, Oxford, 1967.

Fanny Burney: *The Diary and Letters of Mme d'Arblay*, ed. A. Dobson, Macmillan, 1904.
The Journals and Letters of Fanny Burney 1791–1840, ed. J.A. Hemlow, A. Douglas, W. Derry et al, 12 vols, Clarendon Press, Oxford, 1972–4.
Dr Johnson and Fanny Burney, Nigel Wood, Bristol Classical Press, Bristol, 1989.

Isabel Burton: in Lesley Blanch, *The Wilder Shores of Love*, John Murray, 1954. For further information, see books on her husband, Arabist Richard Burton.

Eleanor Butler: see A 'Romantic' Friendship, p. 46

Josephine Butler, Octavia Hill and Florence Nightingale: *Victorian Women who Changed the World*, Nancy Boyd, Macmillan, 1982.

Margery Clarke: in C. Moriarty, ed., *The Voice of the Middle Ages*, Lennard Books, Oxford, 1989.

Hannah Cullwick: *Life and Diaries*, Arthur J. Munby, 1972.

Alexandra David-Néel: *Magic and Mystery in Tibet*, Souvenir Press, 1967. *My Journey to Lhasa*, 1983.

Rosalía de Castro: *Poems of Rolalía de Castro*, ed. and trans. by A. Aldaz, B. Gantt and A. Bromley, State University of New York Press, USA, 1991.

Mary Delany: *Letters from Georgian Ireland*, ed. Angelique Day, Friars Bush Press, Belfast, 1992.

Lucy Duff Gordon: *Letters from Egypt*, L. Duff Gordon, 1865; Virago, 1983.

Emily Eden: *Up The Country: Letters from India*, E. Eden, 1872; Virago, 1983.

Maria Edgeworth: *Letters for Literary Ladies*, M. Edgeworth, 1795.

George Eliot: *George Eliot: A Biography*, Gordon Haight, Oxford University Press, Oxford, 1968.
Selected Letters of George Eliot, ed. Gordon Haight, Oxford University Press, Oxford, 1968.
The George Eliot Letters, ed. Gordon Haight, Yale University Press, Yale, 1954–5.

Elizabeth I: *Original Letters: Illustrative of English History*, H. Ellis, 3 vols., Harding, Triphook and Lepard, 1924. Includes royal letters from Autographs in the British Museum.

An Elizabethan Gentlewoman, R. Weigall, 1911.
Letters of Queen Elizabeth I, 1558–1570, ed. G. Harrison, Greenwood Press, USA, 1935.
The Word of a Prince: A Life of Elizabeth I, Maria Perry, Boydell and Brewer, Woodbridge, Suffolk, 1990.

Elizabeth Elstob: *The English Saxon Homily*, 1709.

Empress Eugénie: *Lettres familières de l'Imperatrice Eugenie, conservées dans les archives du Palais de Liria et publices par les soins du Duc d'Albe*, 1935.

Millicent Fawcett: *Millicent Fawcett*, Ray Strachey, John Murray, 1931.

Ferdinand and Isabella: *Ferdinand and Isabella*, F. Fernández-Arnesto, Weidenfeld, 1975.

Celia Fiennes: *Through England on a Side Saddle in the Time of William and Mary*, C. Fiennes, 1888 (republished as *The Journeys of Celia Fiennes*, ed. Christopher Morris, 1947).

Elizabeth Gaskell: A Portrait in Letters, Manchester University Press, Manchester, 1980.
The Letters of Elizabeth Gaskell, ed. J.A.V. Chapple, Manchester University Press, Manchester, 1967.

Gillian Hanscombe: *Between Friends*, G. Hanscombe, Sheba, 1983.

Mary Hays: *Love Letters of Mary Hays*, ed. A. Wedd, 1925.
Letters and Essays, Moral and Miscellaneous, 1793.

Heber: *Heber Letters*, 1782–1832, Batchworth Press, 1950.

Héloïse: *Epistola*, trans. and ed. B. Radice, vols. i to clxxviii, Penguin, 1974.

Hildegard of Bingen: *Letters of Hildegard of Bingen*, ed. M. Fox, Bear and Co., New York, USA, 1987.

Emily Hobhouse: *M. Fawcett*, R. Strachey, John Murray, 1931.

Isabella of Castile: *Isabel la Católica*, ed. Castalia, Madrid, 1985.

Geraldine Jewsbury: *Selections from the Letters of Geraldine E. Jewsbury to Jane Welsh Carlyle*, ed. A. Ireland, Longman, 1892.

Stéphanie Jullien: Jullien Family Papers, 39 AP 4, Archives Nationales, Paris.

Mary Kingsley: *A Victorian Lady in Africa*, V. Grosvenor Myer, Ashford Press, Shedfield, Hants., 1989.

La Pasionaria: *La Pasionaria*, Robert Lowe, Hutchinson, 1992.

Mary Leapor: 'Epistle to a Lady' in *Poems on Several Occasions*, 1748.

Lady Honor Lisle: *The Lisle Letters*, ed. M. St Clare Byrne, University of Chicago Press, Chicago, 1983; Penguin, 1985.

Madame: *Letters of Madame*, trans. and ed. Gertrude Scott Stevenson, Arrowsmith. 1925.

Katherine Mansfield: *Katherine Mansfield: A Secret Life*, Claire Tomalin, Viking, 1987.

Harriet Martineau: *Harriet Martineau's Autobiography and Memorials of Harriet Martineau*, ed. Maria W. Chapman, Boston, 1877.

Mary Tudor: BL Harleian Ms 444, f. 27; Cotton Ms, Titus CVIII, f. 120.

Elizabeth Montagu: *A Lady of the Last Century: Mrs Elizabeth Montagu*, Dr Doran, 1873.
Mrs Montagu 'Queen of the Blues': Her Letters and Friendships from 1762 to 1800, ed. R. Blunt, Constable, n.d.

Lady Morgan (Sydney Owenson): *O'Donnel: A National Tale*, Irish Novelists Library, 1814; reprinted, London, 1896.

Margaret Cavendish, Duchess of Newcastle: *A Glorious Fame: The Life and Letters of Margaret Cavendish, Duchess of Newcastle*, Kathleen Jones, Bloomsbury Press, 1988.

Florence Nightingale: Letters in the Fawcett Library, London, E1.

Anaïs Nin: *Journals*, ed. G. Stuhlmann, Peter Owen, 1970 and Harcourt Brace, New York, USA. 1967. 10 vols.

Mrs Oliphant: *The Autobiography and Letters of Mrs M.O.W. Oliphant*, ed. Mrs Harry Coghill, W. Blackwood, 1899.

Dorothy Osborne: *Letters of Dorothy Osborne to Sir William Temple*, Everyman, 1914. Republished by Folio Society, 1968 (ed. K. Hart).

Emmeline Pankhurst: *The Fighting Pankhursts*, David Mitchell, Cape, 1967.
Queen Christabel: A Biography of Christabel Pankhurst, ed. David Mitchell, Macdonald, 1977.

The Paston Family: *Selections from the Paston Letters*, ed. Alice D. Greenwood, G. Bell and Sons, 1920.

Lady Pennington: *An Unfortunate Mother's Advice to her Absent Daughters*, The Young Lady's Pocket Library, Dublin, 1790.

Christine de Pisan: *City of Ladies*, C. de Pisan, trans. E.V. Richards, Persea Books, New York, USA, 1982.

Dorothy Richardson: *Writing for their Lives*, eds. G. Hanscombe and V. Smyers, The Women's Press, 1987.

George Sand: *Lettres d'un Voyageur*, Penguin, 1987.
Sand–Flaubert Letters, ed. S. Sherman, Academy Press, Chicago, 1922.
Letters of George Sand, ed. Elizabeth Drew, Routledge, 1930.

Claudia Severa: *Britannia*, vol. XVIII, Society for Roman Studies, 1987.

Madame de Sévigné: *Madame de Sévigné: Choix de Lettres*, ed. N.S. Wilson, Harrap, 1955.
Madame de Sévigné: Selected Letters, trans. L. Tancock, Penguin, 1982.

Anna Seward: *Collected Letters of Anna Seward*, Constable, Edinburgh, New York, 1811.

Mrs Sewell: *Life and Letters of Mrs Sewell*, M. Bayley, 1889.

Edith Sitwell: *Edith Sitwell: Lion Among Unicorns*, Victoria Glendinning, Weidenfeld, 1981.

Charlotte Smith: *Emmeline*, C. Smith, 1788. Oxford University Press, Oxford, 1971.
Lee Smith: *Fair and Tender Ladies*, Macmillan, 1989.

Madame de Staël: *Life of Madame de Staël*, J.C. Herold, Hamish Hamilton, 1959.

Freya Stark: *The Letters of Freya Stark*, eds. C. and L. Moorehead, Compton-Russell, 1974–82, 8 vols.

Ann Martin Taylor: *Correspondence between a Mother and her Daughter*, A. Martin Taylor, 1817.

St Teresa of Avila: *The Complete Works of Saint Teresa of Avila*, trans. Allison Peers, Sheed, 1946.

Maria Theresa: *Maria Theresa*, E. Crankshaw, Longman, 1969.

Hester Thrale: *Intimate Letters 1788–1821*, O. Knapp, 1914.

Flora Tristan: *The London Journal of Flora Tristan*, trans. Jean Hawkes, Virago, 1982.

Marina Tsvetayeva: *Marina Tsvetayeva*, Elaine Feinstein, Penguin, 1989.

Queen Victoria: *Dearest Child: Letters between Queen Victoria and the Princess Royal 1858–1861*, ed. R. Fulford, 1964.
Queen Victoria's Early Letters, ed. J. Raymond, Manchester University Press, Manchester, 1963.
Letters of Queen Victoria, ed. A.C. Benson, 3 vols., John Murray, 1907.

Nellie Weeton: *Miss Weeton: Journal of a Governess*, ed. E. Hall, 1936.

Fay Weldon: *Letters to Alice, on First Reading Jane Austen*, Michael Joseph, 1983.

Jane West: *Letters to a Young Lady*, J. West, 1806.

Rebecca West: *Rebecca West*, Victoria Glendinning, Macmillan, 1985.

Vita Sackville-West: *The Letters of Vita Sackville-West to Virginia Woolf*, eds. L. DeSaho and M. Leaska, Macmillan, 1984.

Edith Wharton: *The Letters of Edith Wharton*, eds. R.W.B. and Nancy Lewis, Simon and Schuster, 1988.

Mary Wollstonecraft: *Collected Letters*, ed. R. Wardle, Cornell, University Press, USA, 1979.
Four New Letters of Mary Wollstonecraft and Helen M. Williams, University of California Press, Los Angeles, 1937.
The Life and Death of Mary Wollstonecraft, Claire Tomalin, Weidenfeld, 1974.

Virginia Woolf: see Vita Sackville-West.

Lady Mary Wortley Montagu: *The Complete Letters of Lady Mary Wortley Montagu*, ed. R. Halsband, Clarendon Press, Oxford, 1965.
Selected Letters were published in paperback by Penguin, 1971.

If the source of a private letter is not stated, it is in private hands.

The following have also been used as general sources:

Aitken, James, *English Letters of the XVIII Century*, Pelican, 1946.
Davidoff, I. and Hall, C., *Family Fortunes: Men and Women of the English Middle Class 1780–1850*, Hutchinson, 1987.
Hanscombe, G. and Smyers, V.L., eds. *Writing for Their Lives*, The Women's Press, 1987.
Hellerstein, Erna Olafson, Hume, L.P. and Offen, K.M., eds., *Victorian Women*, Stanford University Press, 1981.
Hill, Bridget, *Eighteenth Century Women*, Allen and Unwin, 1984.
Howe, Bea, *A Galaxy of Governesses*, Verschoyle, 1954.
Lefkowitz, Mary R. and Fant, M.B., *Women's Life in Greece and Rome*, Duckworth, 1982.

Mavor, Elizabeth, *The Ladies of Llangollen: A Study in Romantic Friendship*, Michael Joseph, 1971.

Moriarty, Catherine, eds., *The Voice of the Middle Ages*, Lennard Books, Oxford, 1989.

Smith, Lee, *Fair and Tender Ladies*, Macmillan, 1989.

Spender, Dale and Todd, Janet, eds., *Anthology of British Women Writers*, Pandora, 1989.

Acknowledgements

I should like to thank the librarians of Morley College and Bradford University for their help. The many friends who lovingly read parts of this manuscript and gave me feedback have been immensely supportive, as have those friends who allowed me to include their own precious letters to me. I should also like to thank the librarian of the Fawcett Library for permission to use this excellent feminist library, and for his generosity in permitting me to publish the hitherto unpublished letter from Florence Nightingale.

The editor has tried assiduously to contact every source, and apologizes, where replies have not been received, if sources stated are not correct. The editor gratefully acknowledges permission to include brief extracts from the following:

Aitken, James, *English Letters of the XVIII Century*. Pelican, 1946.

Bâ, Mariama, *So Long a Letter*, trans. M. Bodé-Thomas, Virago, 1982.

Blanch, Lesley, *The Wilder Shores of Love*. John Murray, 1954.

Chapman, R.W., ed., *Jane Austen: Letters*. Oxford University Press, 1932; New York, 1952.

Chapple, J.A.V., ed., *The Letters of Elizabeth Gaskell*. Manchester University Press, 1967.

Crankshaw, E., *Maria Theresa*. Longman, 1969.

Day, A., *Letters from Georgian Ireland*. Friars Bush Press, 1992.

Davidoff, I. and Hall, C., *Family Fortunes: Men and Women of the English Middle Class 1780–1850*. Hutchinson, 1987.

DeSaho, L., and Leaska, M., *The Letters of Vita Sackville-West to Virginia Woolf*. Macmillan, 1984.

Fernández-Arnesto, F., *Ferdinand and Isabella*. Weidenfeld, 1975.

Fox, M., *Letters of Hildegard of Bingen*. Bear and Co., á USA, 1987.

Gerin, Winifred, *Branwell Brontë*. Hutchinson, 1961.

——, *Charlotte Brontë*. Oxford University Press, 1967.

Glendinning, Victoria, *Rebecca West*. Macmillan, 1985.

Greenwood, Alice D., *Selections from the Paston Letters*. G. Bell and Sons, 1920.

Halsband, R., ed., *The Complete Letters of Lady Mary Wortley Montagu*. Clarendon Press, 1965.

——, *The Selected Letters of Lady Mary Wortley Montagu*. Penguin, 1971.

Haight, Gordon, ed., *George Eliot: A Biography*. Oxford University Press, 1968.

——, *The Selected Letters of George Eliot*. Oxford University Press, 1968.

Hanscombe, G. and Smyers, V.L., eds., *Writing for Their Lives*. The Women's Press, 1987.

Hanscombe, G., *Between Friends*. Sheba, 1983.

Hawkes, Jean, trans., *The London Journal of Flora Tristan*. Virago, 1982.

Hellerstein, Erna Olafson, Hume, L.P. and Offen, K.M., eds., *Victorian Women*. Stanford University Press, 1981. I am particularly grateful to these three editors for their indications of where to ask for further permissions.

Héloïse, *Epistola*, trans and ed., Radice, B., vols. i–clxxviii. Penguin, 1974.

Hill, Bridget, *Eighteenth Century Women*. Allen and Unwin, 1984.

Lefkowitz, Mary R. and Fant, M.B., *Women's Life in Greece and Rome*. Duckworth, 1982.

Lewis, R.W.B. and Nancy, *The Letters of Edith Wharton*. Simon and Schuster, 1988.

Mavor, Elizabeth, *The Ladies of Llangollen: A Study in Romantic Friendship*. Michael Joseph, 1971.

Mitchell, David, *The Fighting Pankhursts*. Cape, 1967.

——, ed., *Queen Christabel: A Biography of Christabel Pankhurst*. Macdonald, 1977.

Moorehead, C. and L., eds., *The Letters of Freya Stark*. Compton-Russell, 1974–82, 8 vols.

Moriarty, Catherine, ed., *The Voice of the Middle Ages*. Lennard Books, Oxford, 1989.

Nin, Anaïs, *Journals*. Peter Owen, 1970.

Palser Havely, C., *The Travels of Isabella Bird*. Century Press, 1971.

Peers, Allison, trans., *Compete Works of Saint Teresa of Avila*. Sheed, 1946.

Perry, Maria, *The Word of a Prince: A Life of Queen Elizabeth*. Boydell and Brewer, Woodbridge, Suffolk, 1990.

Smith, Lee, *Fair and Tender Ladies*. Macmillan, 1989.

Spender, Dale and Todd, Janet, eds., *Anthology of British Women Writers*. Pandora, 1989.

Tancock, L., trans. *Madame de Sévigné: Selected Letters*. Penguin, 1982.

Tomalin, Claire, *The Life and Death of Mary Wollstonecraft*. Weidenfeld, 1974.

——, *Katherine Mansfield: A Secret Life*. Viking, 1987.

Weldon, Fay, *Letters to Alice, on First Reading Jane Austen*. Michael Joseph, 1983.

Wood, Nigel, *Dr Johnson and Fanny Burney*. Bristol Classical Press, 1989.

Index